Lecture Notes in Computer Science 5936

Commenced Publication in 1973
Founding and Former Series Editors:
Gerhard Goos, Juris Hartmanis, and Jan van Leeuwen

Moira C. Norrie   Michael Grossniklaus (Eds.)

Object Databases

Second International Conference, ICOODB 2009
Zurich, Switzerland, July 1-3, 2009
Revised Papers

 Springer

Volume Editors

Moira C. Norrie
ETH Zurich
Department of Computer Science
Zurich, Switzerland
E-mail: norrie@inf.ethz.ch

Michael Grossniklaus
Politecnico di Milano
Dipartimento di Elettronica e Informazione
Milano, Italy
E-mail: grossniklaus@elet.polimi.it

Library of Congress Control Number: 2010931175

CR Subject Classification (1998): H.2, H.4, H.3, H.5, I.2, D.2

LNCS Sublibrary: SL 3 – Information Systems and Application, incl. Internet/Web and HCI

ISSN   0302-9743
ISBN-10   3-642-14680-5 Springer Berlin Heidelberg New York
ISBN-13   978-3-642-14680-0 Springer Berlin Heidelberg New York

springer.com

© Springer-Verlag Berlin Heidelberg 2010
Printed in Germany

Typesetting: Camera-ready by author, data conversion by Scientific Publishing Services, Chennai, India
Printed on acid-free paper   06/3180

Preface

ICOODB 2009 was the second in a series of international conferences aimed at promoting the exchange of information and ideas between members of the object database community. A key feature of the conference was its goal to bring together developers, users and researchers. The conference had three different tracks offered as a tutorial day, an industry day and a research day. In addition, a demo session with contributions from all three communities enabled participants to see the latest and on-going developments in object database technologies, supporting tools and also applications.

The conference proceedings presented as this volume consist of the papers presented in the research track. By publishing these after the conference, authors were given an opportunity to revise and extend their papers based on feedback and discussions held during the conference. Six of the papers were selected from submissions based on reviews by at least three members of the Program Committee. These papers address a number of classic database issues such as query processing, transaction processing, event models and the coupling of data and services in the context of modern object databases.

In addition, the research track included three invited presentations from researchers who were leaders in the field during what might be called the first generation of object databases back in the 1980s and early 1990s. At this time, research in object data models as well as object-oriented databases and persistent programming languages was very active. Over the years, this research became less fashionable and many researchers moved into other fields. However, some continued and as technologies and markets evolved so did their models and systems. With the revival in interest in object databases, it is important that researchers coming into the field are aware of the large body of previous research in the field. At the same time, it is interesting to look back on this research and lessons learned. How have technologies evolved and what remain as open issues? By addressing this question, we can identify future research directions.

The first of these invited papers is from Al Dearle, Graham Kirby and Ron Morrison of the University of St. Andrews, who worked together with Malcolm Atkinson on some of the first persistent programming languages. The goal was for orthogonal persistence and in their paper they revisit this goal, examining efforts to satisfy it through the ages from the earliest persistent programming languages to contemporary object databases.

The second invited paper by Matthias Jarke, Manfred Jeusfeld, Hans Nissen, Christoph Quix and Martin Staudt is a celebration of the 21st birthday of ConceptBase, a deductive object-oriented database system intended for the management of metadata. ConceptBase has been used in numerous projects and the team led by Matthias Jarke of RWTH Aachen and Manfred Jeusfeld of the University of Tilburg has continued to develop the system and add many advanced features over the years. The paper provides an overview of the system and also reports on experiences and impact.

The third invited paper is by Elisa Bertino, Elena Camossi and Michela Bertolotto. Elisa Bertino was a leading researcher in the first generation of object databases and has continued to actively support the field, especially with her work on object data models. The paper shows how an object data model can be extended to represent and query spatio-temporal objects with multiple granularities and concludes with a discussion of open research challenges.

We take this opportunity to thank all those who helped to make this conference a success. First, there are the authors and presenters who of course are an essential part of every conference. It is their enthusiasm and professionalism that makes us confident in the future of object databases. We were pleased to see lots of lively discussions taking place within the conference sessions, during the coffee and lunch breaks and also at ICOODB 2009's social events. We believe that the opportunity for young researchers to interact with not only senior academics but also leading figures in the commercial world was something very special and we are pleased to note that in many cases these dialogues have continued beyond the end of the conference.

We also thank all the members of the program committee who did the reviewing work that plays such an important role in ensuring the scientific quality of a conference. Then there are our fellow organizers Anat Gafni, Stefan Edlich and Roberto Zicari who were key in putting together such an exciting conference program. We also acknowledge the support of the members of the ICOODB Steering Committee who provided valuable advice on the general organization of the conference. Thanks are also due to the many individuals who helped with the local organization of the conference. Last but not least, we thank the sponsors SI-DBTA, Versant and Progress for their financial support: All those who have organized conferences know the difference that this makes.

November 2009   Moira C. Norrie
                                                                Michael Grossniklaus

Organization

General Chair

Moira C. Norrie   ETH Zurich, Switzerland

Program Chairs

Moira C. Norrie   ETH Zurich, Switzerland
Michael Grossniklaus   Politecnico di Milano, Italy

Program Committee

Suad Alagić   University of Southern Maine, USA
Sonia Berman   University of Cape Town. South Africa
Elisa Bertino   Purdue University, USA
Alan Dearle   University of St. Andrews, UK
Giovanna Guerrini   University of Genoa, Italy
Antony Hosking   Purdue University, USA
Geert-Jan Houben   Delft University of Technology,
                         The Netherlands
Matthias Jarke   RWTH Aachen, Germany
Epaminondas Kapetanios   University of Westminster, UK
Gerti Kappel   Vienna University of Technology, Austria
Stefan Keller   University of Applied Sciences Rapperswil,
                         Switzerland
Jessie Kennedy   Napier University, UK
Michele Missikoff   IASI-CNR, Italy
Dennis McLeod   University of Southern Califonia, USA
Oscar Pastor   Valencia University of Technology, Spain
Norman Paton   University of Manchester, UK
Gunter Saake   University of Magdeburg, Germany
Stefano Spaccapietra   EPF Lausanne, Switzerland
Krzysztof J. Stencel   University of Warsaw, Poland
Kazimierz Subieta   Polish-Japanese Institute of Technology,
                         Poland
Bernhard Thalheim   University of Kiel, Germany

Industrial Chairs

Stefan Edlich   TFH Berlin, Germany
Anat Gafni   db4objects, USA

Tutorial Chair

Roberto Zicari   Goethe University, Germany

Local Organization Chairs

Eugenio Lentini   ETH Zurich, Switzerland
Stefania Leone   ETH Zurich, Switzerland
Michael Nebeling   ETH Zurich, Switzerland
Alexandre de Spindler   ETH Zurich, Switzerland

Sponsoring Institutions

SI-DBTA: Special Interest Group on Information Systems, Switzerland
Global Information Systems Research Group, ETH Zurich, Switzerland
Versant Corporation, Redwood City, CA, USA
Progress Software Corporation, Bedford, MA, USA

Table of Contents

Orthogonal Persistence Revisited

Alan Dearle, Graham N.C. Kirby, and Ron Morrison

School of Computer Science, University of St Andrews,
North Haugh, St Andrews, Fife KY16 9SX, Scotland
{al,graham,ron}@cs.st-andrews.ac.uk

Abstract. The social and economic importance of large bodies of programs and data that are potentially long-lived has attracted much attention in the commercial and research communities. Here we concentrate on a set of methodologies and technologies called persistent programming. In particular we review programming language support for the concept of orthogonal persistence, a technique for the *uniform* treatment of objects irrespective of their types or longevity. While research in persistent programming has become unfashionable, we show how the concept is beginning to appear as a major component of modern systems. We relate these attempts to the original principles of orthogonal persistence and give a few hints about how the concept may be utilised in the future.

1 Introduction

The aim of persistent programming is to support the design, construction, maintenance and operation of long-lived, concurrently accessed and potentially large bodies of data and programs. When research into persistent programming began, persistent application systems were supported by disparate mechanisms, each based upon different philosophical assumptions and implementation technologies [1]. The mix of technologies typically included naming, type and binding schemes combined with different database systems, storage architectures and query languages.

The incoherence in these technologies increased the cost both intellectually and mechanically of building persistent application systems. The complexity distracted the application builder from the task in hand to concentrate on mastering the multiplicity of programming systems, and the mappings amongst them, rather than the application being developed. The plethora of disparate mechanisms was also costly in machine terms, in that the code for interfacing them, their redundant duplication of facilities and their contention for resources caused execution overheads. Software architects and engineers observed that it was often much harder and more expensive to build and maintain persistent application systems than was expected, and their evolution was invariably problematic.

Atkinson [2] postulated that, in many cases, the inconsistency was not fundamental but accidental. The various subsystems were built at different times when the engineering trade-offs were different. In consequence, they provided virtually the same services, but inconsistently since they were designed and developed independently. By contrast, Orthogonal Persistence provided the total

M.C. Norrie and M. Grossniklaus (Eds.): ICOODB 2009, LNCS 5936, pp. 1–22, 2010.

composition of services within one coherent design, thereby eliminating these accidental disharmonies.

While research in persistent programming has become unfashionable, it is hard to believe that the situation today has changed much. A recent (2007) quote from Microsoft illustrates this well:

> *"Most programs written today manipulate data in one way or another and often this data is stored in a relational database. Yet there is a huge divide between modern programming languages and databases in how they represent and manipulate information. This impedance mismatch is visible in multiple ways. Most notable is that programming languages access information in databases through APIs that require queries to be specified as text strings. These queries are significant portions of the program logic. Yet they are opaque to the language, unable to benefit from compile-time verification and design-time features like IntelliSense."* [3].

Orthogonally persistent object systems support a *uniform* treatment of objects irrespective of their types by allowing values of *all* types to have whatever longevity is required. The benefits of orthogonal persistence have been described extensively in the literature [2,4,5,6,7,8,9,10,11,12,13,14,15,16,17,18]. They can be summarised as:

- improving programming productivity from simpler semantics;
- avoiding ad hoc arrangements for data translation and long-term data storage;
- providing protection mechanisms over the whole environment;
- supporting incremental evolution; and
- automatically preserving referential integrity over the entire computational environment for the whole life-time of an application.

In this paper we review a selection of the many historical approaches to programming with long-lived data[1] and comment on attempts in the programming language and ODBMS communities to provide various flavours of persistence. We conclude by hinting at how the concept may be utilised in the future.

2   Orthogonal Persistence

In most current application systems there are two domains: the programming language domain and the database domain. The programming language domain presents a Turing-complete programming environment that permits computation over data defined using the programming language type system. In the last twenty years the predominant programming model has become the object-oriented model, usually providing typed objects containing state, methods and (usually typed) references to other objects. This model, and the tools which have

---

[1] Space limitations preclude a full survey of the area; notable omissions include Smalltalk, O2, Galileo, Trellis/Owl, Fibonacci, DBPL and Tycoon.

evolved to support it, has proven to be highly productive in terms of creating and maintaining software.

By contrast, the conceptual database domain is largely unchanged: tables of tuples containing foreign keys identifying tuples in other tables. This remains the pre-eminent long-term storage architecture.

The cost of the conceptual and technological differences between these two models became known as the *impedance mismatch* [19], and was one of the primary motivations for the work on orthogonal persistence, which aimed to remove the conceptually unnecessary distinction between short-term and long-term data [1].

There is a spectrum of possible degrees of integration, as perceived by programmers, between these formats. At one end of this spectrum data formats are completely disparate, and there is no automated support for transformation between them. A programmer has to understand the semantics of multiple representations and the mappings between them, and to write code for data transformations that implement these mappings. The impedance mismatch is strongest at this end of the spectrum. On the other hand, the low degree of integration yields loose coupling between the language and storage domains, which in turn facilitates openness in terms of the persistent data being accessible by routes other than the language.

At the full integration end of the spectrum lies orthogonal persistence, where no distinction between data formats is visible to the programmer. At intermediate points in the spectrum, the mapping between the object and storage domains is partially automated. Typically, the programmer still has to specify the mappings and understand the relationships between the multiple representations, but is relieved of the task of writing explicit translation code.

These differences are crystallised by Fowler, who describes two different architectural patterns that may be applied to persistent systems [20]. These are the *Active Record* and *Data Mapper* patterns. In the first, an object in a programming system represents a row in a database relation. In this pattern the database is wrapped in an object that provides methods to save, update, delete and find objects. Here there is a one-to-one mapping between classes or types in the programming language and relations in the database.

The *Data Mapper* pattern is more general. It comprises (potentially multiple) mappers that move data between the storage layers and maintains the relationships between entities. For example, in an object-relational system there is one mapper and two layers-the language system and the relational database. In a distributed system with caching there might be two mappers maintaining relationships between three layers—the language, the cache and the database.

The degree of integration dictates the extent to which the application programmer must be conscious of these patterns. With orthogonal persistence they are handled entirely by the system. Atkinson and Morrison identified three Principles of Orthogonal Persistence [21]:

– **The Principle of Persistence Independence**
  The persistence of data is independent of how the program manipulates the data. That is, the programmer does not have to, indeed cannot, program to control the movement of data between long term and short term store. This is performed automatically by the system.

– **The Principle of Data Type Orthogonality**
  All data objects should be allowed the full range of persistence irrespective of their type. That is, there are no special cases where objects of a specific type are not allowed to be persistent.

– **The Principle of Persistence Identification**
  The choice of how to identify and provide persistent objects is orthogonal to the universe of discourse of the system[2].

The application of the three principles yields orthogonal persistence. Violation of any of these principles increases the complexity that persistent systems seek to avoid. In the next section we examine these principles in the context of past and current persistent systems.

3   Languages and Persistence

3.1   First Generation Persistence Mechanisms

In the last twenty to thirty years the mechanisms for mapping between the two programming language and database data models have improved considerably. Ironically, this is in part due to technologies that were developed in the typed persistent world, for example strongly typed generative and reflective programming.

In the eighties it was common for programmers to explicitly save and restore programming language objects to the file system. Code was hand-written and tended to be error-prone and time consuming. Furthermore, when the data was changed, the code had to adapt, and more code written to evolve any saved data from previous program incarnations. The need to write such code explicitly was first eliminated by persistent systems such as PS-algol (discussed in the next section) and object-oriented databases.

Java serialization goes some way to reducing the programming effort required to implement object persistence using files, since it allows an entire closure to be written or read in a single operation. Only instances of classes that implement the interface *java.io.serializable* may be serialized. For example:

---

[2] Experience with persistent programming showed that in systems with references, the only mechanism for implementation was persistence by reachability, also known as transitive persistence.

```
FileInputStream f = new FileInputStream("myobject.data");
ObjectInputStream obj_in = new ObjectInputStream(f);
Object obj = obj_in.readObject();
if (obj instanceof Person) {
   Person p = (Person) obj;
   // Do something with p ...
}
```

The above program reads an object from the file *myobject.data* and casts it to the type *Person*. One problem with this style of programming is that the entire closure of an object must be loaded or saved in a single operation. This can make the operations slow for large object closures, and limits the size of closure that can be stored to that of main memory—known as the *big inhale* in early Smalltalk-80 systems. However, more importantly, each time a closure is serialized a new copy of the data is made. This breaks referential integrity since there is no way of matching the identity of objects from different save/load operations. Another problem with the mechanism is that since not all Java classes are *serializable*, some object closures are not consistently saved and restored.

Serialization does not adhere to the first two principles of orthogonal persistence. Data is explicitly written to backing store, violating the principle of independence; only serializable objects may be made persistent, so the principle of data type orthogonality is also violated.

In contrast, to extract data from a database, the programs manipulating persistent data had to perform much string processing. Despite this approach manifesting a high impedance mismatch, it is still common in today's PHP programs. For example:

```
$result = mysql_query("SELECT * FROM Persons");
while($row = mysql_fetch_array($result)) {
   $firstname = $row['FirstName'];
   $secondname = $row['LastName'];
}
```

In this fragment [22], the database access is explicit—the SQL query is embedded as a string in the program, and data is extracted from the database in the form of strings.

The use of strings is also employed in JDBC [23], which provides database independent connectivity between Java programs and databases. The JDBC API permits SQL operations to be performed, by providing three broad classes of operations: establishing connections to a database, performing queries and processing the results of queries. An example is shown below:

```
Connection con = DriverManager.getConnection("jdbc:myDriver:fish",
    "myLogin", "myPassword");
Statement stmt = con.createStatement();
ResultSet rs = stmt.executeQuery("SELECT name,age FROM Persons");
while (rs.next()) {
    String name = rs.getString("name");
    int age = rs.getInt("age");
    ...
}
```

The similarities between the JDBC and PHP examples are striking. Both embed a query in the form of a string in the host program, and both use string matching to extract data from the result set that is delivered by the query. Both mechanisms are a long way from the principles of orthogonal persistence.

3.2 PS-algol

The first language to provide orthogonal persistence was PS-algol [1], which provided persistence by reachability for all data types supported by the language. PS-algol adds a small number of functions to S-algol [24], from which it was derived. These are *open.database*, *close.database*, *commit* and *abort*[3]. A number of functions are also provided to manage associative stores (hash maps), called *tables* in PS-algol. These functions are *s.lookup*, which retrieves a value associated with a key in a table, and *s.enter*, which creates an association between a key and a value in a table. By convention, a database always contains a pointer to a table at its root. Databases serve as roots of persistence and can be created dynamically.

Two slightly modified examples from [1] are shown below to give a flavour of the language. The first example opens a database called "addr.db" and places a person object into a table associated with the key "addr.table" found at its root. Note that the person (denoted by *p*) contains a reference to an address object. When *commit* is called, the updated table, the person and the address objects are written to persistent storage.

```
structure person(string name, phone; pntr addr)
structure address(int no ; string street, town)
let db = open.database("addr.db", "write")
if db is error.record
    do { write "Can't open database"; abort }
let table = s.lookup("addr.table", db)
let p = person("al", 3250, address(76, "North St", "St Andrews"))
s.enter("al", table, p)
commit
```

The second example opens the same database and retrieves the person object before writing out their phone number.

---

[3] Note: dots are legal within identifiers in PS-algol and do not denote dereferencing. Dereferencing is represented by round brackets enclosing a fieldname. There is no explicit new operator; the use of a structure name serves as a constructor.

```
structure person (string name, phone; pntr addr)
let db = open.database("addr.db", "read")
if db is error.record
   do { write "Can't open database"; abort }
let table = s.lookup("addr.table", db)
let p = s.lookup("al", table)
if p = nil then write "Person not known"
else write "phone number: ", p(phone)
```

As described in [25], "the programmer never explicitly organises data movement but it occurs automatically when data is used", a feature shared with many of the object-relational systems. The paper also states "the language type rules are strictly enforced" but is not explicit about how this is achieved, which is a pity, since it is important. PS-algol uses structural type equivalence rather than the name equivalence so prevalent today. Using structural type equivalence, two objects or terms are considered to have compatible types if the types have identical structure. Thus, in the previous examples, the compatible declarations of *person* in the two examples serve to unify the two programs. If the object retrieved from the database is not of (structural) type *person*, the deference of the object will fail.

The type system of PS-algol is more subtle than might appear. Notice that the second program does not require a declaration of the type *address* since that type is never used in the program. It is not necessary since pointers in PS-algol are typed as *pntr*, which is an infinite union over all records. The infinite union facilitates partial and incremental specification of the structure of the data at the expense of a dynamic check. The persistent schema need only be specified within a program up to limit of the *pntr* objects. When one is encountered in a running program, by dereference, a dynamic check ensures the data is of the correct type. The specification within that check need only be to the limit of the subsequent *pntr* types.

A second version of PS-algol incorporated procedures as data objects thereby allowing code and data to be stored in the persistent store.

PS-algol does not support any form of concurrency other than at database level. This often caused problems since it was possible to continue to access objects after *commit*. The addition of explicit syntactic boundaries to control transactions would have addressed this deficiency.

3.3 Napier88

Napier88 attempted to explore the limits of orthogonal persistence by incorporating the entire language support environment within a strongly typed persistent store [12,21,26,27,28,29,30]. The research produced the first integrated, self-contained, type-safe persistent environment.

The Napier88 system provides orthogonal persistence, a strongly typed prepopulated stable store, higher-order procedures, parametric polymorphism, abstract (existential) data types, collections of name-value bindings, graphical data types, concurrent execution, two infinite union types for partial specification, and support for reflective programming. Notable additions over PS-algol include the following:

- the infinite union type *any*, which facilitates partial and incremental specification of the structure of the data
- the infinite union type *environment*, which, in addition to the above, provides dynamically extensible collections of name/L-value bindings—and thereby the dynamic construction of independent name spaces over common data
- parametric polymorphism in a style similar to that later popularised by Java generics, but with computation over truly persistent polymorphic values
- existentially quantified abstract data types for data abstraction
- a programming environment, including graphical windowing library, object browser, program editor and compiler, implemented entirely as persistent objects within the store
- support for hyper-code, in which program source code may contain embedded direct references to extant objects
- support for structural reflection, where a running program may generate new program fragments and integrate these into its own execution

The integrated persistent environment of Napier88 that supported higher-order procedures yielded a new programming paradigm, which is only possible by this means, whereby source programs could include direct links to values that already exist in the persistent environment. The programming technique was termed *hyper-programming* and the underlying representation *hyper-code*.

Hyper-code [31] is a representation of an executing system modelled as an active graph linking source code, existing values and meta-data. It unifies the concepts of source code, executable code and data, by providing a single representation (as a combination of text and hyperlinks) of software throughout its lifecycle. Sharing is represented by multiple links to the same value. Hyper-code also allows state and shared data, and thereby closure, to be preserved during evolution.

The combination of structural reflection, the ability of a program to generate new program fragments and to integrate these into its own execution, and hyper-code provides the basis for type-safe evolution. Within the persistent environment, generator programs may stop part of an executing system (while the rest of the system continues to execute), inspect its state by introspection, change the part as necessary by programming or editing the hyper-code representation, recompiling the new fragment and rebinding it into the executing system.

Unsurprisingly, given their heritage, both PS-algol and Napier88 support all three of the principles of orthogonal persistence.

3.4   Arjuna

The focus of the Arjuna system [32,33] is to support fault-tolerant distributed applications, based upon persistent objects supporting nested atomic actions. Atomic actions control sequences of local and remote operations against abstract datatypes implemented using C++ classes. The file system is used for long-term storage of objects. To support recoverability, a snapshot of object state is taken before an object is modified for the first time within the scope of an atomic action. This mechanism is also used to support persistence, with the new state of an object being used to replace its old state at commit time. A *state manager* provides operations to save and restore the state of object instances.

Since all persistent classes must extend the base class *StateManager*, which provides the mechanisms for persistence and atomic actions, Arjuna does not adhere to the principle of datatype orthogonality. It does not meet the requirements of persistence independence, since the programmer must implement *save_state* and *restore_state* operations for all persistent classes. Finally, for the same reason, it does not support persistence identification by reachability.

3.5   Persistent Java

Several orthogonally persistent versions of Java have been implemented. In PJama [34] the programmer uses an API to associate objects with strings in a persistent map in order to make them persistent. All objects transitively reachable from the map are automatically made persistent. The language syntax itself is unchanged; typically persistence can be introduced to a previously existing application with the addition of a relatively small amount of code making API calls. The compiler and standard libraries are also unchanged. The virtual machine is modified, to move objects to and from a proprietary object store automatically as required. A version of hyper-code has been prototyped using PJama [35].

The emphasis in ANU-OPJ [36] is on promoting inter-operability, by avoiding any modifications to the virtual machine. Instead, read and write barriers are introduced by dynamic byte-code modification. This is achieved by using a customised class loader, making the approach compatible with standard compilers and virtual machines. The programmer's view of persistence is slightly different from PJama, in that no persistence API is involved. Instead, all static fields are implicitly persistent roots. The Shore storage manager [37] provides object storage.

Persistent Java was implemented on the Grasshopper operating system [38]. Unlike the other persistent Java systems, no modifications were made to the abstract machine or to the bytecode generated for a particular application. Instead, orthogonal persistence was achieved by instantiating the entire Java machine within a persistent address space. In this system, like the later ANU-OPJ system, static fields were implicitly roots of persistence.

The three persistent Java systems adhered to the three principles of orthogonal persistence to varying degrees. PJama followed the PS-algol persistence model but could not make some types persistent due to restrictions in the abstract machine. Similarly, ANU-OPJ could not uniformly perform byte code transformation on some system classes. The Grasshopper version did adhere to the three principles, by virtue of making the entire environment persistent.

3.6   OODBs

Object-oriented database systems emerged in the mid 1980s and married persistence to object-oriented languages [39]. In the early systems, the language used tended to be an extension of C++. The Exodus System with its E programming language typified this approach [40].

The Object-Oriented Database Manifesto [41], published in 1989, set out to lay down the ground rules of what was (and what was not) an object-oriented database. It defined a number of mandatory, optional and open issues in OODB design. Space prohibits a full exposition of all the mandatory features (identity, encapsulation, computational completeness, types or classes, class hierarchies, complex objects, overriding, overloading and late binding, extensibility, persistence, secondary storage management, concurrency, recovery and ad-hoc querying); we will therefore comment on what we consider to be the most important here.

The first of these, identity, is perhaps the biggest differentiating feature between an OODB and a relational DB. Relational systems impose identity via primary keys stored as attributes, whereas objects have unique identities formed when they are created and remaining throughout their lifetimes irrespective of their states.

The issue of encapsulation is another feature that distinguishes the relational from the OO world. In a relational system the universe of discourse is made up of relations containing flat tuples, which may be queried using a relational language. By contrast, in an OO system an object has an interface, some state and a procedural component, which implements the interface and may perform operations on the state.

A last issue with OODB systems is whether code should be stored in the database; this issue seems to divide the OODB community. Many feel that putting code in the database has a detrimental effect on performance; the reasons for this are unclear. If code is not stored in the database, well-known semantic anomalies can arise. Richardson [42] describes how a program can populate a database with objects of some type T. Another program can insert into this data-structure an object of type T', a subtype of T. If the original program then accesses the new object and calls methods that have been over-ridden in T', it should of course use the code of the subtype when operations are performed (late binding). However, the code for T' may not be in the static environment (in the file system) of the original program. Indeed, the code may not even exist on the machine on which the program is written. In this case, when the original program invokes an operation on the new object a dynamic failure will result. There are essentially two solutions to this problem: relying on being able to load code from the file system—which is manifestly unsafe—or placing code in the database.

The provision of declarative querying was the primary difference between persistent languages and OODB systems; the latter generally provided querying whilst the former did not. Whilst pointer chasing can be more efficient than some operations, notably outer joins, in database systems, the inability to perform

declarative queries over non-resident data is often cited as the primary reason for
the lack of uptake of OODB and persistent systems. The relatively recent ability
to tightly integrate query languages over objects with a host object-oriented
language [3,43] has addressed much of this criticism.

Another perceived issue with OODB systems is the degree of coupling exhibited. Data in relational systems is loosely coupled; tuples are associated solely
via primary and foreign key values. This permits database schemata to be refactored by database administrators independently of the code base. In an object-
relational system there is also loose coupling between the code and the data.
The object-relational mappings are partial; they specify a degree of compliance
required of the database by the code. Thus database schema changes may not
affect the code in any way. By contrast, this is not true in OODB systems, which
are highly coupled in two respects: the referential integrity of pointers and type
constraints specified in the programming language. Since OODB systems typically rely on being able to follow the transitive closure of objects, changes to the
code and the database must be made in a consistent manner.

Most OODB systems are strongly typed and consequently the types of refer-
ends and referees must be type compliant; resulting in the schema and the code
being highly coupled. A last problem perceived with OODB systems is that it
is often difficult to determine the extent of pointers in the system due to lack of
sufficient encapsulation. Consequently changes to the schema could affect code
in arbitrary locations. However, this problem also applies to relational systems in
which there is a mismatch in the integrity constraints provided by the database
and those expected of the programs that compute over it. Furthermore, in a
pure object-oriented system the integrity of the data may be enforced by encapsulation, which is not true in relational systems. Clearly modern software
engineering tools could be brought to bear on these problems.

3.7   db4o

db4o [44] is a modern OODB system which may be used with both .NET and
Java, via the provision of separate libraries for the two languages. *db4o* requires
no mappings between transient and persistent data to be described by the programmer. Thus the objects stored in the database are real POJOs with no extra
interfaces, extended classes or annotations. The *db4o* model is reminiscent of PS-
algol. To access the database the programmer writes code such as that shown
below.

```
ObjectContainer db = Db4oEmbedded.openFile(Util.DB4OFILENAME);
try {
   Person al = new Person("al", 49);
   db.store(al);
} finally {
   db.close();
}
```

The root of the database is a collection (an *ObjectSet*) of objects. It is possible to access such a persistent collection using *query by example* (QBE), by performing a *get* operation with either a prototypical object or an instance of class *Class* as a parameter. In addition, *db4o* supports both native queries and Simple Object Database Access (SODA). Native queries are constructed using predicates in C# or Java whereas SODA queries are relatively low level, using strings to select fields from objects. Once a root object has been accessed its closure may be traversed using traditional pointer following operations.

By default *db4o* does not load entire closures from persistent storage. *db4o* introduces a concept known as *activation depth*, which determines how much of an object closure is loaded when a parent object is loaded. By default, only the first five levels of objects are loaded from the database. It also includes mechanisms to control activation based on class, via global settings and transparently. Additionally, objects referenced from a loaded object can be loaded by explicitly activating objects as they are loaded.

To update objects stored in the database the programmer has to retrieve an object and call *set* with a top-level object as a parameter (as in the above example). However, like object loading, the entire closure of the object is not written to persistent storage on commit. Instead, the amount of closure written to storage is controlled by a concept known as *update depth* (the default is 1). Like activation depth it is possible to control update depth in a variety of ways. These design decisions have clearly been made for a mixture of implementation and efficiency reasons.

Recent versions of *db4o* support optional *transparent persistence* which is much closer to the ideals of orthogonal persistence. When *transparent persistence* is employed, all objects are transparently loaded from and written to the persistent store and activation is handled automatically by the runtime system. To make use of *transparent persistence* classes must be *enhanced* during the build process. Not all classes can be enhanced, for example, classes containing native methods.

Whenever a container is opened, *db4o* implicitly starts a new transaction and an explicit commit occurs before the container is closed. A *rollback* operation permits transactions to abort. However, this operation is the root of a semantic anomaly. Loaded instances of database objects may be still be accessible yet out-of-sync with the store. To address this problem *db4o* provides a *refresh* operation, which may be applied to objects. It is unclear how the programmer is supposed to know which objects require refreshing; again this deviates from the principles of orthogonal persistence.

The *db4o* system adheres to the principle of data independence. No mappings or annotations are required to indicate which types may be made persistent. Similarly, code may manipulate data independent of its longevity. The concepts of update and activation depth do impact this principle since, for example, a method to determine the length of a list might get the wrong answer if activation depth was not used correctly. This is seen as desirable by the developers who state that *"db4o provides a mechanism to give the client fine-grained control over*

how much he wants to pull out of the database when asking for an object" [45].
The principle of data type orthogonality is adhered to, since any user-defined
data object can be made persistent without any additional code, annotations or
XML specifications.

3.8   Java Data Objects

Java Data Objects was released in 2002 [46], providing a storage interface for
Java objects without the necessity to interact with data access languages such as
SQL. Using JDO, Java objects may be stored in a relational database, an object
database, XML file, or any other technology using the same interface. Since
it enables Java programmers to transparently access underlying data storage
without using database-specific code, it moves considerably towards the goals of
persistent systems. An example of the use of JDO is shown below. Although not
shown in this example, the entire transitive closure of objects is stored in the
database on commit.

```
PersistenceManagerFactory pmf = JDOHelper.
    getPersistenceManagerFactory(..);
PersistenceManager pm = pmf.getPersistenceManager();
Person p = new Person("Bob Smith", 49 );
Transaction tx;
try {
    tx = pm.currentTransaction();
    tx.begin();
    pm.makePersistent(p);
    tx.commit();
} catch (Exception e) {  ... }
```

Although this looks very much like the PS-algol examples, much additional specification is required when using JDO. The relationship between the Java objects
and persistent data is specified using an XML metadata file. A simple example
is shown below, specifying the persistent class *com.xyz.Person*. Field modifiers
may specify a number of attributes, including which fields are primary keys,
whether fields are persistent or transient, how fields are to be loaded, and how
null values should be handled.

```
<?xml version="1.0" encoding="UTF-8"?>
<!DOCTYPE jdo SYSTEM "jdo.dtd">
<jdo>
    <package name="com.xyz">
        <class name="Person">
            <field name="firstname"
            persistence-modifier="persistent"/>
        ...
        </class>
    </package>
</jdo>
```

The query language provided by JDO, JDO Query Language (JDOQL), abstracts over the underlying storage technology. A query interface selects objects from the database irrespective of whether the underlying storage is based on objects or relations. Queries are passed to the persistence manager and operate on either class extents or explicit collections. Filtering is provided by providing Boolean expressions which are applied to instances.

```
Query query = pm.newQuery(Person.class, people,
   "name == \"Malcolm Atkinson\"");
Collection result = (Collection) query.execute();
Iterator iter = result.iterator();
while (iter.hasNext()) {
   Person p = (Person) iter.next();
   ...
}
```

JDO succeeds in abstracting over particular underlying storage technologies. However, in some cases, notably relational databases, the mapping between language objects and storage level objects must be described. When an object-relational mapping is used with JDO, the O-R mappings are described in ORM mapping files.

Persistence of data is independent of the programs manipulating it, provided that appropriate persistence mappings have been described. The principle of data type orthogonality is violated, since only those objects that have a persistent mapping can be made persistent. Furthermore, system classes and some collection classes may not be made persistent.

3.9   Java Persistence API

The Java Persistence API [47] is intended to operate inside or outside a J2EE container, creating a persistence model for (plain old) Java objects. It eliminates much of the complexity required by JDO. For example, the XML mapping tables are no longer required, and the objects that can be made persistent are ordinary Java objects rather than having to implement specified interfaces. In contrast to JDO, which is agnostic to storage technology, the Java Persistence API is explicitly for use in an object-relational context.

```
@Entity
public class Person
   public Person() {}
   @column( name="name" )
   public String getName() {}
   @column( name="age" )
   public int getAge() {}
}
```

The @*Enitity* annotation can be decorated with parameters specifying the name of the table from which data is drawn; by default this is the name of the class. Similarly, the column name may be specified using the @*column* annotation and identity attribute using @*id*. This is clearly not a POJO system, despite being often described as one, since it requires annotations to be made in the Java classes describing the object-relational mappings. Object-relational mappings can be arbitrarily complex, and it is possible to specify that data be drawn from multiple tables using join-based queries.

Queries are defined using (an extension to) Enterprise JavaBeans query language (EJB QL) rather than SQL. The difference is subtle but important: rather than querying over tables in the database, queries are performed on the beans and the relationships between them. These relationships are specified using the attributes embedded within the Java objects.

Using the Java Persistence API the persistence of data is independent of the programs that manipulate data. Additionally, the programmer does not have any explicit control over the movement of data between the store and main memory, thus adhering to the principle of persistence independence. The principle of data type orthogonality is only partially adhered to, since only instances of classes that are decorated with an @*Entity* annotation may be stored in the persistent store. This explicitly precludes most system classes from being persistently stored. The principle of persistence identification is largely adhered, to since the mechanism for identifying persistent objects is not related to the type system.

Despite not being fully compliant with the principles of orthogonal persistence, an application programmer can program against persistent data without the knowledge that the data is persistent. This is very much in the spirit of the aims of orthogonal persistence.

3.10   LINQ

Microsoft, recognizing the problems of embedding queries into programs as strings, has created Language-Integrated Query (LINQ) [3]. Unlike the Java systems described previously, the approach taken by LINQ is to add general-purpose query facilities that may be applied to all information sources. Thus being able to query over relational data is merely a special case of querying. For example, using LINQ it is possible to write a C# program to query over a collection of persons as follows:

```
static void doquery( Person[] people ) {
    IEnumerable<Address> result = from p in people
                                  where p.age == 49
                                  select p.address;
    foreach (Address item in result)
      Console.WriteLine(item.getTown());
}
```

The query selects all the people from the array whose age is 49 and forms an enumeration containing their addresses. Note that the query is integrated with the programming language, making it amenable to static type checking, optimization and—perhaps more importantly—design tools such as refactoring tools.

Relational data stored in a database can also be manipulated using a Visual Studio component called *LINQ to SQL*, which transparently translates LINQ queries into SQL for execution by the database engine. The results are returned in the language level objects defined in the user program. LINQ tracks the relationships between the language objects and the database transparently.

Like the Java object-relational mapping solutions, objects may be labelled with annotations to identify how properties correspond to database columns. Tool support is provided to assist in the translation between extant databases and language level object definitions.

4   Taking Stock

A selection of approaches to programming with persistent data have been outlined. They differ in a number of key attributes, including:

- data-centric or program-centric
- degree of adherence to the principles of orthogonal persistence
- degree of impedance mismatch
- storage technology employed
- whether object identity is automatically preserved
- whether code is stored with data
- support for declarative queries over non-resident data
- support for transactions

Space precludes a full analysis of the various approaches with respect to all of these aspects, but we suggest that the most fundamental is the overall system philosophy. In a data-centric approach it is assumed that pre-existing persistent data is a given, and the issue is how to program over that data. In a program-centric approach, code comes first, and the issue is to provide persistence of program data between executions.

In a data-centric approach the existing data is likely to be large and long-lived, and openness of the data—avoiding lock-in to proprietary technology—is likely to be important. Relational databases have overwhelming advantages in this sector: mature technology resulting from long-term investment in scalability and optimization; widely available expertise; and standard interfaces promoting inter-operability. Approaches in this category include low-level database APIs such as JDBC, and the various object-relational mapping technologies. The constraints imposed by the requirement to inter-operate with existing data—and to cope with changes to both data and meta-data made via other routes to the data—mean that none of these approaches achieve data type orthogonality, and that all involve a significant impedance mismatch. The ORM systems require the programmer to understand and specify the mapping between multiple representations, while low-level APIs also require conversion code to be written.

Designers of program-centric persistence technologies are less constrained in their choice of storage format since they may legitimately assume that the persistent data will be solely accessed via the language infrastructure. The systems that adhere to the principles of orthogonal persistence have all used proprietary closed storage formats. There is no obvious technical reason why this is a necessary choice, although it may well maximise scope for achieving good performance. This may have been one factor behind the lack of commercial adoption of the various successful research prototypes. To invest in significant use of any closed storage system requires a very high level of trust in the long-term viability of the technology and the processes that support it. Other obvious limiting factors are the relatively limited scalability of those systems in terms of size and query performance, inevitable given the resources available.

Object-relational systems have been highly successful, now dominating the field in large applications. It is clear, however, that significant impedance mismatch problems remain. Although the modern programmer is less likely to have to program the transfer of objects to and from long-term storage, they must still deal with a bewildering level of complexity in specifying mappings between objects and relations. The recent emergence of conceptually simpler approaches such as *db4o* is a sign that significant demand remains for the benefits pursued in the original investigations of orthogonal persistence.

It is perhaps also worth reflecting on the current usefulness of the principles of orthogonal persistence, a quarter century after they were first proposed. The principle of persistence independence suggests that data manipulation should be coded in exactly the same way for transient and persistent data, and that the programmer should not have to control data movement between transient and persistent storage. So long as the language is sufficiently rich that all desired data manipulation can be expressed conveniently, there seems no obvious argument against this principle. Of course, adherence to it incurs some implementation effort, hence not all approaches do so.

The principle of data type orthogonality suggests that all objects should be permitted the full range of persistence. Again, as a desirable feature this seems uncontroversial. Again, it raises significant implementation difficulties, leading to few systems achieving full adherence. Even those that claim full orthogonality have tended to have difficulty with objects that depend on external state, such as file descriptors, GUI elements, network channels etc.

The principle of persistence identification has had a more chequered history. The wording of its definition earlier is taken from [21]. In the earlier [1], however, which first proposed principles of orthogonal persistence, the principle is listed but not named. In hindsight, it now seems unclear what, precisely, is mandated by this principle that is not already covered by the principle of persistence independence. This appears to have been recognised in more recent discussion, in which it has been replaced by the more concrete principles of transitive persistence [34] and persistence by reachability [48]. We may perhaps conclude that a more useful general principle might be that it should be possible to identify persistent objects in a convenient way. If doing so via the type system is forbidden by the principle of data type orthogonality, and identifying each object individually is ruled out as too arduous, then persistence by reachability is the only obvious solution.

5   Future Directions

Orthogonally persistent systems will not replace object-relational systems in the foreseeable future. We may, however, speculate on niche areas in which the principles of orthogonal persistence might be usefully carried forward. One possibility is the development of a program-centric approach in which fully orthogonal persistence is implemented using a relational database as the storage engine. This would address the 'closed data format' criticism potentially levelled at previous implementations, since read-only access to the data could be permitted at the relational level.

Another potential avenue for development is to target emerging application styles such as cloud applications. The development of such applications could be significantly simplified by a system supporting programming over resilient distributed objects in a transparent manner, abstracting over replication and physical location in the same way that orthogonal persistence abstracts over storage hierarchy [49].

Another avenue for investigation is how the unique features of orthogonally persistent systems may be exploited to improve current software development technology [18]. For example, the integration of first-class code and data within a persistent store that enforces referential integrity makes the hyper-code paradigm possible. This could be extended with more sophisticated support for application system evolution, analogous to refactoring tools provided by modern IDEs [50]. Hyper-code allows source code to be reliably associated with all code objects. Thus, whereas refactoring tools currently operate separately on a code base or on a database, refactoring within a persistent environment could be applied uniformly to data and the code that operates on it. Evolutionary code could reflect over all of the data bound into the code-base being evolved, as well as the structure of the code-base itself. Arbitrary evolution (or refactoring) of a running application could be performed with complete confidence that all code and data affected by a change could be located and evolved in turn consistently. This would be possible even for data that in conventional systems would be encapsulated within closures and thus inaccessible to evolution code.

6   Conclusions

Orthogonal persistence was proposed to address the impedance mismatch problem. This problem has been with us for 20-30 years and refuses to go away. It has recently been described as the *Vietnam of Computer Science* [51]. Far from being resolved, the impedance mismatch is perhaps getting worse. We now have impedance mismatch across the multiple subsystems concerned with data replication, cache-coherency and distribution. In many of today's enterprise systems the programmer must, by necessity, not only manage mappings from the language to the database but also from the language to the Memcached [52] or DBCache [53] layers, and from those layers to the database. Thus, when we consider the impedance mismatch problem in our systems it is important to recognise that the object-relational mapping is not the only mapping that must be considered. Even if non-relational storage is used, for example Amazon S3 [54], mapping between layers is required. The essential issues are who creates the mappings and how efficiently they can be maintained.

In [19] Maier stated that one of the major problems of OO systems was the lack of integration between bulk operations and the programming language. In this domain good progress has been made in the last few years. LINQ makes great strides in providing a single (sub-) language that operates over objects regardless of their longevity.

The solutions to providing persistence in programming systems have been many, and the road has been long and winding. However, there has been a clear trend towards the ideals of orthogonal persistence. The state of the art has finally moved away from strings containing embedded queries with explicit coercions to values in the programming language space.

In the 1980s orthogonal persistence focussed on the differences between long- and short-term storage. As described above, this is just one of many mappings that an application builder needs to be concerned with; there are many subsystems that require mappings to be maintained, including caching, networks, virtualized hosts, distributed storage, and replication. Furthermore, we are moving towards a world in which applications are self-organising and autonomic. Such autonomic systems are likely to be concerned with data clustering, machine utilisation and the ability to distribute computation and storage. Lastly the scale of application systems is likely to vary enormously from small persistent applications on devices such as iPhones through to extremely large ones to address the scientific challenges of tomorrow. In such a world it seems unlikely that the intellectual burden of managing a plethora of complex mappings can be left in the human domain.

Acknowledgements

Our experience in the design and implementation of persistence systems has benefitted from interaction with so many people that it would be invidious to mention a recently remembered subset. Malcolm Atkinson deserves mention as the inventor of the persistence concept and we would like to thank the community that populated the Persistent Object Systems (POS) and Database Programming Language (DBPL) Workshops where much of this work was reported and digested.

References

1. Atkinson, M.P., Bailey, P.J., Chisholm, K.J., Cockshott, W.P., Morrison, R.: An Approach to Persistent Programming. Computer Journal 26(4), 360–365 (1983)
2. Atkinson, M.P.: Programming Languages and Databases. In: Proc. 4th International Conference on Very Large Databases, West Berlin, Germany, pp. 408–419. IEEE Computer Society Press, Los Alamitos (1978)
3. Kulkarni, D., Bolognese, L., Warren, M., Hejlsberg, A., George, K.: LINQ to SQL:NET Language-Integrated Query for Relational Data (2007), http://msdn. microsoft.com/en-gb/library/bb425822.aspx
4. Atkinson, M.P., Chisholm, K.J., Cockshott, W.P.: PS-Algol: An Algol with a Persistent Heap. ACM SIGPLAN Notices 17(7), 24–31 (1982)
5. Atkinson, M.P., Morrison, R.: Persistent First Class Procedures are Enough. In: Proc. 4th Conference on Foundations of Software Technology and Theoretical Computer Science, Bangalore, India, pp. 223–240. Springer, Heidelberg (1984)
6. Atkinson, M.P., Morrison, R.: Procedures as Persistent Data Objects. ACM Transactions on Programming Languages and Systems 7(4), 539–559 (1985)
7. Morrison, R., Brown, A.L., Bailey, P.J., Davie, A.J.T., Dearle, A.: A Persistent Graphics Facility for the ICL Perq. Software – Practice and Experience 16(4), 351–367 (1986)
8. Morrison, R., Brown, A.L., Carrick, R., Connor, R.C., Dearle, A., Atkinson, M.P.: Polymorphism, Persistence and Software Reuse in a Strongly Typed Object Oriented Environment. Software Engineering Journal 2(6), 199–204 (1987)
9. Atkinson, M.P., Buneman, O.P.: Types and Persistence in Database Programming Languages. ACM Computing Surveys 19(2), 105–190 (1987)
10. Atkinson, M.P., Buneman, O.P., Morrison, R.: Binding and Type Checking in Database Programming Languages. Computer Journal 31(2), 99–109 (1988)
11. Dearle, A., Brown, A.L.: Safe Browsing in a Strongly Typed Persistent Environment. Computer Journal 31(6), 540–544 (1988)
12. Brown, A.L.: Persistent Object Stores. PhD Thesis, University of St Andrews (1989),
http://www.cs.st-andrews.ac.uk/files/publications/download/Bro89.pdf
13. Connor, R.C.H., Brown, A.L., Cutts, Q.I., Dearle, A., Morrison, R., Rosenberg, J.: Type Equivalence Checking in Persistent Object Systems. In: Implementing Persistent Object Bases, Principles and Practice: 4th International Workshop on Persistent Object Systems (POS4), Martha's Vineyard, USA, pp. 151–164. Morgan Kaufmann, San Francisco (1990)
14. Cooper, R.L.: On the Utilisation of Persistent Programming Environments. PhD Thesis, University of Glasgow (1990)
15. Albano, A., Bergamini, R., Ghelli, G., Orsini, R.: An Object Data Model with Roles. In: Proc. 19th International Conference on Very Large Data Bases, Dublin, Ireland, pp. 39–51. Morgan Kaufmann, San Francisco (1993)
16. Connor, R.C.H., Morrison, R., Atkinson, M.P., Matthes, F., Schmidt, J.: Programming in Persistent Higher-Order Languages. In: Proc. European Systems Architecture Conference (Euro-ARCH 1993), Munich, Germany, pp. 288–300. Springer, Heidelberg (1993)
17. Morrison, R., Connor, R.C.H., Cutts, Q.I., Kirby, G.N.C., Stemple, D.: Mechanisms for Controlling Evolution in Persistent Object Systems. Journal of Microprocessors and Microprogramming 17(3), 173–181 (1993)

18. Morrison, R., Connor, R.C.H., Cutts, Q.I., Dunstan, V.S., Kirby, G.N.C.: Exploiting Persistent Linkage in Software Engineering Environments. Computer Journal 38(1), 1–16 (1995)
19. Maier, D.: Representing Database Programs as Objects. In: Proc. 1st International Workshop on Database Programming Languages, Roscoff, France, pp. 377–386. ACM Press/Addison-Wesley (1987)
20. Fowler, M.: Patterns of Enterprise Application Architecture. The Addison-Wesley Signature Series. Addison-Wesley, Reading (2002)
21. Atkinson, M.P., Morrison, R.: Orthogonally Persistent Object Systems. VLDB Journal 4(3), 319–401 (1995)
22. W3 Schools: PHP MySQL Select (2009),
    http://www.w3schools.com/PHP/php_mysql_select.asp
23. Sun Microsystems: JDBC Overview (1998),
    http://java.sun.com/products/jdbc/
24. Morrison, R.: S-Algol: A Simple Algol for Teaching. BCS Computer Bulletin 2(31) (1982)
25. Atkinson, M.P., Bailey, P.J., Chisholm, K.J., Cockshott, W.P., Morrison, R.: PS-Algol: A Language for Persistent Programming. In: Proc. 10th Australian National Computer Conference, Melbourne, Australia, pp. 70–79 (1983)
26. Morrison, R., Connor, R.C.H., Kirby, G.N.C., et al.: The Napier88 Persistent Programming Language and Environment. In: Atkinson, M.P., Welland, R. (eds.) Fully Integrated Data Environments, pp. 98–154. Springer, Heidelberg (1999)
27. Dearle, A.: On the Construction of Persistent Programming Environments. PhD Thesis, University of St Andrews (1988),
    http://www.cs.st-andrews.ac.uk/files/publications/download/Dea88.pdf
28. Connor, R.C.H.: Types and Polymorphism in Persistent Programming Systems. PhD Thesis, University of St Andrews (1990),
    http://www.cs.st-andrews.ac.uk/files/publications/download/Con90.pdf
29. Cutts, Q.I.: Delivering the Benefits of Persistence to System Construction and Execution. PhD Thesis, University of St Andrews (1992),
    http://www.cs.st-andrews.ac.uk/files/publications/download/Cut92.pdf
30. Kirby, G.N.C.: Reflection and Hyper-Programming in Persistent Programming Systems. PhD Thesis, University of St Andrews (1992),
    http://www.cs.st-andrews.ac.uk/files/publications/download/Kir92b.pdf
31. Kirby, G.N.C., Connor, R.C.H., Cutts, Q.I., Dearle, A., Farkas, A.M., Morrison, R.: Persistent Hyper-Programs. In: Persistent Object Systems: Proc. 5th International Workshop on Persistent Object Systems (POS5). Workshops in Computing, San Miniato, Italy, pp. 86–106. Springer, Heidelberg (1992)
32. Parrington, G.D., Shrivastava, S.K., Wheater, S.M., Little, M.C.: The Design and Implementation of Arjuna. USENIX Computing Systems Journal 8(3), 255–308 (1995)
33. Shrivastava, S., Dixon, G.N., Parrington, G.: An Overview of the Arjuna Distributed Programming System. IEEE Software, 66–73 (1991)
34. Atkinson, M.P., Daynes, L., Jordan, M.J., Printezis, T., Spence, S.: An Orthogonally Persistent JavaTM. ACM SIGMOD Record 25(4), 1–10 (1996)
35. Zirintsis, E., Dunstan, V.S., Kirby, G.N.C., Morrison, R.: Hyper-Programming in Java. In: Proc. 8th International Workshop on Persistent Object Systems (POS8), Tiburon, California, pp. 370–382. Morgan Kaufmann, San Francisco (1999)
36. Marquez, A., Zigman, J.N., Blackburn, S.M.: Fast Portable Orthogonally Persistent Java. Software – Practice and Experience, Special Issue on Persistent Object Systems 30(4), 449–479 (2000)

37. Carey, M.J., DeWitt, D.J., Franklin, M.J., Hall, N.E., McAuliffe, M., Naughton, J., Schuh, D.T., Solomon, M.H.: Shoring Up Persistent Applications. In: Proc. ACM SIGMOD International Conference on Management of Data, Minneapolis, MN, USA, pp. 383–394 (1994)
38. Dearle, A., Hulse, D., Farkas, A.: Operating System Support for Java. In: Proc. 1st International Workshop on Persistence for Java, Drymen, Scotland (1996)
39. Dittrich, K., Dayal, U. (eds.): Proc. of the 1986 International Workshop on Object-Oriented Database Systems, Pacific Grove, California, USA. IEEE Computer Society Press, Los Alamitos (1986)
40. Carey, M.: The Exodus Extensible DBMS Project: An Overview. In: Zdonik, S.B., Maier, D. (eds.) Readings in Object-Oriented Database Systems. Morgan Kaufman, San Francisco (1990)
41. Atkinson, M.P., Bancilhon, F., DeWitt, D.J., Dittrich, K., Maier, D., Zdonik, S.B.: The Object-Oriented Database Manifesto. In: Proc. 1st International Conference on Deductive and Object-Oriented Databases, Kyoto, Japan, pp. 223–240. Elsevier Science, Amsterdam (1989)
42. Richardson, J.E., Carey, M.J., Schuh, D.T.: The Design of the E Programming Language. ACM Transactions on Programming Languages and Systems 15(3), 494–534 (1993)
43. Cook, W.R., Rosenberger, C.: Native Queries for Persistent Objects: A Design White Paper (2006), http://www.cs.utexas.edu/users/wcook/papers/NativeQueries/NativeQueries8-23-05.pdf
44. Versant Corporation: db4o: Native Java &.NET Open Source Object Database (2009), http://www.db4o.com/
45. Versant Corporation: db4o Tutorial (2009), http://www.db4o.com/about/productinformation/resources/db4o-6.3-tutorial-java.pdf
46. Java Community Process: Java Data Objects (JDO) Specification (2004), http://www.jcp.org/en/jsr/detail?id=12
47. Sun Microsystems: Java Persistence API (2008), http://java.sun.com/javaee/technologies/persistence.jsp
48. Jordan, M.J., Atkinson, M.P.: Orthogonal Persistence for the Java Platform: Specification and Rationale. Technical Report Report TR-2000-94, Sun Microsystems (2000)
49. Dearle, A., Kirby, G.N.C., Norcross, S.J., McCarthy, A.J.: A Peer-to-Peer Middleware Framework for Resilient Persistent Programming. Technical Report Report CS/06/1, University of St Andrews (2006), http://www.cs.st-andrews.ac.uk/files/publications/download/DKN+06a.pdf
50. Fowler, M., Beck, K., Brant, J., Opdyke, W., Roberts, D.: Refactoring: Improving the Design of Existing Code. Object Technology Series. Addison Wesley, Reading (1999)
51. Neward, T.: Interoperability Happens – the Vietnam of Computer Science (2006), http://blogs.tedneward.com/2006/06/26/The+Vietnam+Of+Computer+Science.aspx
52. Danga Interactive: Memcached: A Distributed Memory Object Caching System (2009), http://www.danga.com/memcached/
53. Altinel, M., Luo, Q., Krishnamurthy, S., Mohan, C., Pirahesh, H., Lindsay, B.G., Woo, H., Brown, L.: DBCache: Database Caching for Web Application Servers. In: Proc. ACM SIGMOD International Conference on Management of Data, Madison, Wisconsin, p. 612 (2002)
54. Amazon: Amazon Simple Storage Service, Amazon S3 (2009), http://aws.amazon.com/s3/

Verification Technology for Object-Oriented/XML Transactions

Suad Alagić, Mark Royer, and David Briggs

Department of Computer Science
University of Southern Maine
Portland, ME 04104-9300
{alagic,mroyer,briggs}@usm.maine.edu

Abstract. Typically, object-oriented schemas are lacking declarative specification of the schema integrity constraints. Object-oriented transactions are also typically missing a fundamental ACID requirement: consistency. We present a developed technology based on object-oriented assertion languages that overcomes these limitations of persistent and database object systems. This technology allows specification of object-oriented integrity constraints, their static verification and dynamic enforcement. Proof strategies that are based on static and dynamic verification techniques as they apply to verification of object-oriented transactions are presented in the paper. Most of this work has been motivated by the problems of object-oriented interfaces to XML that have not been able to express typical XML Schema constraints, database constraints in particular. The components of this technology are an object-oriented constraint language, a verification system with advanced typing and logic capabilities, predefined libraries of object-oriented specification and verification theories, and an extended virtual platform for integrating constraints into the run-time type system and their management.

1 Introduction

Most persistent object and object database technologies lack the ability to express the schema integrity constraints in a declarative fashion, as is customary in conventional data models. The reason is that the mainstream object-oriented languages lack such declarative logic-based specification features. Specification of even the most typical database constraints is beyond expressiveness of object-oriented type systems of mainstream object-oriented languages. This is why the notion of a transaction in most object-oriented technologies does not include a fundamental ACID requirement: consistency. Since object-oriented schemas do not contain specification of general integrity constraints (and often not even keys and referential integrity) requiring that a transaction should satisfy those constraints becomes very problematic.

These limitations emerge when interfacing object-oriented technology with XML. Virtually all object-oriented interfaces to XML, as well as typed XML oriented languages, suffer from the inability to express constraints such as those

M.C. Norrie and M. Grossniklaus (Eds.): ICOODB 2009, LNCS 5936, pp. 23–40, 2010.

available in XML Schema [22]. These constraints include specification of the ranges of the number of occurrences, keys and referential integrity. A core idea behind type derivations in XML Schema is that an instance of a derived type may be viewed as a valid instance of its base type. This includes the requirement that all constraints associated with the base type are still valid when applied to an instance of a derived type.

Overcoming these limitations becomes possible with the proliferation of object-oriented assertion languages, such as JML [14] or Spec# [7]. Object-oriented assertion languages now allow both specification of the integrity constraints in object-oriented schemas and enforcing them when executing database transactions. In addition to specifying constraints that are sufficient for XML types, JML allows specification of mutation (update) of database state. Moreover, the notion of a transaction that updates the database state maintaining the integrity constraints of the database schema can now be specified in this technology. In fact, if the actual Java code is provided, it will be possible to enforce the requirement that a transaction must comply with the integrity constraints.

The availability of constraints makes it possible to use a prover technology for automated reasoning about a variety of properties expressed by constraints. This applies even to application properties that are not expressible in XML Schema. Thus, reasoning and verification are supported in situations when XML data is processed by a transaction or a general purpose programming language. While dynamic enforcement of constraints is a reality in the actual systems, our goal is to use a suitable prover technology to carry out deductions to statically verify properties expressed by constraints.

Our choice of PVS (Prototype Verification System) [15] is based on its sophisticated type system (including subtyping and bounded parametric polymorphism) accommodating a variety of logics with higher-order features. A PVS specification consists of a collection of theories. A theory is a specification of the required type signatures (of functions in particular) along with a collection of constraints in a suitable logic applicable to instances of the theory. Since PVS is a higher-order system it allows embedding of specialized logics as we did for temporal logic, applying the result to Java classes [2].

Our proof methodology for verification that a transaction respects the integrity of a schema equipped with constraintsrequires explicit specification of the frame constraints of a transaction. The frame constraints specify the integrity constraints which the transaction does not affect. In addition, the active part (the actual update) that a transaction performs is specified in a declarative, logic-based style, and the verification is carried out using a proof strategy presented in the paper. This methodology is independent of a particular transaction language [3]. Previous work on transaction verification includes [18,19,8,9,5].

The paper is organized as follows. In Sect. 2 we introduce a motivating example which illustrates the main problems in object-oriented representation of XML Schema constraints. Section 3 presents on overview of the architecture of our underlying software technology for specification, representation and management of constraints and their static and dynamic enforcement. Sections 4, 5, 6, and 7

show how XML Schema constraints and transactions are specified using JML.
In Sect. 8 and 9 we present our techniques for representing JML specifications
in PVS. This is followed by the transaction verification techniques presented
in Sect. 10. Section 11 shows how our extended virtual platform contributes to
the overall technology for management of constraints, and their enforcement in
transaction verification.

2   Motivation: XML Schema Constraints

Although the technology presented in this paper is a general object-oriented
constraint technology, a substantial part of the motivation comes from the problems of interfacing object-oriented persistent and database technology with XML
Schema [13]. A typical XML Schema constraint specifies the range of the number of occurrences of an XML term (an element or a group). This type of a
constraint is illustrated below by a type XMLproject specified according to the
XML Schema formalism.

```
<xsd:complexType name = "XMLproject"
   <xsd:sequence>
    <xsd:element name = "leader" type = "XMLprojectLeader" />
    <xsd:element name = "funds"  type = "xsd:positiveInteger" />
    <xsd:element name = "contract" type = "XMLcontract"
                            minOccurs = "1" maxOccurs = "5" />
   </xsd:sequence>
   <xsd:attribute name = "projectId" type = "xsd:string" />
</xsd: complexType>
```

XML Schema comes with two techniques for type derivation: by extension and
by restriction. Type derivation by extension can be represented using inheritance
in spite of some subtleties. However, object-oriented interfaces to XML cannot
represent type derivation by restriction because this form is, among other subtleties, based on restricting the range constraints of the base type in the type
derived by restriction. This is illustrated below by a type XMLspecialProject
derived by restriction from the type XMLproject. A special project is required
to have exactly one contract.

```
<xsd:complexType name = "XMLspecialProject"
   <xsd:complexContent>
    <xsd:restriction base = "XMLproject" >
     <xsd:sequence>
       <xsd:element name = "leader" type = "XMLprojectLeader" />
       <xsd:element name = "funds"
                     type = "xsd:positiveInteger" />
       <xsd:element name = "contract" type = "XMLcontract"
                              minOccurs = "1" maxOccurs = "1" />
     </xsd:sequence>
    <xsd:attribute name = "projectId" type = "xsd:string" />
   </xsd:complexContent>
</xsd:complexType>
```

A sample application schema in this paper consists of a sequence of projects and
a sequence of contracts. Specification of these two types in the XML Schema
formalism is given below. The range-of-occurrences constraints are such that
representing these types in object-oriented interfaces would not be a problem
using parametric types such as a sequence or a list. But if the range constraints
were more specific like in XMLproject and XMLspecialProject, object-oriented
interfaces could not represent them.

```
<xsd:complexType name = "XMLsequenceOfProjects"
    <xsd:sequence>
     <xsd:element name = "project" type = "XMLproject"
                 minOccurs = "0" maxOccurs = "unbounded" />
    </xsd:sequence>
</xsd:complexType>
<xsd:complexType name = "XMLsequenceOfContracts"
    <xsd:sequence>
     <xsd:element name = "contract" type = "XMLcontract"
                 minOccurs = "0" maxOccurs = "unbounded" />
    </xsd:sequence>
<xsd:complexType>
```

XML Schema also allows specification of typical database integrity constraints
such as keys and referential integrity. Project and contract keys are specified
below according to the XML Schema formalism, so that the attribute projectId
is a key for the sequence of projects and contractNo is a key for the sequence
of contracts. Object-oriented interfaces to XML such as DOM [11], LINQ to
XML [21] and LINQ to XSD [20] are constrained by the limitations of object-
oriented type systems. This is why they have no way of specifying any of these
constraints, because these constraints are not expressible in the standard object-
oriented type systems. The same applies to referential integrity constraints in
XML Schema illustrated below. This referential constraint specifies that the
contract numbers of contracts of a project must be valid, i.e., keys that actually
appear in the sequence of contracts.

```
<xsd:element name= "allContractsAndProjects">
    <xsd:complexType>
        <xsd:sequence>
           <xsd:element name = "Contracts"
                       type ="XMLSequenceOfContracts" />
           <xsd:element name = "Projects"
                       type = "XMLSequenceOfProjects" />
        </xsd:sequence>
    </xsd:complexType>

    <xsd:key name ="contractKey" />
       <xsd:selector xpath="./Contracts/contract" />
       <xsd:field xpath="@contractNo" />
    </xsd:key>
    <xsd:key name ="projectKey" />
```

```
      <xsd:selector xpath="./Projects/project" />
      <xsd:field xpath= "@projectId" />
   </xsd:key>
   <xsd:keyref name = "projectToContract" refer="contractKey">
      <xsd:selector xpath ="Projects/project/contract" />
      <xsd:field xpath ="@contractNo" />
   </xsd:keyref>
</xsd:element>
```

The new proposal for XML Schema 1.1 [22] includes even more general constraints specified as assertions that are based on Xpath expressions. Complex applications naturally contain other types of constraints that cannot be expressed in the XML Schema formalism and well-known object-oriented interfaces to XML cannot represent them either. The problem here is that object-oriented interfaces to XML are used in complex object-oriented software application packages that should enforce the application constraints.

3   Architecture

The underlying support of this technology is an extended virtual platform (XVP) implemented in a related project [17]. This platform allows declarative representation of constraints, introspection by extended reflective capabilities that report constraints along with the type signatures, and interfacing with a program

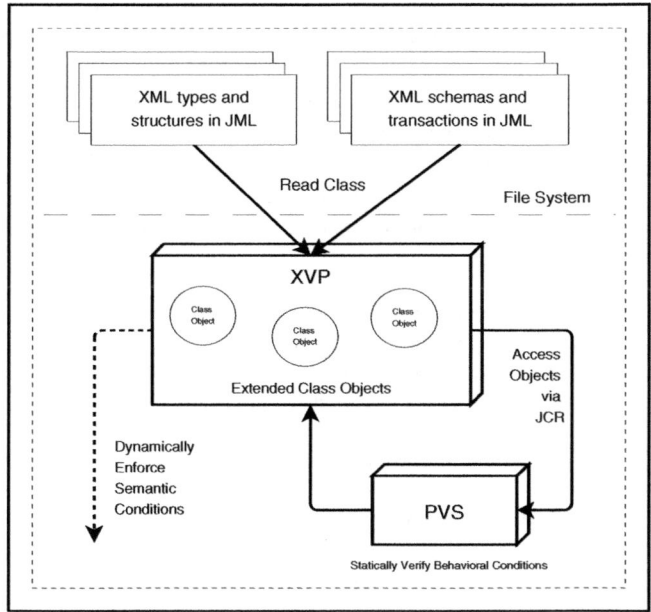

Fig. 1. Components of the technology

verification system. The components of this technology represented in Fig. 1 inter-operate as follows.

- Application schemas are specified in JML by extending our predefined library of JML specifications of the core of XML Schema.
- Application programs and transactions are also specified in JML and implemented in Java, so that JML constraints will be enforced at run-time.
- JML specifications are compiled by a special compiler [17]. The extended virtual platform [17] makes constraints available for introspection and enforcement.
- In order to carry out static verification the PVS theories relevant for the verification task are produced extending our predefined library of PVS theories for the XML Schema core.

This architecture makes a variety of verification techniques possible by combining static and dynamic techniques. If the constraints to be enforced dynamically are taken as assumptions, other constraints, database integrity in particular, may be provable statically. If so, the latter constraints will not have to be verified at run-time, increasing efficiency and reliability of transactions.

4   Object-Oriented Assertions

The JML representation of an XML element XMLproject is specified below. The three components of this specification are: the type information associated with an element type, the type signatures of accessor functions, and the constraints. In fact, the availability of constraints makes this representation possible. A complete and correct representation would not be possible in a type system alone as it requires constraints, like those expressible in JML.

A project element consists of three subelements (leader, contract and funds), and a single attribute (projectId). These are specified in the inner types (classes) ProjectElements and ProjectAttributes. The function elements returns project elements and the function attributes returns project attributes. Usage of parametric types appears in comments because their support in JML is still under development.

```
//    class XMLproject extends XMLelement<XMLcomplex>
public class XMLproject extends XMLelement {
    /*@ ensures this.elements().fundsConstraint() &&
                this.elements().rangeConstraint(); @*/
XMLproject(ProjectElements elements,
                ProjectAttributes attributes) {. . . }
/*@ pure @*/
public ProjectElements elements() { . . . }
/*@ pure @*/
public ProjectAttributes attributes() {. . . }

/*@ ensures \result <==> ((XMLfloat)this.elements().funds().
                value()).floatValue() >= 100000;  pure  @*/
```

```
public boolean fundsConstraint() {. . . }

/*@ ensures \result <==> this.elements().contract().occurs() >= 1
            && this.elements().contract().occurs() <= 5; pure @*/
public boolean rangeConstraint() {. . . }

/* specification of ProjectElements and ProjectAttributes */

/*@ invariant this.fundsConstraint() && this.rangeConstraint(); @*/
}
```

The JML representation technique of type derivation by restriction as defined in XML Schema is illustrated below. The type XMLspecialProject extends the type XMLproject using inheritance as specified in Java. There are no new components of XMLspecialProject in comparison with XMLproject, but the constraints in XMLspecialProject are strengthened with respect to the constraints in XMLproject. This corresponds to the XML Schema notion of type derivation by restriction, except that the constraints in our JML and PVS based technology can be much more general.

```
public class XMLspecialProject extends XMLproject {
// . . .
 /*@ also ensures this.fundsConstraint() <==>
 ((XMLfloat)this.elements().funds().
              value()).floatValue() >= 1000000;  pure @*/
 public boolean fundsConstraint() {. . .}

/*@ invariant this.elements().contract().maxOccurs() == 1; @*/
}
```

5   Application Schemas

A project management application schema XMLprojectManagement contains a sequence of contracts and a sequence of projects. This specification contains two constraints typical for database schemas and available in XML Schema. The **uniqueness** constraint specifies that contract numbers uniquely determine contracts in the sequence of contracts. The **referential** constraint specifies that contracts of projects in the sequence of projects exist in the sequence of contracts. In addition to the above two XML Schema types of constraints, the **ordering** constraint specifies that contracts appear in the sequence of contracts in increasing order of their contract numbers. There is also a self-explanatory **fundsRange** constraint. The **ordering** and the **fundsRange** constraints are samples of typical database constraints. But the advantage of using a general constraint language such as JML is that we can express more general constraints belonging to the application environment and enforce them. Application requirements typically go beyond the expressive capabilities of the constraint language for XML Schema or conventional database management systems.

```
public class XMLprojectManagement implements XMLschema {
/*@ pure @*/
public XMLsequence projects() {. . . }
    // XMLsequence<XMLproject> projects();
/*@ pure @*/
public XMLsequence contracts() {. . . }
    // XMLsequence<XMLcontract> contracts();

/*@ ensures \result <==> (\forall XMLcontract c1,c2;
            contracts().member(c1) && contracts().member(c2) &&
  c1.attributes().contractNo().equals
        (c2.attributes().contractNo()) ==> c1.equals(c2)); pure @*/
public boolean uniquenessConstraint() { . . .}

/*@ ensures \result <==> (\forall XMLproject p;(\forall XMLcontract c;
    projects().member(p) && p.elements(). contract().equals(c) ==>
            (\exists XMLcontract c1; contracts().member(c1) &&
                c.attributes().contractNo().equals
                (c1.attributes().contractNo()))))); pure @*/
public boolean referentialConstraint() { . . . }

/*@ ensures \result <==>(\forall XMLcontract c1,c2;(\forall int n1,n2;
            contracts().member(c1) & contracts().member(c2) &&
    c1.attributes().contractNo() <= c2.attributes().contractNo() &&
                        contracts().get(n1).equals(c1) &&
            contracts().get(n2).equals(c2) ==> n1 <= n2)); pure @*/
public boolean orderingConstraint() { . . . }

/*@ ensures \result <==> (\forall XMLproject p;
    projects().member(p) ==> p.fundsConstraint()); pure @*/

public boolean fundsRangeConstraint() {. . .}

/*@ also ensures \result <==> this.uniquenessConstraint() &&
        this.referentialConstraint() && this.orderingConstraint() &&
        this.fundsRangeConstraint();          pure @*/
public boolean consistent() { . . . }

/*@ invariant this.consistent(); @*/
}
```

6   Data Manipulation via Mutator Methods

Object-oriented interfaces to XML are largely intended for developing applications that manipulate the object-oriented representation of XML data. This is where the availability of constraints is critical to maintain data integrity. The existing object-oriented interfaces such as DOM [11], LINQ to XML [21] and LINQ to XSD [20] have no way of enforcing constraints of XML Schema in data manipulation actions. This becomes possible using object-oriented assertion languages. A few illustrative examples follow.

```
/*@ ensures this.fundsRangeConstraint(); @*/
void updateFunds(XMLelement amount) {. . .}
            // XMLelement<Float> amount

/*@ ensures this.fundsRangeConstraint() &&
            this.referentialConstraint(); @*/
void updateProjects(XMLsequence projects){. . .}
            // XMLsequence<XMLproject>

/*@ ensures this.uniquenessConstraint() &&
            this.orderingConstraint(); @*/
void updateContracts(XMLsequence contracts) {. . . }
            // XMLsequence<XML contract>
```

The above examples demonstrate some of the major advantages of the constraint-based approach with respect to the previous results. Enforcing the integrity constraints is a critical issue for database transactions that perform data manipulation. This cannot be accomplished with other approaches that are not based on constraints, but rather on type systems alone.

7   Transactions

Our JML specification of the class Transaction shares some similarity with the ODMG specification, but the ODMG specification does not have two critical ingredients: constraints and bounded parametric polymorphism [10]. The type constraint says that the actual type parameter must extend the type XMLschema. This is how a transaction is bound to its schema. In spite of all problems related to genericity in Java [1], this form of bounded parametric polymorphism is supported in the recent editions of Java. The JML assertions make it possible to specify the requirements that a transaction must respect the schema integrity constraints.

```
// abstract class XMLtransaction <T extends XMLschema>
abstract public class XMLtransaction {
// . . .
 /*@ pure @*/
 abstract XMLschema schema(); // T schema()
}
```

A specific transaction is specified below. The fact that this transaction is defined with respect to the XMLprojectManagement schema is represented using XMLprojectManagement as the actual type parameter. The constructor takes an instance of the XMLprojectManagement schema and makes it the schema of this transaction returned by the method schema.

The actual update that the transaction performs is specified in the method
update. This method requires that the schema consistency requirements are
satisfied before the update is executed. One of the conditions that this method
ensures after its execution is that the sequences of contracts before and after
execution of update are equal. In other words, this transaction does not affect
the sequence of contracts. In addition, the method update ensures that the
referential integrity constraint of the XMLprojectManagement schema holds after
method execution. The remaining part of the postcondition specifies the actual
update that the transaction performs which is increasing project funds by the
specified amount.

```
// class XMLprojectTransaction
//                        extends XMLtransaction<XMLprojectManagement>
public class XMLprojectTransaction extends XMLtransaction {
 XMLprojectTransaction(XMLprojectManagement schema) {. . . }

 /*@ pure @*/
 XMLprojectManagement schema(){. . . }

 /*@ ensures this.schema().contracts().equals(
                             \old(this.schema().contracts()))
     && this.schema().referentialConstraint() &&
  (\forall int n; 1 <= 1 && n <= this.schema().projects().length();
  ((XMLfloat)((XMLproject)this.schema().projects().get(n)).elements().
                   funds().value()).floatValue() ==
  \old(((XMLfloat)((XMLproject)this.schema().projects().get(n)).
             elements().funds().value()).floatValue()) + 1000 );  @*/
 void update(float increase) {. . . }
 }
```

Note that the result type of the method schema has been overridden covariantly
as in the recent editions of Java. If the method update is implemented in Java,
JML will dynamically enforce the above requirements. In the above example an
obvious question is whether the schema integrity constraints will indeed be satisfied if a transaction behaves according to the above specification. As even this
simple example shows, when the integrity constraints and transaction updates
become more complex, their verification requires support from a suitable prover
technology.

8   PVS Theories

In order to use the PVS prover, JML specifications must be transformed into
PVS theories, preferably by an automated tool. A PVS theory is a specification
of the required type signatures (of functions in particular) along with a collection of constraints in a suitable logic applicable to instances of the theory. Our
core techniques include representation of inheritance, method overriding and
parametric types.

PVS does not support the object-oriented notion of inheritance. Our PVS representation technique for inheritance has the following form:

```
A: THEORY                        B: THEORY
BEGIN A: TYPE                    BEGIN  IMPORTING A
% body of theory A                      B: TYPE FROM A
END A                               % body of theory B
                                 END B
```

In PVS the subtype declaration B: TYPE FROM A is equivalent to

```
B_pred: [A -> bool]
B: TYPE =(B_pred)
```

where (B_pred) denotes a type that satisfies B_pred. This is the PVS notion of predicate subtyping. The implications of the PVS notion of predicate subtyping on modeling inheritance of methods are elaborated in [2].

The PVS notion of predicate subtyping has the following implication on modeling inheritance of methods. A method m of A with the signature

   m: [A,C2,...,A,...,Cm -> A]

will be available in B with exactly the same signature, just like in the Java invariant subtyping rule for signatures of inherited methods. However, since B is a PVS subtype of A, the effect would be as if m is available in B with the signature m: [B,C2,...,B,...,Cm -> A]. Otherwise, overriding the signature of m in B to a signature such as

   m: [B,C2,...,B,...,Cm -> B]

which has covariant change of the result type as in recent editions of Java requires definition of a new function m in B.

Unlike the current version of JML, PVS supports parametric and even bounded parametric polymorphism. A theory representing a parametric type C with a bounded type constraint has the following form:

   C[(IMPORTING B) T: TYPE FROM B]

The fact that a theory K with a bound B for its type parameter T is representing a subclass of a parametric class C is represented in the PVS notation as follows:

```
K [(IMPORTING B) T: TYPE FROM B]
BEGIN
      IMPORTING C[T]
      K: TYPE FROM C[T]
% body of K
END K
```

9   Application-Oriented PVS Theories

Application-oriented PVS theories are illustrated in the specification XMLpro-ject given below. The type information for subelements and attributes is represented by record types. However, because of repetition of the subelement

contract, XMLproject is not represented as a record, since that would not be
an accurate representation with respect to XML. contract is a unique identifier in the record structure, and it gets repeated as the tag of any occurence
of this subelment in the XMLproject element. The repetition is expressed via
minOccurs and maxOccurs constraints and also by specifying the tag language
of XMLproject. In addition to the above two components (type structure and
constraints), the third component consists of accessor functions that apply to an
instance of an XMLproject. Note that the accessor function projectContracts
returns a sequence of XMLcontract elements.

```
XMLproject: THEORY
BEGIN
     IMPORTING  XMLcomplex, XMLcontract, XMLstring
     XMLproject: TYPE+ FROM XMLelement

  XMLprojectElements: TYPE  =  [# leader: string, funds: real,
                                  contract:  XMLcontract #]
  XMLprojectAttributes: TYPE = [# projectId: string #]

  project: [XMLprojectElements, XMLprojectAttributes -> XMLproject]
  elements:    [XMLproject -> XMLprojectElements]
  attributes: [XMLproject -> XMLprojectAttributes]

 p: VAR XMLproject
 leader(p): string = leader(elements(p))
 funds(p): real     = funds(elements(p))
 contract(p): XMLcontract = contract(elements(p))
 projectContracts: [XMLproject -> XMLsequence[XMLcontract]]

 fundsConstraint(p: XMLproject): bool =
                            (funds(elements(p))) >= 1000000

 contractElementsConstraint(p: XMLproject): bool =
         minOccurs(contract(elements(p))) >= 1 AND
         maxOccurs(contract(elements(p))) = unbounded

 elementTags(p: XMLproject): XMLtags =
         conCat(singleton(seq("leader")),
             conCat(singleton(seq("funds")),

                      starPlus(singleton(seq("contract")))) )
END XMLproject
```

Specification of the XMLprojectManagement schema now follows the initial JML
specification. The constraints specify the schema consistency requirements discussed earlier in the PVS notation.

```
XMLprojectManagement: THEORY
```

```
BEGIN
IMPORTING XMLcomplex, XMLcontract, XMLproject, XMLsequence, XMLschema
XMLprojectManagement: TYPE+  FROM XMLschema

   projects:    [XMLprojectManagement -> XMLsequence[XMLproject]]
   contracts:   [XMLprojectManagement -> XMLsequence[XMLcontract]]

M: VAR XMLprojectManagement
p: VAR XMLproject
c: VAR XMLcontract

uniquenessConstraint(M): bool =  (FORALL (c1,c2: XMLcontract):
      member(contracts(M),c1) AND member(contracts(M),c2) AND
      contractNo(contractAttributes(c1)) =
          contractNo(contractAttributes(c2))  IMPLIES c1 = c2)

referentialConstraint(M): bool = (FORALL (p,c):
  (member(projects(M),p) AND contract(elements(p)) = c) IMPLIES
    (EXISTS (c1:XMLcontract):(member(contracts(M),c1) AND
          (contractNo(contractAttributes(c1)) =
                      contractNo(contractAttributes(c))))))

orderingConstraint(M): bool = (FORALL (c1,c2: XMLcontract,
                          n1,n2: below(length(contracts(M)))):
              member(contracts(M),c1) AND member(contracts(M),c2)
          AND  contractNo(contractAttributes(c1)) <=
                      contractNo(contractAttributes(c2)) AND
                      nth(contracts(M))(n1) = c1 AND
                  nth(contracts(M))(n2) = c2 IMPLIES n1 <= n2)

 fundsRange(M): bool = (FORALL (n: below(length(projects(M)))):
                      fundsConstraint(nth(projects(M))(n)))

 consistent(M): bool = uniquenessConstraint(M) AND
                      referentialConstraint(M) AND
                      orderingConstraint(M)  AND
                      fundsRange(M)
END XMLprojectManagement
```

10   Transaction Verification in PVS

A transaction theory XMLprojectTransaction contains specification of both
the frame constraint and the actual update that the transaction performs [3].
The frame constraint specifies the integrity constraints that are not affected by
the transaction. This particular transaction only updates contract funds and
hence it has no impact on the uniqueness, referential, and ordering constraints.
Explicit specification of the frame constraints is essential in our proof strategy
that guides the prover appropriately. The actual update that the transaction

performs is specified in a declarative fashion as a predicate over a pair of object states, the state before and the state after transaction execution. A transaction is then a binary predicate specified as a conjunction of its frame constraint and the actual update constraint.

```
XMLprojectTransaction: THEORY
BEGIN
      IMPORTING XMLtransaction, XMLprojectManagement
      XMLprojectTransaction: TYPE FROM XMLtransaction
      M1,M2: VAR XMLprojectManagement

 frameAx(M1,M2): bool = consistent(M1) AND
        contracts(M1) = contracts(M2) AND referentialConstraint(M2)

 update(M1,M2): bool =  length(projects(M1)) = length(projects(M2))
                  AND  FORALL (n: below(length(projects(M2)))):
                      (funds(elements(nth(projects(M2))(n))) =
                  funds(elements(nth(projects(M1))(n))) + 100000)

 transaction(M1,M2): bool = frameAx(M1,M2) AND update(M1,M2)
END XMLprojectTransaction
```

In order to prove that a transaction which conforms to the above theory maintains the integrity of the XMLprojectManagment database, the following theory is constructed. To simplify the proof, a simple update lemma is proved first. The integrity theorem is then proved using the update lemma [3].

```
VerifyProjectTransaction: THEORY
BEGIN
      IMPORTING XMLprojectTransaction
      M1,M2: VAR XMLprojectManagement

updateLemma: LEMMA fundsRange(M1) AND update(M1,M2)
                        IMPLIES  fundsRange(M2)
Integrity: THEOREM FORALL (M1,M2):
      consistent(M1) AND transaction(M1,M2) IMPLIES consistent(M2)
END VerifyProjectTransaction
```

Consider an example of a characterization of a transaction update that violates the referential integrity constraint and hence its Integrity theorem fails. Let us define badUpdate as

```
badUpdate(M1,M2): bool = length(projects(M1)) > 0 AND
      projects(M2) = projects(M1) AND length(contracts(M2)) = 0
```

This update does not affect the sequence of projects but it deletes all contracts which is an obvious violation of referential integrity. The PVS proof of the updateLema leads to an obvious contradiction demonstrating violation of integrity.

11   Virtual Platform Support

In this section we show an example of combination of static and dynamic verification of a transaction that relies on the support of the extended virtual platform [17]. The main components of an extended virtual platform are given in
Fig. 2.

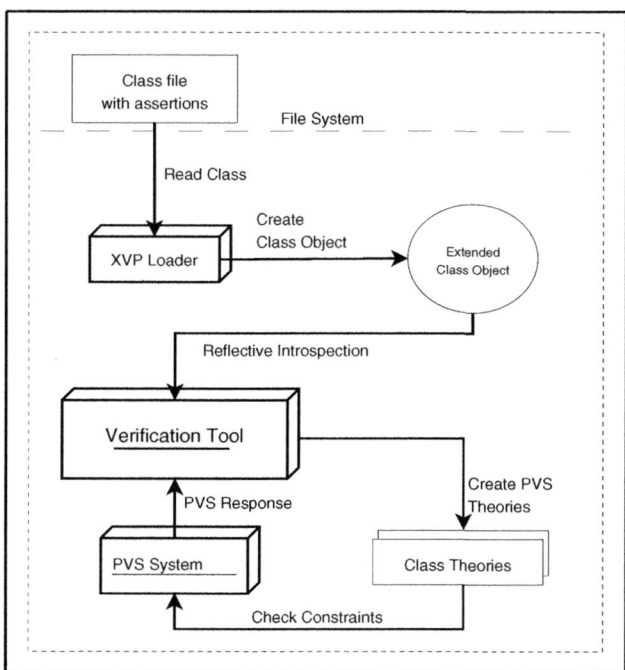

Fig. 2. Verification in the extended virtual platform

The existing Java reflective capabilities allow introspection of type signatures
and the extended virtual platform allows introspection of the constraints associated with those types. Constraints are reported by the extended reflective
capabilities in their logic-based declarative style. This is a major distinction in
comparison with existing virtual platforms, and JML in particular.

This system is designed in such a way that it is independent of a particular constraint language and its underlying logic basis. The program verification
system accesses loaded class objects through a tool that makes use of extended
reflective capabilities. The interface component produces a program verification
theory of a class and the program verification system carries out deduction and
reports the results.

The Java Core Reflection (JCR) classes that have been extended are `Class`,
`Constructor`, and `Method`. These extensions are based on new types such as

Invariant, PreCondition, and PostCondition. With these new types it becomes possible to add method preconditions and postconditions to the class Method, and the class invariant to the class Class. These assertions require further types that make it possible to create objects that represent logical formulas for constraints. In order to achieve independence of a particular constraint language and its logic basis, the types representing logical formulas are specified as abstract classes. These classes must be extended for a particular assertion language as we did for JML.

Additions of the recompiled class Class allow access to the declared and the inherited invariant. The extensions of the class Method allow access to (declared and inherited) preconditions and postconditions. The class Constructor is similarly extended.

```
public final class Class { ...
  public Invariant getInvariant();
}
public final class Method { ...
 public PostCondition  getPostCondition();
 public PreCondition   getPreCondition();
}
```

Each one of the above assertion types is also equipped with the method evaluate for run-time evaluation of the assertion objects. The differences in the signatures of these methods are in their parameters and reflect the nature of the assertions. Postcondition is also equipped with a method to bind parameters taking into account both the object state before and after method execution.

In the example given below, the method executeProjectTransaction is written with the assumption that static verification of the transaction proTransaction has been carried out. Static verification proves that if proManagement is consistent and the transaction proTransaction is executed, proManagement will remain consistent. The consistency predicate is in fact the invariant of the object proManagement.

Dynamic verification requires access to the precondition of the method update of proTransaction and the invariant of the object proManagement. This is done by extended reflection. If these two conditions evaluate to true, the update method is invoked using standard reflection. Upon execution of this method its postcondition is evaluated using extended reflection. If it evaluates to true then we know that the invariant will hold and hence it does not have to be checked dynamically. If the postcondition does not hold the transaction proTransaction is aborted. Otherwise it is committed.

```
executeProjectTransaction(XMLprojectManagement proManagement,
                    XMLprojectTransaction proTransaction,
                    XMLfloat amount) throws Exception
{ proTransaction.start();
  Invariant inv = proManagement.getClass().getInvariant();
  Method update = proTransaction.getClass().getMethod("update",
                        new Class[]{XMLfloat.class});
```

```
Object[] params = new Object[]{amount};
PreCondition preCond = update.getPreCondition();
PostCondition postCond = update.getPostCondition();
postCond.bindPreMethodVars(proTransaction,params);

if (inv.evaluate (proManagement) &&
              preCond.evaluate(proTransaction,params))
    update.invoke(proTransaction,params);

  if (postCond.evaluate(proTransaction,null,params))
    proTransaction.commit();
  else proTransaction.abort();
}
```

12 Conclusions

Specification, representation and enforcement of constraints has been a major factor of the impedance mismatch between object-oriented and data languages. In this paper we showed that interfacing object-oriented database technology with XML technology also stumbles on the problems of constraints, such as those available in XML Schema. Resolving the object-oriented/XML mismatch will be possible only in a constraint-based technology of the kind presented in this paper.

Object-oriented schemas that are based on object-oriented languages and their type systems cannot express the integrity constraints typical for either database schemas or dictated by the semantics of the application environment. The current underlying architecture of object-oriented assertion languages typically allows dynamic enforcement. We make two contributions that are relevant to transactions in particular.

The first contribution is to provide a virtual platform that integrates constraints with the run-time type system making the constraints available by reflection. This makes the integrity constraints of a schema visible by transactions and application programs in general. This platform allows a variety of constraint management and enforcement scenarios.

The second contribution is in the usage of a verification system to statically verify at least some integrity constraints. In fact, it is the combination of dynamic and static verification that that we applied to transactions to decrease the cost of dynamic checking of database integrity constraints.

The complexity of verification systems such as PVS requires development of proof strategies [6] specifically targeted to verification of object-oriented transactions and to interfacing with XML technology. A sample strategy is given in the paper as it applies to transaction verification. These tailored proof strategies and more friendly user interfaces are a key requirement in making these tools accessible to database programmers.

References

1. Alagić, S., Royer, M.: Genericity in Java: Persistent and database system implications. The VLDB Journal (2007), http://www.springerlink.com/content/a0671813x8p28724/
2. Alagić, S., Royer, M., Crews, D.: Temporal verification of Java-like classes. In: Proceedings of FTfJP 2006 (2006), http://www.disi.unige.it/person/AnconaD/FTfJP06/
3. Alagić, S., Royer, M., Briggs, D.: Program verification techniques for XML Schema-based technologies. In: Proceedings of ICSOFT, vol. 2, pp. 86–93 (2006)
4. Alagić, S., Royer, M.: Next generation of virtual platforms, http://www.odbms.org/experts.aspx#article4
5. Alagić, S., Logan, J.: Consistency of Java transactions. In: Lausen, G., Suciu, D. (eds.) DBPL 2003. LNCS, vol. 2921, pp. 71–89. Springer, Heidelberg (2004)
6. Archer, M., Di Vito, B., Munoz, C.: Developing user strategies in PVS: A tutorial. In: Proceedings of STRATA 2003 (2003)
7. Barnett, M., Leino, K.R.M., Schulte, W.: The Spec# programming system: an overview, Microsoft Research 2004. Also in Proceedings of CASSIS 2004 (2004)
8. Benzaken, V., Doucet, D.: Themis: A database language handling integrity constraints. VLDB Journal 4, 493–517 (1994)
9. Benzanken, V., Schaefer, X.: Static integrity constraint management in object-oriented database programming languages via predicate transformers. In: Aksit, M., Matsuoka, S. (eds.) ECOOP 1997. LNCS, vol. 1241, pp. 60–84. Springer, Heidelberg (1997)
10. Cattell, R.G.G., Barry, D., Berler, M., Eastman, J., Jordan, D., Russell, C., Schadow, O., Stanienda, T., Velez, F.: The Object Data Standard: ODMG 3.0. Morgan Kaufmann, San Francisco (2000)
11. Document Object Model (DOM), http://www.w3.org/TR/REC-DOM-Level-1/
12. Fan, W., Simeon, J.: Integrity constraints for XML. Journal of Computer and System Sciences 66, 254–291 (2003)
13. Lammel, R., Meijer, E.: Revealing the X/O impedance mismatch. Microsoft Corporation (2007), http://homepages.cwi.nl/~ralf/xo-impedance-mismatch/paper.pdf
14. Leavens, G.T., Poll, E., Clifton, C., Cheon, Y., Ruby, C., Cook, D., Muller, P., Kiniry, J.: JML Reference Manual, draft (July 2005), http://www.cs.iastate.edu/~leavens/JML/
15. Owre, S., Shankar, N., Rushby, J.M., Stringer-Clavert, D.W.J.: PVS Language Reference, SRI International, Computer Science Laboratory, Menlo Park, California
16. Owre, S., Shankar, N.: Writing PVS proof strategies, Computer Science Laboratory, SRI International, http://www.csl.sri.com
17. Royer, M., Alagić, S., Dillon, D.: Reflective constraint management for languages on virtual platforms. Journal of Object Technology 6, 59–79 (2007)
18. Sheard, T., Stemple, D.: Automatic verification of database transaction safety. ACM Transactions on Database Systems 14, 322–368 (1989)
19. Spelt, D., Even, S.: A theorem prover-based analysis tool for object-oriented databases. In: Cleaveland, W.R. (ed.) TACAS 1999. LNCS, vol. 1579, pp. 375–389. Springer, Heidelberg (1999)
20. LINQ to XSD, Microsoft (2007), http://blogs.msdn.com/xmlteam/archive/2006/11/27/typed-xml-programmer-welcome-to-linq.aspx
21. LINQ to XML, Microsoft (2006), http://www.xlinq.net/
22. XML Schema 1.1, http://www.w3.org/XML/Schema

Compiler Plugins Can Handle Nested Languages: AST-Level Expansion of LINQ Queries for Java

Miguel Garcia

Institute for Software Systems (STS)
Hamburg University of Technology (TUHH), Germany
miguel.garcia@tuhh.de
http://www.sts.tu-harburg.de/people/mi.garcia

Abstract. The integration of database and programming languages is made difficult by the different data models and type systems prevalent in each field. Functional-object query languages contribute to bridge this gap by letting software developers write declarative queries without imposing any specific execution strategy. Although some query optimizers support this paradigm, Java provides no means to embed queries in a seamless and typesafe manner. Interestingly, the benefits of such grammar extension (compile-time type inference and checking, user-friendly syntax) can alternatively be achieved with a *compiler plugin* as discussed in this paper for the LINQ query language and two Java compilers (from Sun and Eclipse). A prototype confirms the benefits of the approach by automating at compile-time (a) the parsing of LINQ queries nested in Java, (b) their analysis for well-formedness, and (c) their rewriting into statements to build Abstract Syntax Trees (ASTs). The technique is also applicable to other languages (JPQL, XQuery) which are handled nowadays by a Java compiler as uninterpreted strings, being thus prone to runtime exceptions due to breaches of static semantics.

1 Introduction

The Microsoft project *Language Integrated Query* (LINQ for short) has raised the bar for data access in mainstream programming languages by introducing query-related constructs as first-class citizens. These constructs include relational operations (*e.g.*, projections, selections, joins) as well as the more fundamental functional operations *map*, *filter*, and *flatMap* (which LINQ calls `Select`, `Where`, and `SelectMany`). The underlying semantic foundation, *list comprehensions* [1], makes LINQ amenable to well-known optimizations [2,3] that compute efficient access plans at runtime. Because of this, a Java integration of LINQ does not involve devising new query compilation techniques but applying instead existing scientific knowledge in the context of language and compiler engineering.

This paper addresses just such engineering problem in a portable manner (across Java compilers from different vendors, across different IDEs) by relying on a *compiler plugin* to extend (but not modify) a Java batch compiler. All

M.C. Norrie and M. Grossniklaus (Eds.): ICOODB 2009, LNCS 5936, pp. 41–58, 2010.

along, the original syntax of LINQ is supported without extending the Java grammar, using the error reporting conventions of the host language. Therefore, our prototype can simply be added to existing toolchains for build automation facilitating real-world adoption. The methodology in question also paves the way for other proofs of concept, for example adapting to Java innovative compilation strategies that straddle the database/virtual machine divide [4,5,6].

Our contributions are twofold. First, we give a denotational semantics for LINQ and make explicit the reasoning behind the translation from LINQ into its lower-level, comprehension-style formulation (*Standard Query Operators*, SQO [7]). The LINQ specification glosses over many of the issues involved and lacks a treatment of the confluence of the rewriting process. We cover these aspects, given their importance for a future standardization of LINQ for Java. As second contribution, a technique is presented to realize compile-time program transformations for Java. Unlike other approaches that demand deep knowledge about the internals of a compiler, the proposed technique enables lightweight language embedding as demonstrated for LINQ query expansion.

The structure of this paper is as follows. Background is provided in Sect. 2 on current approaches to language embedding in Java, an issue relevant to the ODBMS, ORM, and RDBMS communities. The syntax and semantics of LINQ are presented in Sect. 3 thus making the paper self-contained. Section 4 covers the translation of LINQ into SQO building blocks, as well as aspects of language design (side-effects and variable capture). Adapting our approach to other query languages (XQuery, JPQL) is facilitated by the discussion in Sect. 5 of the implementation of our prototype. Finally, the two last sections offer an overview of related work (Sect. 6) and discuss conclusions and areas for future work (Sect. 7). Knowledge is assumed from the reader about database query languages as well as familiarity with compiler terminology.

A prototype (`LINQExpand4Java`) realizing this approach can be downloaded from `http://www.sts.tu-harburg.de/people/mi.garcia/LINQExpand4Java`

2   Language Embedding and Static Semantics

Language extensions, as in the Microsoft implementation of LINQ, require a heavyweight modification of a compiler or the use of a pre-processor. Besides the higher development cost, combining independently developed extensions is impossible, as each front-end rejects all extensions but the one it understands. This explains the renewed interest in *language embedding* for Domain-Specific Languages (DSLs), which fosters an agile approach to language engineering. The original syntax of the host language is kept, while looking for opportunities to express AST building in a visually appealing manner. For example[1]:

```
final Sql sql = Select(ARTICLE.NAME, ARTICLE.ARTICLE_NO)
               .from(ARTICLE)
               .where(ARTICLE.OID.in(named("article_oid")))
               .toSql();
```

---

[1] JEQUEL: SQL embedded in Java, `http://www.jequel.de/`

The previous example not only resembles SQL but moreover is *typesafe*, *i.e.*, the type system of the host language enforces (most) Well-Formedness Rules (WFRs) of the embedded language. Kabanov and Raudjärv [8] provide a comprehensive review of the relevant design patterns (Fluent Interface, Query Builder, reification of the database schema, etc.). Common to all proposals (Native Queries[2], Criteria API[3], etc.) is the limitation that queries are not portable among, say, Java, C#, and Ruby. We reserve the term *nested language* for DSLs that can be reused verbatim across platforms and host languages.

In our context, techniques originally developed for embedded DSLs (EDSLs) are also of interest because *query expansion* takes as input a *nested query* producing statements conforming to an *embedded DSL* (albeit one not intended for direct editing by developers). Thus, the succinctness of nested syntax is combined with the ability to target existing EDSLs.

Both nested and embedded DSLs rely on a facility to import database schema information into the program namespace (*schema awareness*) as an aid to typechecking. This task is made cumbersome by the variety of formats in use today (*i.e.*, the ODMG 3.0 object model [9, Chap. 2] [10], the LINQ Entity Data Model[4], and the JSR-317 Schema Metamodel [11, p. 12] used in `orm.xml`).

Both the nesting and the embedding approach aim at checking at compile time that queries are (a) syntactically correct, (b) well-typed and compliant with the database schema, and (c) robust to cope with *breaking changes* due to schema renamings. Proponents of EDSLs achieve (a) and (b) with library reuse and class generation [8], while (c) is attained by making queries participate in IDE-performed refactorings. However, this IDE functionality cannot be reused for Nested DSLs, their syntax differing radically from that of the host language. Upon breaking schema changes (renamings or others) a compiler plugin signals broken nested queries, for the developer to manually repair. Given our previous work on generators for EDSLs [12] we explored that alternative first, only to realize that encapsulating all well-formedness and schema checks in the compiler plugin (as per the Nested DSL approach) meets all the essential requirements in a modular way, the only shortcomings being the lack of support for refactoring and the fragility resulting from developers tinkering with the generated code.

The code snippet below shows an excerpt of the statements generated by `LINQExpand4Java` before translating into SQO, whose expansion is more verbose.

```
// from entry in contacts select new EmailAddr(entry.name, entry.email)
import static linqtextual.LinqtextualExprBuilder.*; ...
NewExprTraditional newExpr0 = newExprTraditional()
    .fqTypeName("EmailAddr").args(member0, member1).toAST();
SelectClause selClause0 = selectClause().result(newExpr0).toAST();
QueryBody queryBody0 = queryBody().clauses().result(selClause0).toAST();
QueryExpr finalQuery = queryExpr().from(fromClause().var(entry0)
    .inExpr(contacts0).toAST()).body(queryBody0).toAST();
```

---

[2] http://www.db4o.com/about/productinformation/whitepapers
[3] http://in.relation.to/Bloggers/ATypesafeCriteriaQueryAPIForJPA
[4] http://msdn.microsoft.com/en-us/library/bb387122.aspx

3   Syntax and Semantics of LINQ

The state of the art of O/R mapping on the platform Microsoft .NET 3.5 is defined by the combination of three technologies: (1) a functional query language, LINQ; (2) a software component (the Entity Framework [13]) in charge of bidirectional, automatically invertible, O/R mapping [14]; and (3) a LINQ-aware Integrated Development Environment (IDE) offering usability features such as syntax completion. The concepts underlying LINQ are however platform-independent and thus our clean-room implementation for Java based on publicly available specifications only.

The textual syntax of LINQ has been designed for readability and not for direct evaluation, which requires a previous translation step. For example, the query `from x in numbers where x>0 select 2*x` actually stands for the following C# code: `numbers.Where(x => x>0).Select(2*x)`. LINQ can query data sources that behave as streams (*i.e.*, that support a minimal *open/next/close* iterator interface). In the example, each number `x` is tested (with the predicate given by the lambda expression `x => x>0`) to decide whether to include `2*x` in the result (another stream).

The expressiveness of functional-object query languages [15] calls for optimization techniques to achieve performance competitive with manually tuned "native" queries (in the dialect supported by a particular persistence engine). For read-only queries all the techniques devised to speed up the evaluation of list comprehensions are applicable: deforestation [16, Chap. 7], removal of nested loops [3], join graph isolation [17], and memoization [18], to name a few. Optimizations for the main-memory case have also been devised [2,19,20].

3.1   Syntax

In its simplest form, a LINQ query begins with a `from` clause and ends with either a `select` or `group` clause. In between, zero or more *query body clauses* can be found (`from`, `let`, `where`, `join` or `orderby`). Queries may be nested: the collection over which a `from` variable ranges may itself be a query. A similar effect can be achieved by appending `into variable` S_2 to a subquery S_1: with that, S_1 is used as generator for S_2. The fragment `into variable` S_2 is called a *query continuation*.

A `join` clause tests for equality the key of an inner-sequence item with that of of an outer-sequence item, yielding a pair for each successful match. An `orderby` clause reorders the items of the incoming stream using one or more keys, each with its own sorting direction and comparator function. The ending `select` or `group` clause determines the shape of the result in terms of variables in scope.

The detailed structure of LINQ phrases is captured by the grammar in Tab. 1 (listing LINQ-proper productions, with *QueryExp* being the entry rule) and in Tab. 2 (listing other syntactic domains). In order to save space, well-known productions have been omitted (*e.g.*, those for arithmetic expressions). The notation conventions in the grammar follow Turbak and Gifford [21]. Terminals are enumerated (*e.g.*, for the syntactic domain *Direction*). Compound syntactic

Table 1. LINQ-related production rules

$$Q \in \text{QueryExp} ::= F_{from} \;\; QB_{qbody}$$

$$F \in \text{FromClause} ::= \text{from} \;\; T_{type}^{0..1} \;\; V_{var} \;\; \text{in} \;\; E_{in}$$

$$QB \in \text{QueryBody} ::= B_{qbclauses}^{0..\,*} \;\; SG_{sel\_gby} \;\; QC_{qcont}^{0..1}$$

$$B \in \text{BodyClause} = (\text{FromClause} \cup \text{LetClause} \cup \text{WhereClause}$$
$$\cup \; \text{JoinClause} \cup \text{JoinIntoClause} \cup \text{OrderByClause})$$

$$QC \in \text{QueryCont} ::= \text{into} \;\; V_{var} \;\; QB_{qbody}$$

$$H \in \text{LetClause} ::= \text{let} \;\; V_{lhs} \;\; \text{=} \;\; E_{rhs}$$

$$W \in \text{WhereClause} ::= \text{where} \;\; E_{booltest}$$

$$J \in \text{JoinClause} ::= \text{join} \;\; T_{type}^{0..1} \;\; V_{innervar} \;\; \text{in} \;\; E_{innerexp}$$
$$\text{on} \;\; E_{lhs} \;\; \text{equals} \;\; E_{rhs}$$

$$K \in \text{JoinIntoClause} ::= J_{jc} \;\; \text{into} \;\; V_{result}$$

$$O \in \text{OrderByClause} ::= \text{orderby} \;\; U_{orderings}^{1..\,*\; <separator:,>}$$

$$U \in \text{Ordering} ::= E_{ord} \;\; Direction_{dir}$$

$$Direction \in \{ \text{ascending, descending} \}$$

$$S \in \text{SelectClause} ::= \text{select} \;\; E_{selexp}$$

$$G \in \text{GroupClause} ::= \text{group} \;\; E_{e1} \;\; \text{by} \;\; E_{e2}$$

domains are sets of phrases built out of other phrases. Such domains are annotated with *domain variables*, which are referred from the right-hand-side of productions. References, *e.g.* $QC_{qcont}^{0..1}$ (which ranges over the *QueryContinuation* domain) are subscripted with a *label* later used to denote particular child nodes in the transformations rules. The superscript of a reference indicates the allowed range of occurrences.

LINQ is mostly implicitly typed: only variables in `from` or `join` clauses may optionally be annotated with type casts. Several ambiguities have to be resolved with arbitrary lookahead (*e.g.*, to distinguish between a *JoinClause* and a *JoinIntoClause*) requiring rule priorities or syntactic predicates [22].

3.2   Semantics

The "official" semantics of LINQ is given by translation into query operators [7] whose counterparts in the `Data.List` Haskell library make for a viable denotational semantics [21]. Still, a LINQ-level semantics is useful to determine (a) whether two queries are equivalent, or (b) whether a rewritten SQO formulation is semantically equivalent to the original LINQ query. The denotational

Table 2. Other syntactic domains

$Id,\ V \in \text{Identifier} = (\ (\texttt{[a-zA-Z][a-zA-Z0-9]}*) - \text{Keyword}\ )$

$SG \in (\text{SelectClause} \cup \text{GroupByClause})$

$E \in \text{Exp} = (\text{QueryExp} \cup \text{ArithExp} \cup \text{BoolExp} \cup \text{UnaryExp}$
$\qquad\qquad \cup \text{BinaryExp} \cup \text{PrimaryExp} \cup \text{DotSeparated} \cup \dots)$

$EL \in \text{ExpOrLambda} = (\text{Exp} \cup \text{Lambda})$

$P \in \text{PrimaryExp} = (\text{Application} \cup \text{QueryExp} \cup \text{NewExp} \cup \text{PrimitiveLit} \cup \dots)$

$T \in \text{TypeName} ::= Id_{fragments}^{1..*\ <separator:.>}$

$D \in \text{DotSeparated} ::= P_{pre}\ .\ P_{post}$

$A \in \text{Application} ::= Id_{head}\ Cast_{cast}^{0..1}\ (\ EL_{args}^{0..*\ <separator:,>}\ )$

$L \in \text{Lambda} ::= (\ Id_{params}^{0..*\ <separator:,>}\ )\ \texttt{=>}\ E_{body}$

---

semantics of LINQ given in this section (originally outlined by Wes Dyer[5]) is also necessary to guarantee that each LINQ → LINQ simplification step (Sect. 4) is semantics preserving. Determining the equivalence of two arbitrary queries is in general undecidable [23, Chap. 8], but the proof is simpler for a transformation affecting a sub-expression in a compositional manner. Automated proof of query equivalence for a functional-object language (Entity SQL) is addressed by Mehra *et al.* [24].

The semantic foundation of LINQ, list comprehensions, is summarized next.

In the list comprehension $[e \mid e_1 \dots e_n]$ each e_i is a qualifier, which can either be a generator of the form $v \leftarrow E$, where v is a variable and E is a sequence-valued expression, or a filter p (a boolean valued predicate). Informally, each generator $v \leftarrow E$ sequentially binds variable v to the items in the sequence denoted by E, making it visible in successive qualifiers. A filter evaluating to *true* results in successive qualifiers (if any) being evaluated under the current bindings, otherwise 'backtracking' takes place. The *head* expression e is evaluated for those bindings that satisfy all filters, and taken together these values constitute the resulting sequence. A *let* expression in a comprehension provides local bindings visible in successive qualifiers (generators, filters, let expressions) as well as in the head of the comprehension. For example [1], the SQL query `select dept, sum(salary) from employees group by dept` is expressed in Haskell as:

```
let depts = asSet [ dept | (name, dept, salary) <- employees ]
in [ (dept, sum[salary | (name, dept', salary) <- employees,
     dept == dept']) | dept <- depts ]
```

---

[5] http://blogs.msdn.com/wesdyer/archive/2006/12/26/
a-model-for-query-interpretation.aspx

The denotational semantics of LINQ gives meaning to a query in terms of its syntax components. An auxiliary definition and two kinds of valuation functions are needed. A *binding-set* $\mathcal{B} \equiv \{v_1 \mapsto t_1, \ldots\}$ is a finite map from non-duplicate variables v_i to values t_i. We write $v_i \mapsto t_i$ as a shorthand for the pair (v_i, t_i). LINQ forbids declaring a variable whose name would hide another, so a non-ordered map is enough. As usual, an expression E can be evaluated *in the context of* $\mathcal{B}$ by induction on its syntactic structure, with a non-defining occurrence of variable v evaluating to its image t under $\mathcal{B}$.

The kinds of valuation functions are: (1) $[\![Q]\!] envs$ denotes the sequence of binding-sets generated by Q (a query body) given the *incoming* sequence of binding-sets $envs$; while (2) $[\![E]\!](env)$ denotes the evaluation of E in the context of the single binding-set env. To simplify the formulation of the valuation functions, a query is regarded as a sequence S of body clauses Q, resulting from having desugared query continuations into subqueries (Sect. 4).

The valuation $[\![Q]\!] envs$ denotes simply the (sub-)query results when Q is a *SelectClause* or a *GroupByClause*:

$$[\![\texttt{select } E_{selexp}]\!] envs \stackrel{\text{def}}{=} [\ [\![selexp]\!](env) \mid env \leftarrow envs\ ] \tag{1}$$

Informally speaking, `group result by key` returns a *grouping*, i.e. a finite *ordered* map with entries $key \mapsto cluster$, a cluster being a sequence of results. The valuation of *GroupByClause* involves a left-fold, taking an empty grouping as initial value and progressively adding the valuation of *result* to the cluster given by the valuation of *key*. Using Haskell,

$$[\![\texttt{group } E_{result} \texttt{ by } E_{key}]\!] envs \stackrel{\text{def}}{=} \texttt{foldl cf [] } envs \tag{2}$$

where `cf`, the combining function, captures the provided result selector and key extractor, has type *Grouping* $\rightarrow$ *BindingSet* $\rightarrow$ *Grouping*, and is defined as:

```
cf g bs = let r = [[result]](env) in
          let k = [[key]](env) in
          if hasKey g k then appendToCluster g k r
                        else append g [(k,[r])]
```

For Q other than `select` or `groupby`, $[\![Q]\!] envs$ denotes a sequence of binding-sets which constitute the $envs$ in effect for the next clause in S, the first Q in S being evaluated with an empty incoming $envs$.

$$[\![\texttt{from } V_{var} \texttt{ in } E_{srcSeq}]\!] envs \stackrel{\text{def}}{=} [env' \mid env \leftarrow envs,\ item \leftarrow [\![srcSeq]\!](env),$$
$$let\ env' = env \cup \{var \mapsto item\}\ ] \tag{3}$$

$$[\![\texttt{let } V_{var} = E_{exp}]\!] envs \stackrel{\text{def}}{=} [env' \mid env \leftarrow envs,$$
$$let\ env' = env \cup \{var \mapsto [\![exp]\!](env)\ \}\ ] \tag{4}$$

$$[\![\texttt{where } E_{test}]\!] envs \stackrel{\text{def}}{=} [env \mid env \leftarrow envs, [\![test]\!](env)\ ] \tag{5}$$

The valuation of an *OrderByClause* permutes the incoming binding-sets, sorting the sequence *envs* according to the multi-key given by expressions key_i and sort directions dir_i. In terms of the Haskell function `Data.List.sortBy`,

$$\llbracket \texttt{orderby } key_1 \, dir_1 \, \ldots \, key_n \, dir_n \rrbracket envs \overset{\text{def}}{=} \texttt{sortBy comp envs} \tag{6}$$

where `comp` is a comparison function (specific to the given key_i and dir_i, $i = 1 \ldots n$) between two binding-sets `bsA` and `bsB`, returning one of `GT`, `EQ`, `LT`. First, $\llbracket key_1 \rrbracket(bsA)$ and $\llbracket key_1 \rrbracket(bsB)$ are compared taking dir_1 into account. If they are not equal that's the outcome of `comp bsA bsB`. Otherwise, $\llbracket key_2 \rrbracket(bsA)$ and $\llbracket key_2 \rrbracket(bsB)$ are compared taking dir_2 into account, and so on. If no `GT` or `LT` is found for $i = 1 \ldots n$, `EQ` is returned.

The semantics is defined over a core syntax where explicit type annotations have been desugared into type casts (in `from` and `join` clauses) as discussed in Sect. 4.

$$\llbracket \texttt{join } V_{innerVar} \text{ in } E_{isrc} \text{ on } E_{outerKey} \text{ equals } E_{innerKey} \rrbracket envs$$
$$\overset{\text{def}}{=} [ienv \mid env \leftarrow envs, innerItem \leftarrow \llbracket isrc \rrbracket(env) ,$$
$$let \, ienv = env \cup \{ \, innerVar \mapsto innerItem \, \} ,$$
$$\llbracket outerKey \rrbracket(env) = \llbracket innerKey \rrbracket(ienv)] \tag{7}$$

$$\llbracket \texttt{join } V_{innerVar} \text{ in } E_{isrc} \text{ on } E_{outerKey} \text{ equals } E_{innerKey} \text{ into } V_{resVar} \rrbracket envs$$
$$\overset{\text{def}}{=} [renv \mid env \leftarrow envs,$$
$$let \, group = [\, innerItem \mid innerItem \leftarrow \llbracket isrc \rrbracket(env)$$
$$let \, ienv = env \cup \{ innerVar \mapsto innerItem \},$$
$$\llbracket outerKey \rrbracket(env) = \llbracket innerKey \rrbracket(ienv)],$$
$$let \, renv = env \cup \{ \, resVar \mapsto group \, \}] \tag{8}$$

4   Rewriting from LINQ to Query Operators

The translation *LINQ textual syntax* $\rightarrow$ *Standard Query Operators* [25, §7.15.2] is defined in terms of 18 simpler structural transformations. By structural it is meant that they recursively traverse an input AST leaving most nodes unchanged. Surprisingly, the C# specification does not label each transformation with a unique tag, so Tab. 3 cross-references them by listing a brief description for each rule as well as the section in [25] where it is covered.

In this section a notation is put forward to specify LINQ $\rightarrow$ SQO using LINQ itself (Sect. 4.1) and a precise formulation of rewriting order is given (Sect. 4.2). In order to be useful, a set of rewriting rules should be (a) *confluent* (*i.e.*, rule application terminates in a finite number of steps), (b) *deterministic* (*i.e.*, for any input AST just one output AST exists), and (c) free from multiple applicable rules during any intermediate step. Moreover, the rewrite rules should be (d) *semantics preserving*. In Sect. 4.3 we explain how the transformation rules fare with regard to these properties. Section 4.4 reviews the consequences (as for the semantics of Java with embedded LINQ) of our design choice to favor the query-shipping paradigm.

Table 3. Catalog of structural transformations in the $LINQ \rightarrow SQO$ translation

ID	Phase	Description			§ in C# spec.
T1	1	Inline query continuation			7.15.2.1
T2		*FromClause*			
T3	2	*JoinClause*	type annotation		7.15.2.2
T4		*JoinIntoClause*			
T5	3	Identity query			7.15.2.3
T6		*FromClause FromClause*	*SelectClause*		
T7			otherwise		
T8		*FromClause JoinClause*	*SelectClause*		
T9			otherwise		
T10		*FromClause JoinIntoClause*	*SelectClause*		7.15.2.4
T11			otherwise		
T12	4		*OrderByClause*		
T13			*WhereClause*		
T14			*LetClause*		
T15		*FromClause*	non-identity *SelectClause*		7.15.2.5
T16			identity *SelectClause*		
T17			non-identity *GroupByClause*		7.15.2.6
T18			identity *GroupByClause*		

4.1 Notation

To clarify notation, Tab. 4 lists for transformation T1 (a) its informal formulation (from [25, §7.15.2]); (b) its applicability condition, in terms of the productions in Tab. 1; and (c) its functional definition, using LINQ itself. For completeness, Fig. 1 depicts the parse tree of the resulting query.

In contrast to the cursory presentation in [25], the notation in Tab. 4 is precise (facilitating conformance across different implementations) and seems therefore well suited as an ingredient for a JSR standardizing LINQ for Java. As another advantage, this notation is closer to the logic formalism of model-checkers, which can be used to validate the translation algorithm (*i.e.*, to certify that the resulting ASTs are well-formed, for all valid input ASTs [26]) and to test the algorithm's implementation against an *oracle* (*i.e.*, to corroborate whether an implementation produces for some given input the result expected by the declarative specification). Also based on that specification, a model-checker can generate input datasets for tests, achieving larger coverage than manual testing.

4.2 Phases

Transformations T1 - T18 are not applied all at once but in phases. The first phase comprises just T1 ("inline query continuations"), recursively rewriting subqueries to eliminate this syntax shorthand.

After the second phase (T2 - T4) all explicit type annotations have been reformulated in terms of *Application* and *Cast* productions (shown in Tab. 2).

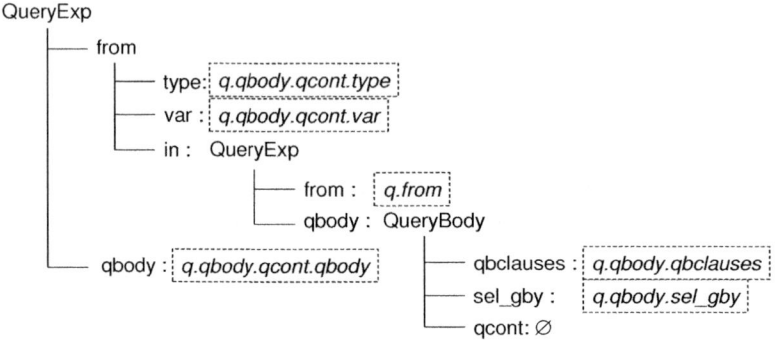

Fig. 1. Template of parse trees resulting from applying T1

The third phase rewrites identity queries (of the form `from x in srcSeq select x`) into `srcSeq.Select( x => x )`. In main-memory evaluation, returning items as in the first query would expose the object identities of the base data. In contrast, the second formulation allows an overridden `Select` to return clones of the items, clones that can be mutated later at will. In the query shipping scenario both formulations denote the same result.

The fourth phase iteratively applies the bulk of the transformations (T6 - T18). In each iteration, T6 to T18 are tried *in that order*, innermost queries first. After successful application of a rule, the next iteration tries again from T6 onwards.

4.3   Confluence and Determinism

Regarding confluence and determinism, each of phase 1 and 3 involves applying only one rewriting whereby a construct is consumed (*i.e.*, not copied to the output). Phase 2 involves three rules, whose applicability conditions are disjoint (each rule matching *one* of the constructs *FromClause*, *JoinClause*, and *JoinIntoClause*). While the same kind of clause will be copied to the output, it will not match again as the explicit cast has been removed. As can be seen, the first two phases are confluent and lead to a deterministic result for finite input.

Following a similar reasoning, Phase 3 can be shown to be well-behaved. And due to the fact that rewritings reduce syntax shorthands, there is no doubt that the output queries are semantically equivalent to the original queries.

The analysis of Phase 4 must consider more subcases. To recap, the shape of the input to this phase is: (a) because of T1, a legal query expression can now only end in either a `select` or a `groupby` clause, and (b) because of none of Phases 1 to 3 touches them, the initial mandatory `from` clause(s) are still there.

Table 4. Definition of transformation T1

(a)	T1: inline query continuation
	    `from x1 in e1 ... into x2 ...`
	    `→ from x2 in (from x1 in e1 ...) ...`

(b)	`function T1 ( q : QueryExp ) : QueryExp` when `q.qbody.qcont ≠ ∅`

```
new QueryExp {
from = new FromClause {
        type = q.qbody.qcont.type,
        var = q.qbody.qcont.var,
        in = new QueryExp {
          from = q.from
          qbody = new QueryBody {
                  qbclauses = q.qbody.qbclauses,
                  sel_gby = q.qbody.sel_gby
        }   }   }
qbody = q.qbody.qcont.qbody
}
```
(row (c))

The translation sidesteps the issue of non-unique rule applicability by forcing the order T6-T18 on rewriting. A visual inspection of columns 3 and 4 in Tab. 3 reveals that the subcases partition the set of valid queries. To prove confluence, it suffices to show that each rule strictly diminishes a progress measure. This measure is the number of clauses in the query.

1. The rules that bring an outermost query into its final SQO form are T6, T8, T10, and T15 to T18. They have in common that the input query ends in a *GroupByClause* (T17 and T18) or a *SelectClause* (the rest).
2. In contrast, T7, T9, and T11 to T14 result in a non-SQO query, but diminish the number of clauses by one: T7 consumes a *FromClause*, T9 a *JoinClause* without `into`, and T11 a *JoinIntoClause*.
3. Finally, T12, T13, and T14 consume one `orderby`, `where`, and `let` clause resp.

The clauses that each of T7, T9, T11, and T14 consume happen to declare range variables. In order to avoid those usages becoming dangling in the output query, they are prepended with a prefix (a so called *transparent identifier*) to access hidden identifiers, as follows. The input to any of these rules starts with two clauses (the first of them a *FromClause*) that introduce two variables x_1 and x_2. In all cases, those two clauses are reduced to a single `from` *prefix* in *srcSeq*, where *prefix* is a fresh name and *srcSeq* denotes a sequence of pairs (x_1, x_2), *i.e.*, the labels for the tuple components match the old variable identifiers. Pairs (x_1, x_2) result from instantiating an *anonymous type*, as done with the C# code `new {` `x1 = `E_{x1}`, x2 = `E_{x2}`}`. With this name choice, usages of x_1 can be rewritten to *prefix*.x_1 (similarly for x_2) thus making the output query well-formed.

The analysis of semantic equivalence for T6-T18 remains as future work, on the basis of the denotational semantics introduced in Sect. 3.2 for LINQ.

4.4   Language Integration Aspects

In the Microsoft implementation, the behavior of an SQO method chain is determined by the receiver object at its head. Depending on the runtime type of the receiver the following will happen:

- for an in-memory collection (an instance of `IEnumerable`) an iterator is configured to reel off results as they are found when traversing the object graph on the heap. The iterator idiom simulates lazy evaluation from functional languages, and the applicable optimizations are only those that the C# compiler and the virtual machine (VM) know about.
- for an `IQueryable`, an AST is built for shipping to a *LINQ provider*, which mediates the interaction with a DBMS engine. Any or both of provider and engine may optimize the AST.

In our prototype we focus only on the query shipping case, which implies:

- When evaluating queries on the heap (*LINQ to Objects*) C# does not restrict query constituents in any way: calls to `Thread.Sleep()` may appear, custom comparators may be given as arguments to sorting operators (in the spirit of `java.util.Comparator`); *i.e.*, constructs may be used which in general cannot be translated into a DBMS native language. Such translation could be successfully performed *in some cases* with the help of bytecode inspection and rewriting techniques [27], but we find the supported LINQ textual syntax to be expressive enough for all practical purposes. In our implementation, constructs that cannot be translated are rejected.
- The LINQ grammar includes a production invoking *expression*, the most general syntactic category for expressions in C# [25, §B.2.4]. This defeats any hope of faithfully supporting 100% of the LINQ grammar (short of reimplementing the C# compiler). As done in the NLinq open-source project[6] (where LINQ capabilities are back-ported to previous versions of .NET) our grammar covers as large a subset of *expression* as practical.

Favoring the query shipping scenario results in two other behaviors of *LINQ to Objects* not being exhibited by our translation: (a) side-effects, and (b) variable capture. We argue in what follows that these behaviors are more a consequence of VM-semantics than desirable properties of a database query language.

Side-effects are possible in *LINQ to Objects*, *e.g.*, `index++` in the query:

```
int index = 0;
List<Customer> top10 = (from c in customers
                        where index++ < 10   select c).ToList();
```

Besides rendering most optimizations useless, the stateful `index++` makes the query prone to race conditions, in case `index` can be accessed from other threads.

Variable capture occurs when a lambda expression refers to a variable in scope not hidden by a parameter. For example[7], the following C# code prints 10 five times and not 0, 2, 4, 6, 8:

---

[6] http://www.codeplex.com/nlinq
[7] http://lorgonblog.spaces.live.com/Blog/cns!701679AD17B6D310!689.entry

```
List<Func<int>> actions = new List<Func<int>>();
for (int i = 0; i < 5; ++i) { actions.Add( () => i * 2 ); }
foreach (var act in actions) { Console.WriteLine( act() ); }
```

because all five instances of the `Func` objects created by the lambda capture a reference to the same mutable variable instance `i`. McNamara goes on to say,

> [As in] every language that has both mutable variables and closures ... the lambda captures the mutable variable now, but gets evaluated later, after further mutations may have occurred. This is an instance of how "lazy evaluation" and "side effects" don't always mix nicely.

In the query shipping scenario, no DBMS can callback the client VM to retrieve the then-current value of a captured variable. In our implementation, such variable references are re-formulated as copy by-value parameter passing (and thus evaluated once, just before query shipping).

5   Rewriting of Compiler-Level Trees

A Java compiler operates in phases, progressively decorating Abstract Syntax Trees (ASTs) and populating symbol tables with information needed for successive analyses. JSR-269 (Pluggable Annotation Processing) allows third-parties to provide *compiler plugins* to interact with any Java compiler during the early phases of compilation, for example to *rewrite* an AST. After rewriting an AST in phase N, a compiler plugin may (a) reconstruct the state that previous phases would have computed up to that point; or (b) pretty-print the updated AST and launch the compilation task anew. Depending on the amount of information required from surrounding nodes (the *program context*) transformations range from *desugaring* (performed based on the contents of a subtree alone) to *whole-program* (requiring knowledge of several compilation units).

The phases of the OpenJDK `javac` (Fig. 2) are representative of those in other compilers. Rather than describe each phase in detail (as done in [28]) we review first the whole process, focusing afterwards on the contract between the *Annotation Processing* and the *Analyze and Generate* phases where our plugin gets activated. During the first phase (*Parse and Enter*), externally-visible information about each compilation unit is entered into symbol tables. Next, *Annotation processing* calls one or more annotation processors which may generate new source or class files, causing a compilation restart until no new files are created. The last phase, *Analyze and Generate* encapsulates several complex stages: (1) *Attribute* includes type checking and constant folding. Additionally, names, expressions and other elements in the AST are resolved to their corresponding type and symbol nodes. (2) *Flow* checks for definite assignment to variables and for unreachable statements, based on a class-level dataflow analysis. (3) *Generics erasure* is followed by (4) *Desugar* (*e.g.*, simplification of nested and inner classes into normal ones, expansion of "foreach"); concluding with (5) *Generate*.

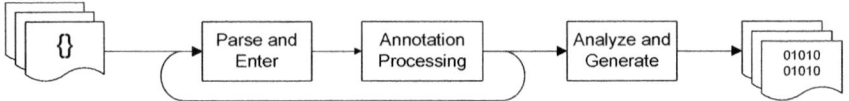

Fig. 2. Compilation workflow realized by `javax.tools.JavaCompiler`

5.1   Prototype

Annotation processors, standardized for Java 6 in JSR-269, access functionality from packages `javax.annotation.processing.*` and `javax.lang.model.*`. A custom processor (a subclass of `AbstractProcessor`) may declare interest in handling all compilation units, be they annotated or not[8]. With that, a method overriding `AbstractProcessor.process()` may inspect a set of `TypeElement`, for example to look up enclosed `ExecutableElement` elements, which stand for methods, constructors, or initializers of a class or interface. Still, no access is provided to the subtrees of their associated statement blocks, as necessary for detecting LINQ queries nested as strings. At least not through that interface, but in practice such navigation is possible for both the Sun and Eclipse compilers by downcasting an `elem` AST-node reference to its specific type in the compiler tree API, along the lines of:

```
if (elem.getKind() == ElementKind.CLASS) {
  String cName = elem.getClass().getName();
  if (cName.startsWith("org.eclipse.jdt.internal.compiler")) { ...
  } else if (cName.startsWith("com.sun.tools.javac.tree")) { ...
```

A factory provides at startup compiler-specific visitors (based on the runtime type of the obtained `javax.tools.JavaCompiler`). These visitors are later used to detect LINQ queries, expand them, and instantiate AST nodes. The first and last visitors admittedly require porting to each supported compiler, however the bulk of the plugin functionality (LINQ → SQO) is compiler-independent. Moreover, the AST hierarchies between compilers exhibit variations mostly in naming conventions, while their organization always reflects the Java Language Specification (*e.g.*, `JCMethodDecl` vs. `MethodDeclaration`). Because of this, the porting effort is kept to a minimum.

Instead of letting compilation proceed on the rewritten AST, the compilation unit may be pretty-printed into a textual file (option `-printsource` in `javac`). This arrangement is convenient in conjunction with an IDE, where the project builder internal to the IDE picks up the output file as part of the build process. In this case, generated code can be inspected in read-only mode.

Our LINQ query expander gets activated immediately after Java ASTs have been built and performs a desugaring, without restarting the compilation task. Each statement block of the form `{JL.expand("<LINQ query>");}` is replaced with another containing invocations to SQO factory methods. In a typical arrangement, a method is declared for each LINQ query, whose expansion will constitute

---

[8] `@SupportedAnnotationTypes("*")`.

the method body, with method arguments corresponding to query parameters. As to the return type, the developer-provided dummy placeholder (*e.g.*, `Object`) is overwritten with the specific type computed for the query result.

5.2 Static Semantics and Schema Awareness

Once expanded, the resulting queries are well-formed (*i.e.*, guaranteed not to cause syntax errors when shipped to a persistence engine) and immune to *injection attacks* (that is, for LINQ queries provided by the developer at compile-time). These guarantees result from (a) the checks performed by the compiler plugin; (b) the wrapping of query parameters as arguments to strongly-typed factory methods; and (c) the checks performed later during the *Attribute* phase of the compilation task.

Regarding the *runtime* assembly of LINQ queries immune to injection attacks, that capability can be achieved by directly building an AST using factory methods, rather than by concatenating strings[9].

Our design decision does not prevent others from adapting our compiler plugin to target other query EDSLs or different DBMS drivers. Rather, it simplifies that customization by relieving them from performing the aforementioned well-formedness checks at the level of generated EDSL statements. Irrespective of the compile-time analyses performed, still there will be some queries that generate exceptions upon evaluation (*e.g.*, division by zero, or attempting to obtain the `single()` element of a non-singleton sequence). These queries would also have raised exceptions in the Microsoft implementation of LINQ.

Incidentally, it is not necessary for the generated code to serve simultaneously the purposes of (a) checking well-formedness, and (b) building the AST of its translation. As an extreme example, our compiler plugin might have generated code to null out at runtime the AST just built, only to send the original query string to a LINQ provider (*à la* JDBC, JPQL, etc.) Unlike its JDBC counterpart, such plugin would still statically guarantee well-formedness.

6   Related Work

Several grammar-centered approaches promote language extensibility, with case studies reporting typesafe nesting of SQL based on an *Attribute Grammar* formalism as implemented by the `Silver` system [29]. Similar extensions are reported for the `JastAdd` system [30]. These systems act as frontend processors, performing AST-to-AST transformations that are later fed to a standard Java compiler. As our prototype shows, non-trivial transformations can be achieved without the extra machinery offered by these systems. If needed, a compiler plugin can also perform elaborate rewriting, with the MatchO library [31].

---

[9] http://blogs.msdn.com/swiss_dpe_team/archive/2008/06/05/
    composable-linq-to-sql-query-with-dynamic-orderby.aspx

The closest to a grammar-centered approach being addressed by Java compiler vendors is the *OpenJDK Compiler Grammar Project*[10], an experimental version of the `javac` compiler based on a grammar written in `ANTLR v3`. Modifications to `javac` were ruled out by our design objectives. This decision will be revisited in case the Compiler Grammar Project graduates to release status.

Ideally, a standard API should be available to process ASTs (as intended by JSR-198), an idea that has not gained support among compiler and IDE vendors. AST manipulation is supported in Java by IDE-specific frameworks, *e.g.*, Jackpot for NetBeans[11] and LTK [32] for Eclipse.

Embedded DSLs leverage the compiler to perform *impact analysis* upon changes to the object-oriented schema, as such code does not type-check when the classes involved in queries have been refactored. An early example of a tool reifying the schema is *Safe Query Objects* [27].

DSLs which do not assume an object model (*e.g.*, XQuery) may have well-formedness constraints that cannot be captured by the Java 5 type system. Such DSLs can still be embedded in a typesafe manner, given that the *Checker Framework*[12] of JSR-308 supports the implementation of custom static analyses in compiler plugins. Besides its current use cases (*e.g.*, enforcing non-null references) JSR-308 can thus play a key role in improving language embedding.

7   Conclusions and Future Work

Rather than shoehorning a query language to stay within the confines of Java syntax (which raises new problems, *e.g.*, extracting declarative queries from imperative code [6]) we have attempted instead to balance the desire for dedicated syntax with the realities of standard compiler infrastructure.

The work reported in this paper is part of a larger project on language engineering, aiming at efficiently supporting in one of the traditionally distinct execution environments (Virtual Machine, Database Manager) useful abstractions originating in the other. While functional queries were originally applied to main-memory object populations, their adoption in the DBMS setting is gaining momentum. In the other direction, ACID transactions are finding a new home in virtual machines with *Software Transactional Memory* [33].

Finally, we believe that while individual improvements (as addressed in this paper for nested query languages) contribute to advancing the case for Object Database Management Systems (ODBMSs), it is still necessary not to lose sight of a more encompassing research and engineering agenda if ODBMSs are to become a strategic technology for software development.

Acknowledgement. Kaichuan Wen proficiently contributed to the implementation of the prototype as part of his course project on query language translation.

---

[10] http://openjdk.java.net/projects/compiler-grammar/
[11] A framework for Java source code reengineering, http://jackpot.netbeans.org/
[12] http://groups.csail.mit.edu/pag/jsr308/

References

1. Jones, S.P., Wadler, P.: Comprehensive Comprehensions. In: Proc. of the ACM SIGPLAN Workshop Haskell 2007, pp. 61–72. ACM Press, New York (2007), http://research.microsoft.com/~simonpj/papers/list-comp/list-comp.pdf
2. Bruno, N., Castro, P.: Towards declarative queries on adaptive data structures. In: ICDE, pp. 1249–1258. IEEE, Los Alamitos (2008)
3. Grust, T., Scholl, M.H.: Translating OQL into Monoid Comprehensions—Stuck with Nested Loops? Technical Report 3a/1996, Database Research Group, Univ Konstanz (September 1996)
4. Cooper, E., Lindley, S., Wadler, P., Yallop, J.: Links: web programming without tiers. In: de Boer, F.S., Bonsangue, M.M., Graf, S., de Roever, W.-P. (eds.) FMCO 2006. LNCS, vol. 4709, pp. 266–296. Springer, Heidelberg (2007)
5. Manolescu, D., Beckman, B., Livshits, B.: Volta: Developing distributed applications by recompiling. IEEE Softw. 25(5), 53–59 (2008)
6. Wiedermann, B., Ibrahim, A., Cook, W.R.: Interprocedural query extraction for transparent persistence. SIGPLAN Not. 43(10), 19–36 (2008)
7. Microsoft Corporation: Standard Query Operators Overview (2009), http://msdn.microsoft.com/en-us/library/bb397896.aspx
8. Kabanov, J., Raudjärv, R.: Embedded typesafe domain specific languages for Java. In: PPPJ 2008: Proc. of the 6th Intnl. Symp. on Principles and Practice of Programming in Java, pp. 189–197. ACM, New York (2008), http://www.ekabanov.net/kabanov-raudjarv-pppj08.pdf
9. Berler, M., Eastman, J., Jordan, D., Russell, C., Schadow, O., Stanienda, T., Velez, F.: The object data standard: ODMG 3.0. Morgan Kaufmann Publishers Inc., San Francisco (2000)
10. Bierman, G., Trigoni, A.: Towards a formal type system for ODMG OQL. Technical Report 497, University of Cambridge Computer Laboratory (September 2000), http://research.microsoft.com/~gmb/papers/tr497.pdf
11. Garcia, M.: Formalizing the well-formedness rules of EJB3QL in UML + OCL. In: Kühne, T. (ed.) MoDELS 2006. LNCS, vol. 4364, pp. 66–75. Springer, Heidelberg (2007)
12. Garcia, M.: Automating the embedding of Domain Specific Languages in Eclipse JDT. Eclipse Technical Article (2008), http://eclipse.org/articles/article.php?file=Article-AutomatingDSLEmbeddings/index.html
13. Adya, A., Blakeley, J.A., Melnik, S., Muralidhar, S.: Anatomy of the ADO.NET Entity Framework. In: SIGMOD 2007: Proc. of the 2007 ACM SIGMOD Intnl. Conf. on Mgmt. of Data, pp. 877–888. ACM, New York (2007)
14. Melnik, S., Adya, A., Bernstein, P.A.: Compiling mappings to bridge applications and databases. In: SIGMOD 2007: Proc. of the 2007 ACM SIGMOD Intnl. Conf. on Mgmt. of Data, pp. 461–472. ACM, New York (2007)
15. Gray, P.M.D., Kerschberg, L., King, P.J., Poulovassilis, A. (eds.): The Functional Approach to Data Management: Modeling, Analyzing, and Integrating Heterogeneous Data. Springer, Heidelberg (2004)
16. Jones, S.P.: The Implementation of Functional Programming Languages. Prentice-Hall, Inc., NJ (1987), http://research.microsoft.com/en-us/um/people/simonpj/papers/slpj-book-1987/
17. Grust, T., Mayr, M., Rittinger, J.: XQuery join graph isolation. In: Proc. of the 25th Intnl. Conf. on Data Engineering (ICDE 2009), Shanghai, China, March/April (2009), http://arxiv.org/abs/0810.4809

18. Diao, Y.: Implementing memoization in a streaming XQuery processor. In: Bellahsène, Z., Milo, T., Rys, M., Suciu, D., Unland, R. (eds.) XSym 2004. LNCS, vol. 3186, pp. 35–50. Springer, Heidelberg (2004)
19. Willis, D., Pearce, D.J., Noble, J.: Caching and incrementalisation in the Java Query Language. In: OOPSLA 2008: Proc. of the 23rd ACM SIGPLAN Conf. on Object-oriented Programming Systems, Languages and Applications, pp. 1–18. ACM, New York (2008)
20. Garcia, M., Möller, R.: Incremental Evaluation of OCL Invariants in the Essential MOF Object Model. In: Kühne, T., Reisig, W., Steimann, F. (eds.) Modellierung 2008. GI-Edition Lecture Notes in Informatics, vol. 127, pp. 11–26 (2008)
21. Turbak, F.A., Gifford, D.K.: Design Concepts in Programming Languages. MIT Press, Cambridge (2008)
22. Parr, T.: The Definitive ANTLR Reference: Building Domain-Specific Languages. The Pragmatic Programmers (2007)
23. Moerkotte, G.: Building Query Compilers, Draft (2009), http://pi3.informatik.uni-mannheim.de/~moer/querycompiler.pdf
24. Mehra, K.K., Rajamani, S.K., Sistla, A.P., Jha, S.K.: Verification of object relational maps. In: SEFM 2007: Proc. of the Fifth IEEE Intnl. Conf. on Software Engineering and Formal Methods, Washington, DC, USA, pp. 283–292. IEEE Computer Society, Los Alamitos (2007)
25. Microsoft Corporation: C# version 3.0 language specification (2007), http://msdn.microsoft.com/en-us/vcsharp/aa336809.aspx
26. Garcia, M.: Formalization of QVT-Relations: OCL-based Static Semantics and Alloy-based Validation. In: Proc. of the 2nd Workshop on MDSD Today, October 2008, pp. 21–30. Shaker Verlag (2008), http://www.sts.tu-harburg.de/people/mi.garcia/pubs/2008/qvtr/QVTRelationsFormalization.pdf
27. Cook, W.R., Rai, S.: Safe Query Objects: statically typed objects as remotely executable queries. In: ICSE 2005: Proc. of the 27th Intnl. Conf. on Software Engineering, pp. 97–106. ACM, New York (2005)
28. Erni, D., Kuhn, A.: The Hacker's Guide to javac. Technical report, Software Composition Group (SCG), University of Bern, Switzerland (August 2008), http://www.iam.unibe.ch/~scg/Archive/Projects/Erni08b.pdf
29. Wyk, E.V., Krishnan, L., Bodin, D., Schwerdfeger, A.: Attribute grammar-based language extensions for Java. In: Ernst, E. (ed.) ECOOP 2007. LNCS, vol. 4609, pp. 575–599. Springer, Heidelberg (2007)
30. Ekman, T., Hedin, G.: The JastAdd extensible Java compiler. In: OOPSLA 2007: Proc. of the 22nd ACM SIGPLAN Conf. on Object Oriented Programming Systems and Applications, pp. 1–18. ACM, New York (2007)
31. Visser, J.: Matching Objects without Language Extension. Journal of Object Technology 5(8), 81–100 (2006)
32. Frenzel, L.: LTK: an API for automated refactorings in Eclipse IDEs (2006), Technical Article, http://www.eclipse.org/articles/Article-LTK/ltk.html
33. Jones, S.P.: 24 (Beautiful Concurrency). In: Beautiful Code: Leading Programmers Explain How They Think. O'Reilly Media, Inc., Sebastopol (2007)

Active Components as a Method for Coupling Data and Services – A Database-Driven Application Development Process

Beat Signer[1] and Moira C. Norrie[2]

[1] Vrije Universiteit Brussel
Pleinlaan 2
1050 Brussels, Belgium
bsigner@vub.ac.be
[2] Institute for Information Systems, ETH Zurich
CH-8092 Zurich, Switzerland
norrie@inf.ethz.ch

Abstract. In the area of highly interactive systems, the use of object databases has significantly grown in the past few years due to the fact that one can, not only persistently store data in the form of objects, but also provide additional functionality in terms of methods defined on these objects. However, a limitation of such a tight coupling of objects and their methods is that parts of the application logic cannot be reused without also having instances of these objects in the new application database. Based on our experience of designing multiple interactive cross-media applications, we propose an approach where we distinguish between regular database objects containing the data and so-called *active components* storing metadata about specific services. Active components are first class objects which, at activation time, can perform some operations on the server as well as on the client side. Since active components are standalone lightweight components, they can be dynamically bound to single objects or semantically grouped sets of objects and be automatically invoked by different forms of database interactions. The database-driven development of arbitrary client and server-side application functionality not only simplifies the design of highly interactive systems, but also improves the reuse of existing components across different systems.

1 Introduction

In recent years, there has been a rapid growth in the number of applications where the same data can be accessed by different input modalities as well as from a variety of input devices. These types of highly interactive applications generally require an adaptation of the content as well as the form of interaction in order to become accessible from different client devices. Nevertheless, the database is often seen purely as a storage container for data, with any complex interaction handled and implemented in an application-specific manner.

M.C. Norrie and M. Grossniklaus (Eds.): ICOODB 2009, LNCS 5936, pp. 59–76, 2010.
© Springer-Verlag Berlin Heidelberg 2010

If, however, a database can not only store data but also some general application logic, this functionality can be reused in the development process of a specific application, thereby simplifying the design of new applications in terms of time and cost. Furthermore, by reusing existing application logic, the corresponding functionality gets refined and optimised over time leading to more stable and less error-prone applications.

Of course, the idea of modular software development and the reuse of components is not a new one and there exists a variety of different solutions for component-based software development such as the OSGi Service Platform[1]. Also Web Services and service-oriented architectures (SOAs) offer a method for loosely coupling different distributed components and composing complex applications out of simple building blocks and services.

However, for many existing solutions, the configuration and use of the services still requires substantial programming skills and often the solutions are too heavyweight for applications that should run on devices with limited resources. They are based on a simple remote method invocation (RMI) mechanism where a client-side proxy component offers the functionality of a remote service. While this simplifies the development of applications with a distributed application functionality, it does not really provide a method for designing reusable components for more complex client-server interaction. Based on our experience in developing multiple interactive cross-media applications and working together with, not only programmers, but also designers and artists, we identified a need for a less programming intensive solution for reusing functionality in the development of these kinds of applications. We present a solution where application functionality can not only be executed remotely on the server but also run on the client side and enable complex interaction between client and server-side application functionality.

In this paper, we show how database-driven application development can be simplified through the concept of active components. Some motivational examples for database-driven client and server-side functionality are provided in Sect. 2. Related work in terms of solutions for reusing component-based application functionality in software engineering and also active databases is discussed in Sect. 3. In Sect. 4, we introduce the concept of active components and outline the basic idea of storing data as well as services in an object database. We then present our architecture for executing active components in Sect. 5 and provide some details about the prototype implementation of our new active component-based approach in Sect. 6. Different active component use cases are presented in Sect. 7 before providing concluding remarks in Sect. 8.

2   Motivation

To motivate our approach, we will first provide some application scenarios where data managed by a database system is accessed through a combination of database-driven client- and server-side services. We will later show how this kind

---

[1] http://www.osgi.org

of database-driven client-server interaction can be realised based on our active component solution for coupling data and services.

If we think about the evolution of the Web and how rich Internet applications (RIAs) are nowadays used to mimic the behaviour of desktop applications within a browser, we can see that a similar behaviour can be achieved by using some form of active database content that is deployed to and executed on the client side. RIAs normally need a browser plug-in or a virtual machine to run the client-side components, which is the equivalent of a runtime environment for active components deployed to the client side as introduced later in this paper. If we implement an active component runtime environment as a browser plug-in, we can execute the client-side active component directly within a web browser for the access to and manipulation of any remote data stored in an object database.

While in most service-oriented architectures there is an explicit remote execution of services offered by a server, we would like to introduce a scenario where services are executed implicitly by accessing database objects. A service could for example be associated with specific object instances, object types or semantic collections of database objects. If such a database object with an associated active component is accessed, the linked active component is automatically loaded by an active component runtime environment. An example where active components are associated with specific media on the type level is shown in Fig. 1.

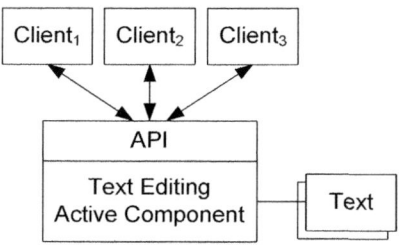

Fig. 1. Media service component

The idea is that specific applications (clients) no longer directly deal with raw media types but rather use services offered by active components coupled to these media types. In the example shown in Fig. 1, all objects of type text have been associated with a special text editing active component. This text editing component provides some basic text editing functionality such as the insertion or deletion of a set of characters within a text which can be reused and shared by different client applications. Of course we would easily have the possibility to run different text editing active component implementations at remote sites while still having control over who is currently accessing a specific text resource based on a given server-side text editing component. The text editing component could be used by standard word processors (e.g. Microsoft Word) as well as browser-based text editors or a basic editing active component executed within the active component runtime environment of small portable devices.

Since the text editing functionality is not implemented as methods on the text data objects themselves, we could still exchange the services provided for specific classes or instances of media types by simply dynamically reconfiguring the associated active components. Another advantage is that we could provide editing functionality for rich media types out of the database and the number of supported formats could be extended in a flexible way. The active component runtime environment would be in charge of providing a layer for the basic functionality by running the media service active components whereas specific input and output devices might provide different user interfaces on top of these media service components. Since we can not only define active component services on a type level but also use role-driven service invocation based on object classification, our text objects in Fig. 1 could be dynamically reconfigured over time and bound to other services (e.g. a logger service) based on their classification. Note that type-based as well as role-driven service invocation is a powerful mechanism for automatically triggering any object-related functionality which otherwise would have to be explicitly accessed by static library method calls.

Another use case we would like to address is the processing of data generated by physical objects such as sensors. In today's "Internet of Things" where more and more physical objects become integrated with the digital world by sensing for example some environmental parameters, it becomes important that input from these objects can be easily integrated with digital information spaces as represented by a database. If we can guarantee that some kind of active component runtime environment is available for the augmented physical objects, then the client-server active component communication provides a lightweight solution for updating sensor data in a database. At initialisation time, a physical object could query for a specific active component which would then define the application logic on the client and server side and provide functionality for database updates.

In the next section, we present related work in terms of solutions for active databases as well as component-based and service-oriented architectures. We then introduce our database-driven and active component-based development process for applications such as the ones presented in this section.

3   Related Work

In component-based software engineering (CBSE) [1], the emphasis is on building modular components with well-defined interfaces which can then be composed to develop more complex systems. This allows components to be aggregated in a distributed manner as well as within a single local system. More recent technologies for software components in distributed computing are Web Services [2] and service-oriented architectures (SOAs) [3]. While these technologies provide a solution for language independent reuse of business logic as well as data exchange, there is still quite some effort required for a developer to register and make use of existing Web Services. Also, data exchange over the transport layer is well suited to standard business applications, but does not suit the processing of real-time and streaming data as produced, for example, by different types of physical sensors. More recently there have also been some efforts to apply SOA principles to DBMSs to provide loosely-coupled database services [4], but in this case the principles are applied to the DBMS rather than to the applications.

While Web Services mainly focus on digital services, there exist other approaches trying to integrate physical devices as elements of a component-based architecture. For example, as part of a research project, the OSGi model has been generalised to support the "Internet of Things" by turning physical devices and objects into loosely coupled software modules that interact with each other through service interfaces [5]. Since OSGi can use direct method invocations without requiring a transport layer, it is much faster than a Web Service approach. In contrast to Web Services, OSGi components can also directly react to the appearance and disappearance of new services. However, the extended OSGi model deals with integration on a rather low level in terms of different transport protocols such as Bluetooth and is less concerned with higher level concepts directly supporting the application developer.

The connection and integration of devices with a service oriented architecture is the idea of the Service-Oriented Device Architecture (SODA) [6] and some of its implementations such as DBNet [7]. The SODA solution is effective for connecting powerful client devices but less suited to realising lightweight services as required by devices with limited computing and communication resources.

Database systems were traditionally designed to store application data which was then accessed and manipulated by one or more application programs. While the data was managed by the database system, the application logic normally formed part of a specific application accessing the database. The handling of any application logic outside of the database potentially results in a replication of functionality if multiple applications are going to use the same data and implement the same or similar functionality. Of course, this often led to maintenance problems if parts of the application logic had to be updated at a later stage since changes to different implementations were necessary.

The idea to move functionality from the application layer into the database was originally introduced to perform integrity checks within the database. Nowadays almost all commercial relational database systems support triggers as a form of automatically executing some functionality, for example implemented as stored procedures [8], within the database. Triggers are usually represented as event-condition-action (ECA) rules which were adopted as the main means of representing business logic in the paradigm of active database systems [9]. The event describes the happening, inside or outside of the database, to which a rule might respond. Upon a specific event, the condition part of an ECA rule is checked and, if necessary, the corresponding action is executed.

There were also proposals to extend object databases with ECA rules to support the active database paradigm. For example, the TriGS system [10] was an active object database based on GemStone [11]. In these systems, the application-specific interaction with data is often defined by methods on the data objects and the ECA rules are mapped to invocations of these methods.

In contrast to active object databases, we propose a clear distinction between regular data objects and active components providing services based on these data objects. This is mainly due to the fact that functionality provided by the active components is sometimes closely related to the interaction with different input and output modalities. Therefore, this functionality should not be implemented as methods on the class level since this would restrict its reuse across different classes of database objects without (mis)using inheritance. However, this additional extrinsic object behaviour should not be implemented via various static library calls but be designed as active components that are bound to data objects and can access and update any information managed by these data objects and also create new data objects.

Furthermore, an active component should not only be able to be triggered by a single event but also process successive events if required. These long-lived interactions—note the similarity to long-lived transactions—are very helpful in the design of more complex types of interactions with data where the single triggering of a method is not sufficient since additional input data (e.g. streaming data) should be processed by an active component. While active object databases support the execution of methods on database objects, our active component-based solution also provides a mechanism to deploy and run parts of the application functionality on the client side, thereby enabling rich types of long-lived interactions between client- and server-side active components.

4   Approach

The active component concept was originally developed as part of a general link server for cross-media information management [12]. While the server initially supported the cross-linking of arbitrary types of digital and physical resources, we were looking for a way to integrate, not only data and information in terms of different resources such as web pages, movie clips and sounds, but also services as represented by small software components that would be executed when a link is activated.

The concept of active components has been generalised and can now be instantiated as an *active component runtime environment* on top of an existing object database system. The activation of active component services is managed by the active component runtime environment. In addition to the set of regular database objects $\mathcal{O} = \{O_1, O_2, \ldots, O_m\}$, the database now also has to persistently handle a set of active components $\mathcal{A} = \{A_1, A_2, \ldots, A_n\}$.

The active component runtime layer enables the definition of associations or links l_i between arbitrary database objects O_j and active components A_k. The active component runtime environment shown in Fig. 2 checks for any associated active components after each query processed by the database system. If a returned object O_i has an associated active component A_j, the active component service is started and gets a handle to the database object O_i. Note that, in the current version, only queries resulting in single database objects may also trigger an associated active component service. Result sets are currently treated without the additional active component features but we plan to investigate how this could best be handled in future research. The coupling of database objects with active component services can be achieved on the *instance level* as well as on the *schema class* level. Let us assume that our object database contains the classes or types $\mathscr{T} = \{T_1, T_2, \ldots, T_n\}$. A link l_i can then be defined between a type T_j and an active component A_k which implies that the active component service is also bound to all the subtypes of T_j. For example, an association l_i can be defined between a type `contact` and a service A_k that operates on objects of a contacts database. Each time a contact object is accessed, the active component runtime layer ensures that the associated service is started and gets access to the contact object.

Our object-model further distinguishes between the typing of objects for representing behavioural properties and the semantic classification of objects by grouping them into collections [13]. Therefore, a third possibility for the service binding is to define an association l_i between an active component A_j and one or multiple of these semantic collections $\mathscr{C} = \{C_1, C_2, \ldots, C_n\}$ resulting in *role-driven service invocation*. Since these role-driven services are no longer bound to the object type, objects can easily gain and lose service functionality over time by simple reclassification (service evolution). Note that the kind of implicit service invocation presented in this section is not available in most service-oriented architectures where services have to be invoked explicitly.

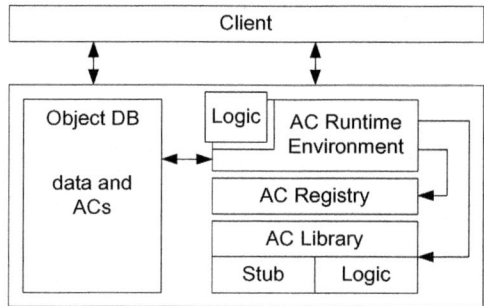

Fig. 2. Active component runtime environment

A second way of accessing a service offered by an active component is to query the active component directly by its name (shown in Fig. 3). After a query is sent to the database, the active component runtime environment checks whether the returned object is an active component A_i. In the case that the database returns an active component, the object is not forwarded to the requester but instead the corresponding service is invoked. Note that in this direct form of service invocation, the active component will not get a handle to any linked data object O_j.

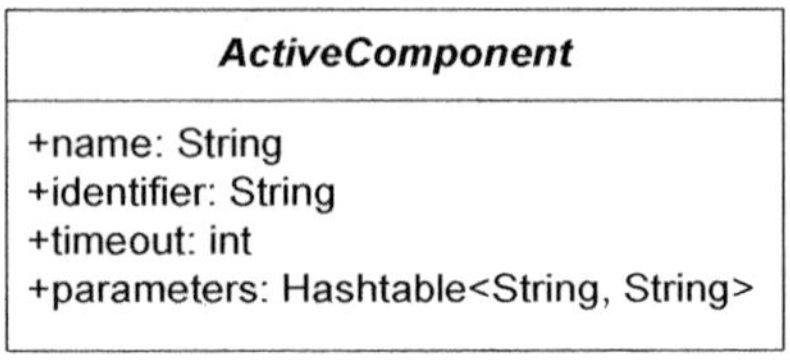

ActiveComponent
+name: String +identifier: String +timeout: int +parameters: Hashtable<String, String>

Fig. 3. Active component database object

Since an active component only contains some data about the service to be invoked, we need a way of getting access to the actual program code to be executed. The `identifier` field provides a unique identifier which is used to lookup the corresponding stub and logic classnames in an *active component registry* and fetch the classes from the *active component library*. An example of an entry in the active component registry is shown in Fig. 4. After a classname has been retrieved from the active component library, the Java reflection mechanism is used to dynamically load the corresponding Java class and initialise it with any data provided by the active component database object.

identifier	org.ximtec.iserver.activecomponent.BROWSER
stub	org.ximtec.iserver.activecomponent.stub.BrowserStub
logic	org.ximtec.iserver.activecomponent.logic.BrowserLogic

Fig. 4. Active component registry entry

Due to the fact that some active components will deal with multiple input events and we can never be sure whether further data has to be processed, an active component may have an optional `timeout` field that defines after how many milliseconds without a new input event an active component should be terminated. Last but not least, each active component can contain an arbitrary number of properties in terms of key/value string pairs defining different parameters of the service to be invoked.

By decoupling the functionality offered by an active component service and the data object stored in the database, one gains flexibility in reusing the corresponding functionality since it is no longer implemented as a class method and therefore no longer tightly coupled to a specific class of objects. Furthermore, through the use of the active component registry and library, the implementation of a specific service offered by an active component can be easily updated or replaced at any time. The introduction of active components as first-class objects eliminates the need to introduce artificial class hierarchies just for the sake of reusing some application functionality and leads to a cleaner and more flexible integration of data and the corresponding services.

5   Architecture

As stated earlier, our active component-based solution enables not only the remote invocation of server-side services but also more complex and richer types of interaction with any database content. Often it is not sufficient for an active component to react to and process a single event, but instead it needs to establish some long-term interaction with a client application or device. In addition to the active components managed by the active component runtime layer in combination with the DBMS (active component logic), we therefore also support the concept of active components that are deployed to the client side by the database (active component stub) as highlighted in Fig. 5.

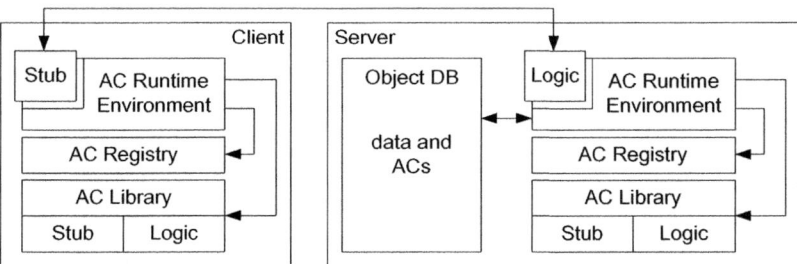

Fig. 5. Client-server active component runtime environment

In this new client-server active component scenario, the first phase is still the same. After the active component runtime environment has detected that an active component has been returned as a result of a query, the corresponding active component logic is instantiated and initialised on the server side. In the next step, a representation of the active component including its unique identifier and all the other fields is sent to the client side. The active component response is detected by the client-side active component runtime environment and, after a lookup in the active component registry, the corresponding active component stub class is fetched from the active component library and executed on the client side. In Fig. 5, the active component registry as well as the active component library are part of the client environment. However, these two lookup services could also be accessed remotely.

An interesting aspect of the client-server active component approach is that the active component stub can take over the control over any input from the client and communicate directly with the server-side active component logic instance. It is up to the implementation of a specific active component stub to define any criteria for the termination of an active component service by calling a special setDone() method. Note that the terms client and server are to be interpreted on a conceptual level and do not necessarily imply that the active component stub and logic instances have to run on remote sites. It is even possible that an active component stub interacts with an active component logic within the same virtual machine.

We can basically distinguish three different types of active component services that can be driven by the database. If only data has to be created, updated or deleted on the database side, an active component logic instance can be used to implement this kind of functionality as shown in Fig. 6. After a database request has been processed, the corresponding active component logic is loaded and a confirmation message (OK) is sent to the client. Note that the confirmation for the client can either be sent after the active component stub has been successfully initialised or after the execution of the active component logic has finished. This solution is closely related to the AOODB approach with the difference that interactions may also be driven explicitly from outside rather than being based only on the internal database state. An example of such a server-side active component service could be an active component that provides some business logic and updates multiple database objects when invoked.

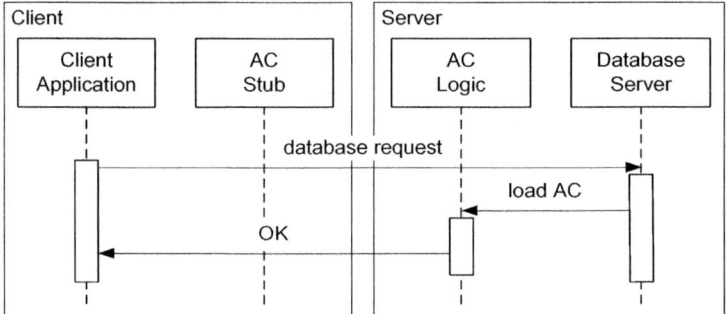

Fig. 6. Server-side application functionality

The second type of service involves the client component only. In this case, illustrated in Fig. 7, the server-side active component logic just sends an active component specification to the client side without executing any application functionality. The client-side active component runtime environment loads the corresponding active component stub instance and executes its functionality. An example of a client-side active component could be a Movie active component that is deployed to the client together with the URI of a movie clip as a parameter and opens the movie in the client's default movie player.

The advantage of this database-driven execution of client-side functionality is that it becomes easier to deploy specific functionality to different client devices. As long as a client device provides an active component runtime environment, an active component stub can be executed on different devices. Another advantage of the database-driven deployment of client-side services is that we can avoid any redundant installation and update of services on different client devices since the functionality is deployed to these devices on demand.

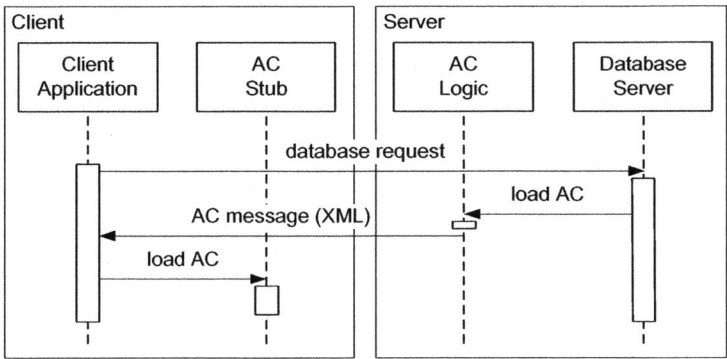

Fig. 7. Client-side application functionality

The most powerful active component service solution involves the combined execution of application functionality on the server as well as on the client side and potential communication between the client- and server-side active components as highlighted in Fig. 8. This flexible approach supports a variety of use cases ranging from consistency checks on the client side before sending update queries to the database to the filtering and streaming of real-time data. In Sect. 7, we will provide some examples of how this client-server active component approach has been used for implementing highly interactive user interfaces to databases.

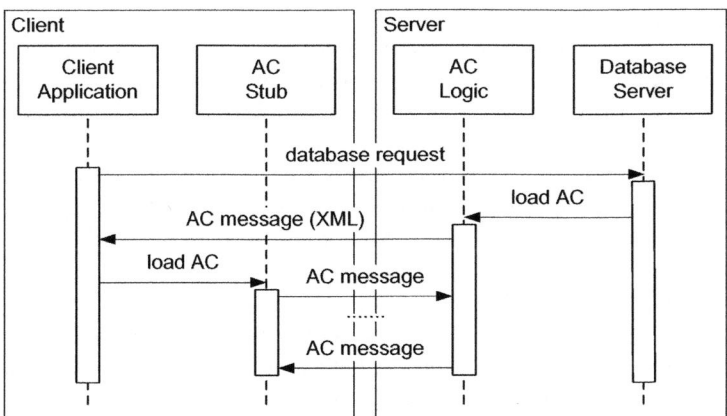

Fig. 8. Client- and server-side application functionality

Note that the second as well third type of active component services, where part of the active component functionality is executed on the client side, are not supported by AOODB solutions or Web Service approaches.

6   Implementation

A first prototype of the active component framework for database-driven services has been realised in Java on top of our own object-oriented data management framework [14]. However, the presented concepts are general enough to be implemented in other programming languages and environments. Since our application scenario was mainly dealing with various client devices accessing and interacting with information stored within our object-oriented database system, we have chosen a classical client-server architecture where the client communicates with the server over the HTTP protocol. The active component communication does not have to be limited to a single protocol and different configurations are possible.

While our OODBMS stores active components in terms of database objects containing the relevant information to initialise the services at request time, it is up to the client- and server-side active component runtime environments to start the corresponding services. For each uniquely identifiable service, the corresponding stub and logic Java classes have to be registered in the active component registry. The client- and server-side active component runtimes use this information provided by the active component registry to dynamically load the classes.

The active component logic and stub classes share some common features such as all the metadata provided by the active component database object as well as an initialisation method as shown in Fig. 9. After an active component stub has been loaded, its `init()` method is invoked. The active component metadata is then serialised in XML and sent to the client-side active component runtime environment. After deserialising the XML message, an active component stub is instantiated on the client side. The active component stub provides an enhanced initialisation method where the component gets not only access to its configuration data (`ACConfiguration`) but also a handle to the client (device) initiating the interaction. Subsequent events are processed by the `processEvent()` method and there might be some potential communication with the server-side active component logic. Any request from an active component stub to its corresponding active component logic is sent in XML format and processed by the active component logic's `handleActionRequest()` method which generates an appropriate response.

It is up to the client-side active component to decide when its work has to be finished and the component has to be unloaded. As soon as the active component stub's `setDone()` method gets invoked as part of the component's program logic, the active component stub is unloaded by the client-side active component runtime environment. Note that before its removal from the system, there is an upcall to the active component's `finish()` method. This enables the active component developer to perform any necessary cleanup and release of acquired resources such as database or network connections. In addition, a client- or server-side active component has an optional timeout parameter and is terminated automatically if it has been idle for longer than a given amount of time.

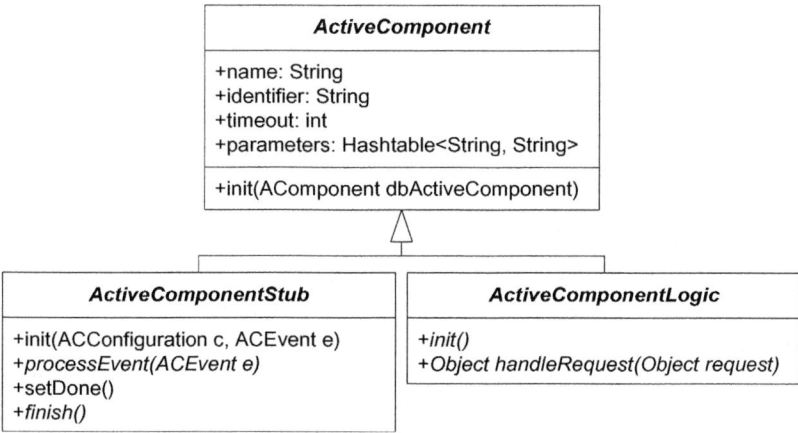

Fig. 9. Active component stub and logic

There are some *resource-specific active components* which require additional information from the client triggering the active component. These components can be reused in different applications but they always have to be used in combination with a client providing the appropriate input data. On the other hand, *generic active components* do not depend on any additional information from the client. An example of a generic active component is a `Browser` active component opening the system's default web browser with a given URI parameter.

Note that while the current implementation is based on Java, it is also possible to support active components implemented in other programming languages. It would even be possible to have stub and logic components that are implemented in different languages given that the communication could, for example, be over XML. It is up to the active component registry and active component library to provide access to an active component in the required programming language based on the active component identifier. Of course in order to support active components implemented in other programming languages, we would also have to implement additional active component runtime environments.

By providing the corresponding active component runtime environment on top of our data management framework, we also plan to implement some of the examples introduced earlier in Sect. 2..

7 Use Case

A major advantage of having the active components as first class objects within the system rather than implementing the corresponding functionality within a method that is tightly bound to a specific database object is that it becomes easier to reuse functionality of existing active components by inheritance. To illustrate this, we provide an example of several active components that build on top of each other and have been implemented as part of our interactive paper platform (iPaper) [15,16] for processing digital pen input. Digital pen and paper technology[2] enables the continuous capturing of a pen's position on ordinary paper augmented with a position encoding pattern. The captured digital information can, for example, be processed by an active component and used to trigger digital actions and services. Note that we only show the details for the stub components since, for this specific task, most of the interaction takes place on the client side.

As part of a specific iPaper application, we wanted to capture pen stroke information from a digital pen, perform intelligent character recognition (ICR) on the captured handwriting and output the recognised text using a text-to-speech (TTS) engine. Instead of implementing this functionality as a monolithic piece of program, the active component-based approach enabled us to separate the functionality into several reusable active components highlighted in Fig. 10.

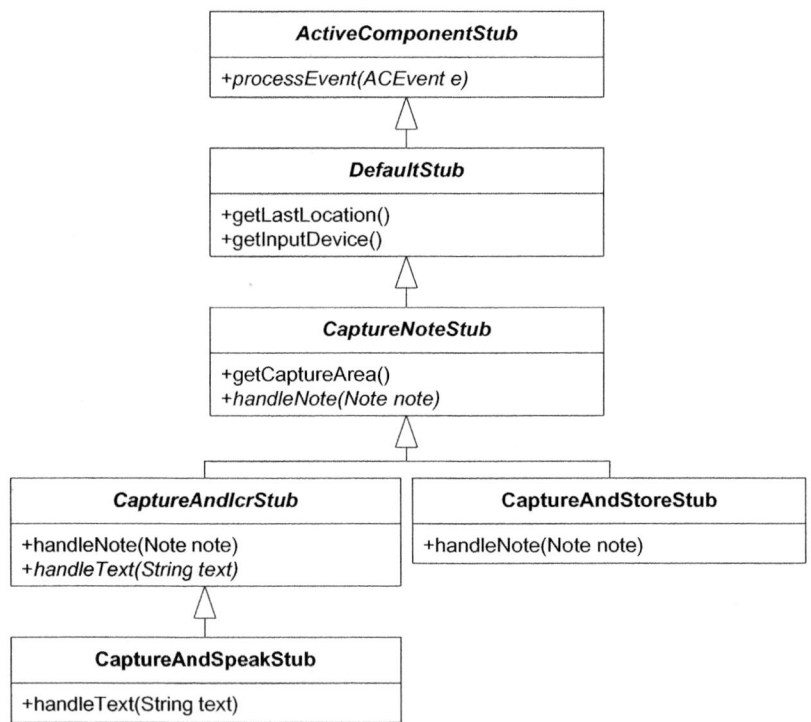

Fig. 10. Active component examples

A first client-side active component is the DefaultStub, an extension of the ActiveComponentStub providing some general functionality required by many interactive paper active components. For example, the DefaultStub provides access to the last pen position (getLastLocation()) that was processed by the

---

[2] http://www.anoto.com

active component or offers a handle to the buffered input device. Note that the
`DefaultStub` is an abstract class and therefore it is not possible to directly
instantiate any `DefaultStub` active component.

The `CaptureNoteStub` active component extends the `DefaultStub` class and
offers the functionality to capture handwritten notes. For example, the
`CaptureNoteStub` communicates with its server-side logic component to get information about the capture area from the interactive paper database. This
information is accessible via the `getCaptureArea()` method and is used as a
criteria to finish the capture process and terminate the active component as
soon as the pen leaves the predefined capture area. The `CaptureNoteStub` is
still an abstract class which can be accessed by other services that would like
to build on top of a capture service. As a result of the capture process, there is
an upcall to the abstract `handleNote()` method with the captured note as an
argument, as soon as the capture process finishes. Note that the configuration
of a `CaptureNoteStub` active component contains a variety of other key/value
properties to, for example, define whether a captured note should be cropped.

A simple active component that makes use of the `CaptureNoteStub` service
is defined in the `CaptureAndStoreStub` class. By overriding the `handleNote()`
method, the `CaptureAndStoreStub` active component gets access to the captured note and stores it in the local file system. The configuration parameters
of the `CaptureAndStoreStub` component include information about the format
of the document to be stored (e.g. jpeg or gif) as well as the path and filename.

This example of an active component storing the captured note in the file
system was only introduced to show that an active component's functionality,
in this case the one of the `CaptureNoteStub`, can be reused by many different active components. Our goal is to further process the capture information
and therefore we implement a `CaptureAndIcrStub` that takes the output of the
`CaptureNoteStub` component, performs some intelligent character recognition
on the stroke data and returns a text in string form. The `CaptureAndIcrStub`
is again an abstract class and the `handleText()` method has to be overridden
by any concrete subclass.

Last but not least, the `CaptureAndSpeakStub` class is an extension of the
`CaptureAndIcrStub` component implementing the `handleText()` method and
feeding the text to a text-to-speech engine. A summary of the method upcalls
within the inheritance hierarchy of the `CaptureAndSpeakStub` class is shown in
Fig. 11.

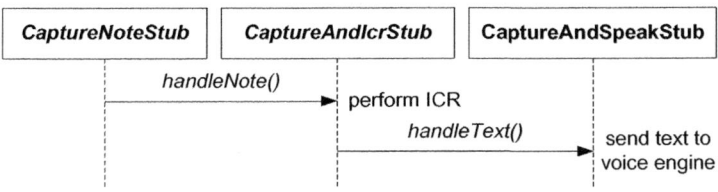

Fig. 11. Active component method calls

Figure 12 outlines the interaction between the `CaptureAndSpeakLogic` and `CaptureAndSpeakStub` components as part of a capture process. After the `CaptureAndSpeakLogic` and `CaptureAndSpeakStub` components have been initialised, the `CaptureAndSpeakStub` sends a request to the server-side active component to get information about the capture area. The `CaptureAndSpeakStub` then autonomously processes any positional input from the digital pen until the pen leaves the predefined capture area. It finally applies an intelligent character recognition (ICR) algorithm to the captured data and sends the resulting string to a text-to-speech (TTS) engine. While it was not the goal of this active component to store the captured information, this functionality can be easily realised by sending a message with the captured data to the server-side active component. This server-side storage of captured information based on active components was used in the EdFest interactive paper-based festival guide [17] for sharing comments. In the EdFest application, active components were not only used to persistently store captured information but also to send requests to external databases.

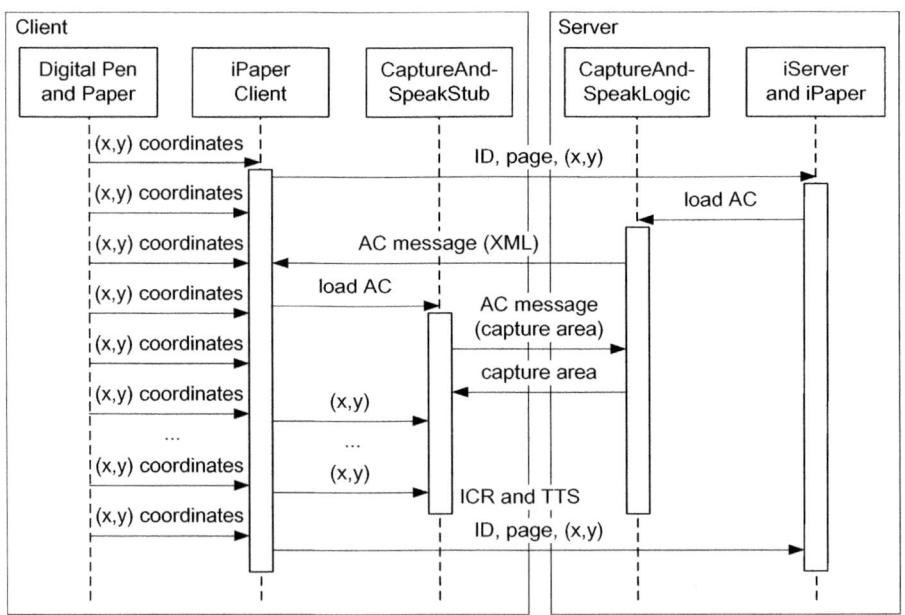

Fig. 12. Client and server active component interaction

To achieve the task of capturing some pen-based input, recognising the handwritten information and producing the corresponding voice output, we have defined four reusable components. There are several advantages of this fine granularity of functionality offered by the different active components. First of all, the frequent reuse of the components should enhance the overall quality of the components over time. Since there is a growing set of active components, it also becomes easier for the developer to design and implement extensions of existing active components. Another advantage is that the code size of a single active component is relatively small and therefore it is easy to understand the functionality that it offers. Furthermore, we gain flexibility by storing the active component configurations in a database since all of its parameters can easily be adapted at runtime without a recompilation of the source code. However, the reusability of active component functionality within and across applications is only one aspect. As we have shown, another important benefit is the definition of modular and component-based client-server interaction which goes far beyond the "simple" remote service invocation offered by other solutions.

Our database-driven application development process based on active components has been successfully used to realise multiple highly interactive cross-media applications. These applications included artistic installations [18] as well as a variety of interactive paper applications [16,19].

8   Conclusions

We have presented a database-driven approach for developing highly interactive applications based on active components. While many systems focus on the integration of services on the protocol level, our approach provides a high-level lightweight solution for an application developer to implement and reuse modular services. The clear separation of data objects and services provided by active components further simplifies the reuse of services with various types of data. Since active components are first-class database objects, their associated services can easily be configured within the database. A service provided by an active component can be flexibly associated with data objects on the instance, type or classification level. Role-driven service invocation provides a flexible mechanism for runtime object evolution in terms of services that are bound to a specific object. Further, the client-server active component runtime environment provides a powerful solution for executing parts of the application on the client side and for establishing a client-server service communication. While service-oriented architectures allow for executing remote services, our active component-based approach enables the definition and execution of autonomous and encapsulated client-server services. The automatic deployment of services to the client side not only simplifies the installation and maintenance of new functionality but also enables a richer form of interaction between client-side services and application data that is stored on the server side.

Acknowledgements

We would like to thank Samuel Willimann and Philipp Bolliger for their work on the prototype implementation of the active component framework. We would further like to thank Stefania Leone and Alexandre de Spindler for their valuable comments on the paper.

References

1. Szyperski, C.: Component Software: Beyond Object-Oriented Programming. Addison-Wesley Professional, Reading (2002)
2. Papazoglou, M.: Web Services: Principles and Technology. Prentice Hall, Englewood Cliffs (2007)
3. Krafzig, D., Banke, K., Slama, D.: Enterprise SOA: Service-Oriented Architecture Best Practices. Prentice Hall, Englewood Cliffs (2004)
4. Subasu, I.E., Ziegler, P., Dittrich, K.R., Gall, H.: Architectural Concerns for Flexible Data Management. In: Proc. of SETMDM 2008, EDBT Workshop on Software Engineering for Tailor-made Data Management, Nantes, France (March 2008)
5. Rellermeyer, J.S., Duller, M., Gilmer, K., Maragkos, D., Papageorgiou, D., Alonso, G.: The Software Fabric for the Internet of Things. In: Floerkemeier, C., Langheinrich, M., Fleisch, E., Mattern, F., Sarma, S.E. (eds.) IOT 2008. LNCS, vol. 4952, pp. 87–104. Springer, Heidelberg (2008)
6. de Deugd, S., Carroll, R., Kelly, K., Millett, B., Ricker, J.: SODA: Service Oriented Device Architecture. IEEE Pervasive Computing 5(3), 94–96 (2006)
7. Tok, W.H., Bressan, S.: DBNet: A Service-Oriented Database Architecture. In: Proc. of DEXA 2006, 17th Intl. Conference on Database and Expert Systems Applications, Krakow, Poland, September 2006, pp. 727–731 (2006)
8. Eisenberg, A.: New Standard for Stored Procedures in SQL. ACM SIGMOD Record 25(4), 81–88 (1996)
9. Paton, N.W., Díaz, O.: Active Database Systems. ACM Computing Surveys (CSUR) 31(1), 63–103 (1999)
10. Kappel, G., Retschitzegger, W.: The TriGS Active Object-Oriented Database System – An Overview. ACM SIGMOD Record 27(3), 36–41 (1998)
11. Bretl, R., Maier, D., Otis, A., Penney, J., Schuchardt, B., Stein, J., Williams, E.H., Williams, M.: The Gem–Stone Data Management System. In: Object Oriented Concepts, Databases and Applications. ACM Press, New York (1989)
12. Signer, B., Norrie, M.C.: As We May Link: A General Metamodel for Hypermedia Systems. In: Parent, C., Schewe, K.-D., Storey, V.C., Thalheim, B. (eds.) ER 2007. LNCS, vol. 4801, pp. 359–374. Springer, Heidelberg (2007)
13. Norrie, M.C.: Distinguishing Typing and Classification in Object Data Models. Information Modelling and Knowledge Bases VI 26, 399–412 (1995)
14. Kobler, A., Norrie, M.C.: OMS Java: A Persistent Object Management Framework. In: Java and Databases. Hermes Penton Science, May 2002, pp. 46–62 (2002)
15. Norrie, M.C., Signer, B., Weibel, N.: General Framework for the Rapid Development of Interactive Paper Applications. In: Proc. of CoPADD 2006, 1st Intl. Workshop on Collaborating over Paper and Digital Documents, Banff, Canada, November 2006, pp. 9–12 (2006)
16. Signer, B.: Fundamental Concepts for Interactive Paper and Cross-Media Information Spaces. PhD thesis, ETH Zurich, Dissertation ETH No. 16218 (May 2006)
17. Signer, B., Grossniklaus, M., Norrie, M.C.: Interactive Paper as a Mobile Client for a Multi-Channel Web Information System. World Wide Web Journal 10(4), 529–556 (2007)
18. Vogelsang, A., Signer, B.: The Lost Cosmonaut: An Interactive Narrative Environment on Basis of Digitally Enhanced Paper. In: Subsol, G. (ed.) ICVS-VirtStory 2005. LNCS, vol. 3805, pp. 270–279. Springer, Heidelberg (2005)
19. Signer, B., Norrie, M.C.: PaperPoint: A Paper-Based Presentation and Interactive Paper Prototyping Tool. In: Proc. of TEI 2007, First Intl. Conference on Tangible and Embedded Interaction, Baton Rouge, USA, February 2007, pp. 57–64 (2007)

Optimization of Object-Oriented Queries Involving Weakly Dependent Subqueries

Michał Bleja[1], Tomasz Kowalski[2],
Radosław Adamus[2], and Kazimierz Subieta[3,4]

[1] Faculty of Mathematics and Computer Science, University of Łódź, Poland
`blejam@math.uni.lodz.pl`
[2] Computer Engineering Department, Technical University of Łódź, Poland
`{tkowals,radamus}@kis.p.lodz.pl`
[3] Polish-Japanese Institute of Information Technology, Warsaw, Poland
[4] Institute of Computer Science, Polish Academy of Sciences, Warsaw, Poland
`subieta@pjwstk.edu.pl`

Abstract. A new static optimization method in object query languages is presented. We introduce a special kind of subqueries of a query referred to as "weakly dependent subqueries". A subquery is weakly dependent if it depends from an external query operator only on an expression returning the result of an enumerated type. If a query contains such subqueries then we rewrite it to an equivalent form which guarantees much better performance. Our method is based on the stack-based approach (SBA) and its query language SBQL (Stack-Based Query Language) implemented in the ODRA system. SBA is relevant for a general object model and for its specific variants. Clean formal semantics and abstract implementation of SBQL, integration with the constructs of programming languages and advanced data structures give the possibility to investigate different areas that are related to query optimization techniques. The paper presents examples how the optimization method works. General and detailed features of the implemented algorithm are also presented.

Keywords: query optimization, weakly dependent subquery, stack-based approach, SBQL, object-oriented database, strong typing.

1   Introduction

In the past optimization of object-oriented queries attracted many researchers, see for example [4,6]. Recently, however, the attention of the research community to object databases is much lower thus the problem is a bit forgotten. There are even opinions that nothing essential in this respect has been done and is expected. Fortunately, this is not true. In our research and implementation devoted to object-oriented databases we treat query optimization very seriously. We have developed and implemented several methods, including query rewriting and indices [10]. Some of them we adopted and generalized from relational systems,

M.C. Norrie and M. Grossniklaus (Eds.): ICOODB 2009, LNCS 5936, pp. 77–94, 2010.

but the majority of them are totally new. This paper presents one of such new powerful methods.

Query optimization based on the analysis of weakly dependent subqueries belongs to optimization methods that are based on query rewriting. It is static optimization entirely performed before a query is executed. Rewriting means transforming a query q1 into a semantically equivalent query q2 ensuring better performance. It is accomplished according to rewriting rules, which are based on detecting parts of a query matching some pattern. These parts are to be replaced according to the rewriting rule by other parts. Such optimizations are compile-time actions, hence the optimization processes do not affect run-time performance of database applications. For very large databases the gain from query rewriting can be significant, sometimes the orders of magnitude shorter query response time.

One of the most important rewriting optimization techniques is the method of independent subqueries. It is known from relational systems and SQL in a less general variant [8,9]. Using the method, some subquery can be factored out from a loop implied by a query operator if the subquery result is the same for each cycle of the loop. In the stack-based approach [1,17,18,19] this method is generalized (see [13,14,15,18]) for any kind of non-algebraic query operators and for a general object-oriented database model that includes arbitrarily complex objects, collections, classes and methods, cardinalities associated to any database entity, static and dynamic inheritance, associations, encapsulation, polymorphism, etc. Non-algebraic operators include selection, join, projection/navigation (dot), quantifiers, ordering and transitive closures. In such cases an independent subquery is evaluated only once and its result is used in each loop iteration. The method was successfully implemented in different systems. The last implementation concerns the ODRA system [2,11,12] deployed in two large European projects, eGov Bus and VIDE [20], and in several local projects.

In the research that is presented in this paper we generalize the independent subqueries method. It may happen that the result of some subquery is dependent from the nearest non-algebraic operator (the result can be different in each loop cycle of the operator), but the dependency is specifically constrained. The dependency concerns a name that is typed by enumeration. Consider the query (*Get females earning more than the average for women and males earning more than the average for men*):

$$(Emp \textbf{ as } e) \textbf{ where } e.sal > \textbf{avg}((Emp \textbf{ as } f \textbf{ where } e.sex = f.sex).f.sal) \quad (1)$$

In this case the subquery

$$\textbf{avg}((Emp \textbf{ as } f \textbf{ where } e.sex = f.sex).f.sal) \quad (2)$$

is not independent from the first *where* operator because it contains the name e that is bound in the second section of the environment stack, which is just opened by the first operator *where*. However, it makes little sense to evaluate it thousands of times because it is clear that it can be evaluated only two times: once assuming $e.sex = $ "male" and next one assuming $e.sex = $ "female". How such cases can be generally formalized and how the corresponding rewriting algorithm should look like?

A subquery like (2) we call "weakly dependent", because it depends on the enumerated type { "male", "female"} only. The idea of our rewriting rule is based on converting weakly dependent subqueries into independent subqueries and then, optimizing it by the already developed independent subqueries method. The advantage of the mentioned above optimization method is that the number of evaluations of a weakly dependent subquery is equal to the number of values of the enumerated type that the subquery depends on. Usually the number of values of an enumerated type is much lower than the number of objects in a collection visited by a query operator like selection. Thus the performance gain can be very essential. The method can also be associated with some query evaluation cost model or with some heuristics if we assume very large enumerated types which do not justify straightforward application of the method.

Implementation of the weakly dependent subqueries method is strictly related to an enumerated types. This kind of types has been implemented by us in the ODRA system. We hope that this optimization method will also be useful in other object-oriented database management systems that involve non-trivial nested queries. The method can also be extended to dictionaries that are kept in databases and to some kind of queries that address jointly very big and very small collections in a database.

The rest of the paper is organized as follows. In Sect. 2 we briefly present main concepts of the Stack-Based Approach that are important for our optimization method. Section 3 gives an overview of the method based on factoring out independent subqueries. Section 4 describes the general idea of the weakly dependent subqueries method. Section 5 presents the corresponding algorithm that we have implemented, including its pseudocode. Section 6 presents the results of simple experiments with the method. Section 7 presents conclusions and future work.

2 Main Concepts of the Stack-Based Approach (SBA)

The Stack-Based Approach (SBA) and its Stack-Based Query Language (SBQL) are the result of investigations into a uniform conceptual platform for integrated query and programming languages for object-oriented databases [1,17,18,19]. The approach is universal and abstract, what makes it relevant to a very general object model. SBA assumes that a query language is a special case of a programming language. The basic paradigm of SBA is known as the *naming, scoping* and *binding*. Each *name* in a query or program code is *bound* according to its scope to a suitable run-time entity (e.g. object, attribute, variable, procedure, method, view, etc.).

Environment stack (ENVS), known also as *call stack*, is an important concept of SBA. The stack is responsible for binding names, scope control, procedure and method calls, parameter passing and other features of object-oriented query and programming languages. In SBA the stack has a new role: processing non-algebraic operators. In contrast to stacks implemented in (practically all) well-known high-level programming languages, in SBA the stack does not store objects (or variables). It stores *binders*, that is, some structures built upon names, object identifiers and values. SBA assumes full internal identification:

each run-time entity that can be separately retrieved or updated must possess a unique internal identifier. SBA assumes no differences in defining types and queries addressing transient and persistent data (this is known as *orthogonal persistence* [3]). SBA assumes the *object relativity* principle which claims no syntactic, semantic and pragmatic differences of queries addressing objects stored at any level of object hierarchy.

In SBA results of functional methods and procedures belong to the same semantic category as results of queries. Thus such methods and procedures can be called in queries. SBQL is semi-strongly typed, which means that a type can be associated with a cardinal number like [0..1] or [0..*] (known from UML), where lower number 0 denotes that an object can be absent (similar to a *null value* known from relational systems) or a collection can be empty. Types are used for static code checking, dynamic checking of objects structures and for query optimization. The following three sets are used to define objects:

- I – the set of unique internal identifiers
- N – the set of external data names
- V – the set of atomic values, e.g. strings, integers, blobs, etc.

Atomic values include also codes of procedures, functions, methods, views, etc. Let $i, i_1, i_2 \in I$, $n \in N$, and $v \in V$. Objects are modeled as triples: *atomic objects* as $\langle i, n, v \rangle$; *link objects* as $\langle i_1, n, i_2 \rangle$; *complex objects* as $\langle i, n, S \rangle$, where S denotes a set of objects. This definition is recursive—it is possible to create complex objects with any number of hierarchy levels. Relationships are represented through link objects. To represent collections SBA does not assume the uniqueness of external object names at any level of object hierarchy.

Queries in SBQL return structures built upon object identifiers, names and values. In SBA classes are understood as prototypes, which means that they are objects, but their role is different. A class object stores invariants (e.g. methods) of the objects that are instances of that class. A special relationship—instantiation—between a class and its instances is introduced. Inheritance between classes is supported.

Example database. An SBA object store is specified in the UML-like class diagram presented in Fig. 1. The schema defines five classes: *Person, Student, Emp, Project*, and *Dept. Person* is the superclass of the classes *Student* and *Emp*. The classes *Project, Student, Emp* and *Dept* model students implementing projects, which are supervised by employees working in departments. An *Emp* object can contain multiple complex *prev_job* subobjects (previous jobs). Names of classes (attributes, links, etc.) are followed by cardinality numbers, cardinality [1..1] is dropped. Attributes *sex* of *Person* and *position* of *Emp* are of an enumerated type. The first one takes values (*"male"*, *"female"*), the second one takes values (*"analyst"*, *"programmer"*, *"tester"*).

SBQL is described in detail in [1,12,18,19]. It has several implementations, in particular for the ODRA system. The syntax of SBQL is as follows:

- A single name or a single literal is an (atomic) query. For instance, *Emp, name, salary, x, y, "John", 1000*, etc, are queries.

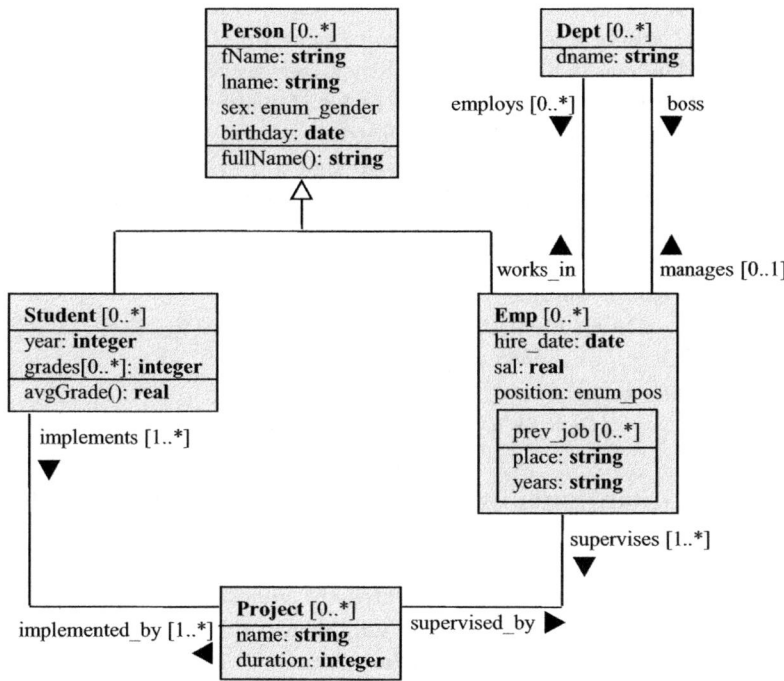

Fig. 1. A schema (class diagram) of an example database

- If q is a query, and σ is a unary operator (e.g. *sum, avg, count, distinct, cos, sqrt*), then $\sigma(q)$ is a query.
- If q_1 and q_2 are queries, and θ is a binary operator (e.g. *where, dot, join, +, =, and*), then $q_1 \, \theta \, q_2$ is a query.

Semantics of SBQL queries follows the *compositionality* principle, which means that the semantics of a query is a function of the semantics of its components, recursively, down to atomic queries (names and literals). In principle, all operators that are used to build queries are unary or binary. Big syntactic and semantic patterns, such as *select...from...where...group by...having...* etc., are avoided. This feature much simplifies implementation and supports query optimization.

SBQL operators are subdivided into *algebraic* and *non-algebraic*. The main difference between them is whether they modify the state of ENVS during query processing or not. If an operator does not modify ENVS then it is algebraic. The algebraic operators include string and numerical operators and comparisons, Boolean *and, or, not*, aggregate functions, bag and sequence operators and comparisons, structure constructors, etc. Very useful algebraic operators are *as* and *group as* which name query results. Operator *as* names each element in a bag or sequence returned by a query, while *group as* names the entire query result.

Evaluation of the non-algebraic operators requires further notions. If we have a query $q_1\,\theta\,q_2$, where θ is a non-algebraic operator, then q_2 is evaluated in the context of q_1. The context is determined by a new section on ENVS opened by θ for an element returned by q_1. Thus the order of evaluation of subqueries q_1 and q_2 is important. The non-algebraic operators include: selection (q_1 **where** q_2), dependent join (q_1 **join** q_2), projection/navigation ($q_1.q_2$), quantifiers ($\forall q_1(q_2)$ and $\exists q_1(q_2)$), ordering and transitive closures. Path expressions are compositions of the dot operator, e.g. $q_1.q_2.q_3.q_4.q_5$ is understood as $(((q_1.q_2).q_3).q_4).q_5$. All features of currently implemented SBQL can be found in [1,12,18,19]. Below we present sample SBQL queries:

"Get employees earning more than 2000"

$$Emp \textbf{ where } sal > 2000 \qquad (3)$$

"Get departments together with their bosses"

$$(Dept \textbf{ as } d) \textbf{ join } (d.boss.Emp \textbf{ as } b) \qquad (4)$$

3 Query Optimization by Factoring Out Independent Subqueries

The following example in SBQL illustrates the general idea of the independent subqueries method. The query (5) gets employees who earn more than Clark.

$$Emp \textbf{ where } sal > ((Emp \textbf{ where } name=\text{"Clark"}).sal) \qquad (5)$$

Note that the subquery

$$(Emp \textbf{ where } name=\text{"Clark"}).sal \qquad (6)$$

due to the loop implied by the first *where* operator, is evaluated for each *Emp* object in the database. However, it is enough to evaluate the subquery only once, because its result is the same in each loop cycle. The idea of the independent subqueries method assumes two phases: detecting subqueries that are independent and then, rewriting the entire query by pushing independent subqueries out of loops.

Detecting independent subqueries is accomplished by the analysis in which section of the environment stack the names occurring in a subquery are to be bound. If none of the names of the subquery is bound in the stack section opened by the currently evaluated non-algebraic operator, then the subquery is independent and can be evaluated outside the loop. In our example the subquery (6) is independent from the first *where* operator of the query (5). Hence the method factors (6) out of the *where* operator in the following steps:

- A new unique auxiliary name is introduced to name the result of (6)
- Query (6) is named with that name, put before the entire query (5), and connected to (5) by the dot operator
- The auxiliary name is put in the original place of (6)

In the result of the above rewriting rules we get the following query:

$$((Emp \textbf{ where } name=\text{"Clark"}).sal \textbf{ group as } aux).(Emp \textbf{ where } sal > aux) \qquad (7)$$

Note that for naming the subquery we use the operator *group as* (nesting) rather than *as*. In this way the method is much more general, because we need not to care what type of the result the subquery returns. In particular, it can return bags, sequences or any other data structures that are provided by the typing system.

Although the idea seems to be simple, the general algorithm is quite sophisticated. It is connected with the strong type checker, which (besides typical actions) augments a query abstract syntax tree (AST) by order numbers of the environment stack sections. A number is assigned to all non-algebraic operators and to all names occurring in a query and denotes a section opened by a non-algebraic operator or a section in which a given name is to be bound, correspondingly. Then, AST is traversed recursively to find the largest subquery having all the numbers different than the number assigned to a non-algebraic operator processing the subquery. After discovering such a subquery the AST is reorganized, as shown in our example above. The optimization method is repeated, to detect next and next subqueries to be pushed out of loops. Some subquery can be independent from several loops, hence in each step of the method the subquery is pushed out of a next loop. The process is finished when no nontrivial independent subquery is detected. (Trivial queries are literals and single names, with exception of names of procedures, methods and views.).

The architecture for query processing is presented in Fig. 2. Query optimizer acts on three structures: a metabase (compiled form a database schema), a static environment stack S_ENVS and a static query result stack S_QRES. These structures are compile-time counterparts of run-time structures: an object store, an environment stack ENVS and a query result stack QRES, correspondingly. The static stacks contain typing signatures. These stacks are managed by the strong type checker, which simulates run-time computations for the given query by calculating type signatures of run-time entities (objects, in particular). Each non-algebraic operator occurring in a query augments S_ENVS according to the stack-based semantics of SBQL and each name occurring in the query is statically bound on S_ENVS returning the signature of a corresponding run-time entity.

Figure 3 presents a part of the schema from Fig. 1 and the corresponding metabase. It consists of nodes, that represent particular entities in the schema, and edges that represent associations between nodes. Three kinds of associations are provided: inheritance (arrows with white ends), subordination of objects (arrows with black ends) and pointer links (arrows with broken lines). The metabase is organized as an object-oriented database, in particular, each node has a unique identifier. The metabase is queried by regular SBQL queries.

Now we can give a precise definition of the concept of typing signature (set T); the definition is recursive:

1. Names of atomic types (e.g. **integer**, **real**, **string**, **date**, etc.) belong to T.
2. Literals belongs to T (to take into account enumerated types).
3. All identifiers of the metabase graph nodes (e.g. i_{Emp} and i_{Dept}) belong to T. Identifiers of graph nodes represent types defined in the database schema.
4. If x belongs to T and n is an external name, then the pair $n(x)$ belongs to T. Such a pair will be called *static binder*.

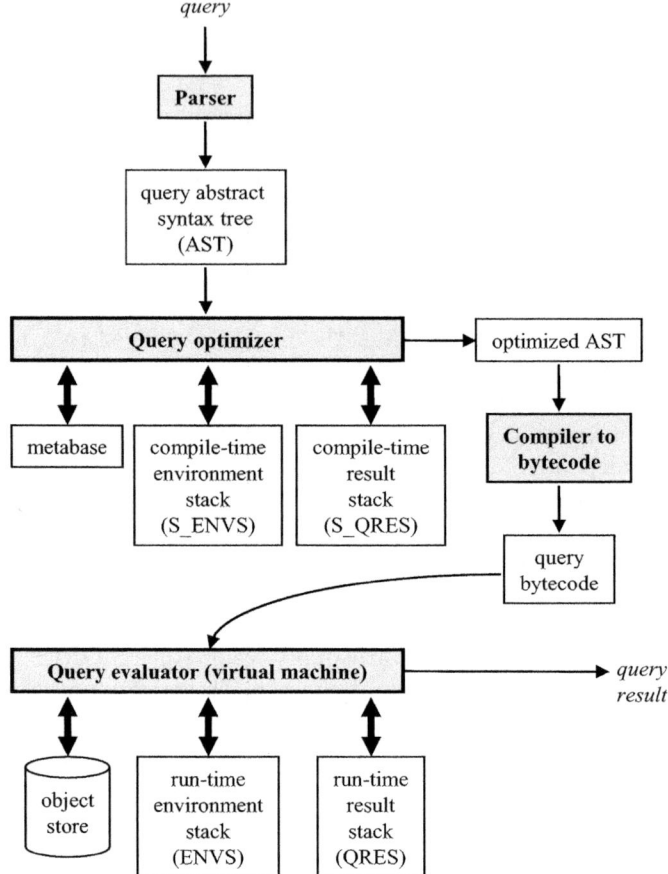

Fig. 2. Architecture of SBQL query processing

5. If $x_1, x_2, \ldots, x_n$ belong to T, then **struct**$\{x_1, x_2, \ldots, x_n\}$ and **variant**$\{x_1, x_2, \ldots, x_n\}$ belong to T. A **variant** is used when the type of an expression cannot be determined at the given stage of compilation (for instance, for processing elliptic queries).
6. If x belongs to T, then **bag**$\{x\}$ and **sequence**$\{x\}$ belong to T. Signatures **bag** and **sequence** reflect bags and sequences processed by the query engine.

There are next rules defining the set T. A function *static_nested* (a compile-time counterpart of the run-time function *nested*) is used during the static type check of queries when a non-algebraic operator is processed. The function refers to the metabase and returns static binders subordinated to a processed metabase node. S_ENVS contains static binders that correspond to actual binders processed during run-time. S_QRES contain signatures that correspond to types of entities that are returned by a query. The strong typechecking mechanism processes these signatures according to the stack-based semantics of SBQL.

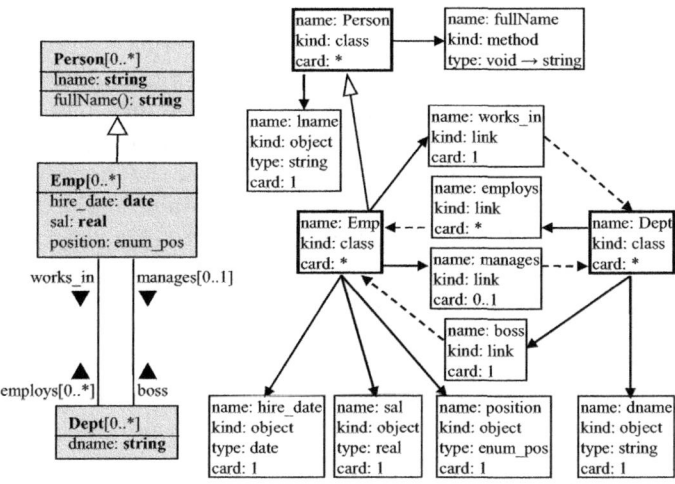

Fig. 3. Database schema and the corresponding metabase

In this way each non-algebraic operator occurring in AST is associated with the number of a stack section that it opens, and each name occurring in AST is associated with the number of a stack section in which it is bound during runtime. Because of the relativity of the stacks (query evaluation can start with any previous state of the stacks) all sections that existed prior to query evaluation are denoted by the number 1. For example, for query (5) these numbers are presented below:

$$Emp \textbf{ where } sal > ((Emp \textbf{ where } name=\text{``Clark''}) \;.\; sal) \tag{8}$$
$$\quad 1 \qquad 2 \quad\; 2 \qquad\quad 1 \qquad 3 \quad\; 3 \qquad\qquad\; 3\; 3$$

Now we can see that the first operator *where* opens the 2nd stack section, but no name occurring in the subquery (6) is bound in this section. Hence the subquery is independent from the loop implied by the *where* operator and can be factored out of the loop, as shown in (7).

After determining that a given subquery is independent from the nearest left-side non-algebraic operator, the general query rewriting rule is the following. Let $q_1 \, \theta \, q_2$ be a query with a non-algebraic operator θ. Let $q_2 = \phi_1 \circ q_3 \circ \phi_2$, where ϕ_1, ϕ_2 are some query parts (perhaps empty), $\circ$ is concatenation of strings, q_3 is a subquery for which θ is the nearest left-side non-algebraic operator and q_3 is independent from this operator. Let *aux* be a unique name that is chosen automatically and is internally marked (to avoid naming clashes). Then the query:

$$q_1 \, \theta \, \phi_1 \circ q_3 \circ \phi_2 \tag{9}$$

can be rewritten to:

$$(q_3 \textbf{ group as } aux) \;.\; (q_1 \, \theta \, \phi_1 \; aux \; \phi_2) \tag{10}$$

Note the generality of this rewriting rule. The rule holds for any data model, including the relational model, the XML model and any version of the object-oriented model. Moreover, it makes no difference concerning which non-algebraic operator is considered—it works for selection, projection, navigation, quantifiers, transitive closures, ordering and any other non-algebraic operator (assuming it will be invented). Note also that the rule makes no assumptions concerning how an independent subquery is complex: it may include any operators, including aggregate functions, method calls, algebraic and non-algebraic operators, etc. The rule makes also no assumptions concerning what the independent subquery returns: it may return a single value, a reference to an object, a structure, a collection of values, a collection of references, a collection of structures, etc. Finally, the rule makes no assumption how the independent subquery is connected with its left and right context (ϕ_1 and ϕ_2).

We claim that such a general and fundamental for query optimization rewriting rule is impossible to express in any other formalism, including the relational algebra and calculus, their object-oriented counterparts, monoid comprehensions calculus, F-logic, etc. Only the stack-based approach presents the right theory that is able to solve the problem in its full generality.

Query optimization rules that are presented in this paper strictly depend on type processing. Calculations performed on type signatures and the management of stacks S_ENVS and S_QRES are fundamental for detecting independent subqueries. Hence, the typing mechanism should strongly involve the semantics of a given query language. Because previous approaches to strong typing of object-oriented query/programming languages do not consider the query semantics at all (e.g. ODMG ODL [5], F-bounded polymorphism, etc.), we claim they are unacceptably limited. Query optimization is much more important function of a typing system than discovering typing errors. For very large databases we can live without a compile-time strong type checking (cf. SQL), but a query language without optimization is unacceptable for the users. Again, only the stack-based approach with its strong typing based on the compile time simulation of runtime actions [7,16,18] presents the right idea which deals either with strong type checking and with query optimization.

4   Query Optimization Involving Weakly Dependent Subqueries

As in case of independent subqueries, weak dependence of subqueries is considered in the context of non-algebraic operators. A subquery is called weakly dependent if there is a name (names) which can be statically bound to an enumerated type and is in the scope opened by the currently evaluated non-algebraic operator. Other names in the subquery should not be in this scope. As previously, finding weakly dependent subqueries consists in analyzing in which sections of ENVS particular names are bound. Hence the static analysis does the following:

- For each non-algebraic operator occurring in a query assigns the order number of a section which it opens. Note that for store models AS1, AS2 and AS3 [19] there may be several sections opened by a non-algebraic operator. Without loss of generality we can assume that all of them are assigned by the same number.

- For each name that is bound in a query assigns the order number of a stack section in which the name is bound (binding level). Note that names after *as* and *group as* are not bound on the stack, hence they are omitted.

The following example illustrates the general idea of the method. The query gets employees which are men and earn more than Smith and women earning more than 2000. For the query below we determine the stack size and the binding level for each name and the order number of a section opened by non-algebraic operators.

$$Emp \textbf{ as } e \textbf{ where } e \, . \, sal > ((2000 \textbf{ where } e \, . \, sex = \text{``female''}) \textbf{ union} \qquad (11)$$
$$\quad 1 \qquad\qquad 2 \quad 2\,3\;3 \qquad\qquad 3 \quad 2\,4\;4$$

$$(Emp \textbf{ where } e \, . \, sex = \text{``male''} \textbf{ and } lName = \text{``Smith''}) \, . \, sal)$$
$$\quad 1 \qquad 3 \quad 2\,4\;4 \qquad\qquad\qquad 3 \qquad\qquad 3\;3$$

Consider the following subquery of query (11).

$$((2000 \textbf{ where } e.sex = \text{``female''}) \textbf{ union} \qquad\qquad\qquad (12)$$
$$(Emp \textbf{ where } e.sex = \text{``male''} \textbf{ and } lName = \text{``Smith''}).sal)$$

The subquery (12) is not independent from the first *where* in query (11) because name e in expressions $e.sex$ is bound in the scope opened by the *where* operator. However subquery (12) is weakly dependent w.r.t. the operator. The name *sex* in both expressions $e.sex$ is typed to an enumerated type. Hence the expression $e.sex$ can take only two values: "male" or "female". Denote (12) by *wdq(e.sex)*. Then, the original query (11) $Emp \textbf{ as } e \textbf{ where } e.sal > wdq(e.sex)$ can be rewritten to (13):

$$Emp \textbf{ as } e \textbf{ where if } e.sex = \text{``male''} \textbf{ then } e.sal > wdq(\text{``male''}) \qquad (13)$$
$$\textbf{else } e.sal > wdq(\text{``female''})$$

After unfolding (13) we obtain the following query:

$$Emp \textbf{ as } e \textbf{ where if } e.sex = \text{``male''} \qquad\qquad\qquad\qquad (14)$$
$$\textbf{then } e.sal > ((2000 \textbf{ where } \text{``male''} = \text{``female''}) \textbf{ union}$$
$$(Emp \textbf{ where } \text{``male''} = \text{``male''} \textbf{ and } lName = \text{``Smith''}).sal)$$
$$\textbf{else } e.sal > ((2000 \textbf{ where } \text{``female''} = \text{``female''}) \textbf{ union}$$
$$(Emp \textbf{ where } \text{``female''} = \text{``male''} \textbf{ and } lName = \text{``Smith''}).sal)$$

If an enumerated type has more than two values, we can use several *if* operators or some *case* or *switch* operator. Note that we put *if* directly after the first *where* operator on which the subquery depends. This is conscious decision, because in this way we can collectively resolve several weakly dependent subqueries that may occur in the scope of a non-algebraic operator and depend on the same name.

Is our transformation beneficial for performance? In (11) the expressions $e.sex$ is under two operators *where*. Therefore we had to perform many evaluations (e.g. bindings, opening new sections) of expression $e.sex$. For instance, if the database contains 500 employees we process the expression $e.sex$ 250500 times. Query (14) requires only 500 times, because $e.sex$ is under the external *where* operator only.

Moreover, query (14) is a good starting point for further optimizations. Our static analysis mechanism can calculate comparison of literals and change them into *true* or *false*. Then, these truth values can be removed, together with some parts of the entire query (14). In the result, (14) can be transformed to the form:

Emp **as** e **where if** $e.sex$ = "male"   (15)
　　then $e.sal$ > $(Emp$ **where** $lName$ = "Smith").sal **else** $e.sal$ > 2000

In (15) the subquery $(Emp$ **where** $lName$="Smith").sal is now independent from the first where operator, hence it can be optimized by the independent subquery method:

　　$((Emp$ **where** $lName$ = "Smith").sal **group as** aux).   (16)
　　$(Emp$ **as** e **where if** $e.sex$ = "male" **then** $e.sal$ > aux **else** $e.sal$ > 2000)

If there is a dense index for $lName$ in the Emp collection, then the query can be further optimized by involving the index $(Emp\_lName\_Index$ is a function returning a reference to a proper object according to the parameter being the index key):

　　$((Emp\_lName\_Index($"Smith").sal **group as** aux).   (17)
　　$(Emp$ **as** e **where if** $e.sex$ = "male" **then** $e.sal$ > aux **else** $e.sal$ > 2000)

The form (17) terminates the optimization action—no further optimization is possible.

In some cases the weakly dependent subqueries method does not generate independent subqueries. Consider the query (18) (*Get departments together with the number of their employees having the position of their boss*):

　　$Dept$ **join count**($employs$. Emp **where** $position$ = $boss$. Emp . $position$)   (18)
　　　　1　　2　　　　　　2　　3　3　　　3　　　3　　　　2　4　4　4　　　4

The above query contains the *subquery boss.Emp.position* which is weakly dependent from the *join* operator (name *boss* is bound in the 2nd stack section opened by the join). The subquery can take three values (*"analyst"*, *"programmer"*, *"tester"*). According to our method we get the following query:

　　$Dept$ **join**   (19)
　　　　(**if** ($boss.Emp.position$="analyst")
　　　　then (**count**($employs.Emp$ **where** $position$="analyst"))
　　　　else (**if** ($boss.Emp.position$="programmer")
　　　　　　then (**count**($employs.Emp$ **where** $position$="programmer"))
　　　　　　else (**count**($employs.Emp$ **where** $position$="tester"))))

Query (19) does not contain an independent subquery, hence its optimization is terminated. However, the optimization brings the essential gain. In (19) *boss.Emp.position* is processed only in the loop implied by *join*. Providing there is 20 departments and 500 employees, query (18) evaluates *boss.Emp.position* 10000 times, while query (19) only 20 or 40 times.

If the method of independent subqueries would be used before the method of weakly dependent subqueries, the situation is different. The subquery *boss.Emp. position* is independent from the nearest *where* operator, thus the subquery can be factored out of its scope:

　　$Dept$ **join** ($boss.Emp.position$ **group as** aux).   (20)
　　　　(**count**($employs.Emp$ **where** $position$ = aux)))

The query (20) cannot be further optimized. However, we have concluded that (20) is less optimal than (19). In order to evaluate (20) we must do many bindings to the aux name. Unlike statically bound programming languages, bindings in SBQL are dynamic, hence cost some processing time. In (19) we have another situation: conditions under *where* contain constant values (*"analyst"*, *"programmer"*, *"tester"*), which do not require binding. This example suggests that the method of weakly dependent subqueries should be used before the method of independent subqueries, but this requires more examples and experiments on real applications.

The general rewriting rule for queries having weakly dependent subqueries can be formulated as follows. Let $q_1 \, \theta \, q_2$ be a query connecting two subqueries by a non-algebraic operator θ. Let $ET = \text{enum}\{v_1, v_2, \ldots, v_k\}$ be an enumerated type, $k \geq 2$. Let $q_2 = \phi_1 \circ wdq(q_3) \circ \phi_2$, where ϕ_1, ϕ_2 are some query parts (perhaps empty), $\circ$ is concatenation of strings, $wdq(q_3)$ is a weakly dependent query that has a part q_3 that depends on θ and has the type ET. Then the query:

$$q_1 \, \theta \, \phi_1 \circ wdq(q_3) \circ \phi_2 \tag{21}$$

can be rewritten to:

$$q_1 \, \theta \; \textbf{if} \; q_3 = v_1 \; \textbf{then} \; \phi_1 \circ wdq(v_1) \circ \phi_2 \tag{22}$$
$$\textbf{else if} \; q_3 = v_2 \; \textbf{then} \; \phi_1 \circ wdq(v_2) \circ \phi_2$$
$$\ldots$$
$$\textbf{else} \; \phi_1 \circ wdq(v_k) \circ \phi_2$$

It may happen that after this rewriting $\phi_1 \circ wdq(v_i) \circ \phi_2$ has still a next weakly dependent subquery. In this case such a rewritten query can be the subject of next analysis and rewriting, according to the same rule.

The rewriting rule is correct in the general case. The idea of the method is to build a proper conditional statement. The conditions of the statement are based on all the values of an enumerated type. The statement is put directly after the non-algebraic operator in relation to which the weakly dependence is investigated. All the names occurring in the query before and after transformation are bound in exactly the same ENVS sections. Therefore the binding results before and after that transformation are exactly the same. We conclude that our method cannot change the result of a query. This conclusion is confirmed by experiments on the implemented prototype.

As in the case of the method based on factoring out independent subqueries we underline that the method is very general. It does not depend on a data or object model, a kind of a non-algebraic operator, complexity of weakly dependent subqueries, complexity of their output and the contexts in which weakly dependent subqueries occur. This kind of generality is possible only in the stack-based approach to query and programming languages.

In trivial cases the method gives no result. Assume the query:

$$Emp \; \textbf{where} \; sex = \text{``male''} \tag{23}$$

Query (23) contains the weakly dependent subquery $sex = \text{``male''}$, so we can rewrite it to the following form:

$$Emp \; \textbf{where} \; (\textbf{if} \; sex = \text{``male''} \; \textbf{then} \; \text{``male''} = \text{``male''} \; \textbf{else} \; \text{``female''} = \text{``male''}) \tag{24}$$

We see there is no gain. To avoid such cases we provide the following rule:

- Check whether an expression typed to an enumerated type is under the scope of another non-algebraic operator (we call it internal operator) which is under the scope of the non-algebraic operator for which weakly dependence is investigated (we call it external operator).

- Check the number of cycles in the loop implied by the internal operator. If the number is greater than some threshold (e.g. 1) then the query can be transformed, otherwise should be left without changes.

The number of cycles can be estimated according to some cost model, which involves estimated sizes of collections in the store. The number can be also deduced from cardinalities that are associated to collection types. In (23) the subquery *sex* = "male" is under external *where* operator only and the query does not contain an internal non-algebraic operator. According to the criteria above it should not be rewritten. Returning to example (18) we see that *boss.Emp.position* is under the internal *where* operator. The number of cycles can be very large, because the cardinality of the *Emp* collection is *. Hence this query should be rewritten.

5   Algorithm of the Weakly Dependent Subqueries Method

In this section we describe the general algorithm of the method. Optimization is performed by means of four recursive procedures:

- *optimizeQuery(q:ASTtype)* – it applies the procedure *weaklyDependentSubqueryMethod* to AST node *q* as long as possible;
- *weaklyDependentSubqueryMethod(q:ASTtype)* – it recursively traverses AST from node *q* and applies the *applyWeaklyDependentSubqueryMethod* procedure to it;
- *applyWeaklyDependentSubqueryMethod(q:ASTtype)* – it analyzes AST *q* and performs query rewriting; *q* is an AST node with a non-algebraic operator.
- *checkWeakDependence(q:ASTtype):ASTtype[0..*]* – responsible for detecting weakly dependent subqueries starting from AST node *q*. It returns AST nodes that are roots of weakly dependent subqueries.

The procedure *weaklyDependentSubqueryMethod* traverses AST of a query starting from its root. If the procedure meets a non-algebraic operator θ then its right and left queries are visited by the same procedure, recursively. At first we want to rewrite weakly dependent subqueries which are under the scope of the most nested non-algebraic operators. *weaklyDependentSubqueryMethod* calls *applyWeaklyDependentSubqueryMethod* for the encountered operator θ. In turn it invokes *checkWeakDependence* to check whether the right subquery of θ contains names which are to be bound to an enumerated type in the scope of θ. If such names occur in the subquery then *checkWeakDependence* method returns nodes of a subtree (right subquery of θ) containing the names which will be bound to enumerators. On the basis of these names the proper *if* or *switch* statement is inserted into the AST depending on number of values enumerated type. The right subtree of the operator θ will be replaced by earlier created *if/switch* statement. The subqueries in the *if/switch* statement are built through replacing the nodes returned by the *checkWeakDependence* procedure. Nodes will be replaced through the values of the given enumerated type. If the query has been rewritten then its static analysis is performed at the end of *applyWeaklyDependentSubqueryMethod* method. Static analysis is required to determine signatures, binding levels for names and scope numbers for non-algebraic operators.

When *weaklyDependentSubqueryMethod* method have rewritten at least once the original query, then the method of independent subqueries is to be applied, as well as other methods.

Pseudocodes of the procedures

```
procedure optimizeQuery(q : ASTtype)
  begin
    loop
      weaklyDependentSubqueryMethod(q);
      if  q has not been rewritten  then break;
      end if;
    end loop;
    if  q has been rewritten at least once  then
      independentSubqueryMethod(q);
    end if;
end.

procedure weaklyDependentSubqueryMethod(q : ASTtype)
  begin
    traverse AST starting from q;
    if  non-algebraic θ operator is met  then
      weaklyDependentSubqueryMethod(left subquery of θ);
      weaklyDependentSubqueryMethod(right subquery of θ);
      applyWeaklyDependentSubqueryMethod(ASTofθ);
    end if;
end.

procedure applyWeaklyDependentSubqueryMethod(ASTofθ : ASTtype)
    nodes : array of ASTtype;
  begin
    nodes := checkWeakDependence(ASTofθ);
    /* the nodes array contains the parts of the right subquery of θ
       which are to be bound to an enumerated type */
    if  nodes array is not empty  then
      q : ASTtype := nodes[0];
      enumerators : array of ASTtype := getEnums();
      /* the enumerators array contains the values of the given
         enumerated type */
      ifStatement, elseIfStatement : ASTtype;
      ifStatement := (if q = enumerators[0] then
        replaceDependentPart(nodes,enumerators[0]));
       /* the parts in the right subquery of ASTofθ which are to be bound
          to the enumerated type (elements of the nodes array) will be
          replaced by enumerators[0] */
      for  i = 1  to  enumerators.size  do
```

```
    /* iterate through the values of the enumerated type starting from
       the second */
    elseIfStatement := (else if q = enumerators[i]
                           then replaceDependentPart(
                           nodes,enumerators[i]));
    add the i-th else-if part to ifStatemnt and
    set it to elseIfStatement;
    end for;
    set the right subquery of ASTofθ to ifStatement;
    determine signatures, binding levels for names
    and scope numbers for the new form of the query;
    end if;
end.
```

```
function checkWeakDependence(ASTofθ₁ : ASTtype) : ASTtype[0..*]
    nodes : array of ASTtype;
    threshold : integer := 10;
  begin
    traverse AST of the right subquery of θ₁
    starting from its root;
    if  visited node is a name  then
      if  the name is bound to an enumerated type  then
        if  (the name is under non-algebraic operator θ₂ which is under
             the scope of θ₁) and (number of cycles in the loop implied
             by θ₂ is greater then threshold)  then
          add the name to nodes;
        end if;
      end if;
    end if;
end.
```

6   Optimization Gain

The algorithm is experimentally implemented and tested within the ODRA system. Figure 4 presents the average times of execution and optimization gain for query (11). For instance, the gain for a collection of 1000 employee objects is 361 times faster execution and the gain for 10000 employee objects is 3940 times faster execution.

7   Conclusions and Future Work

We have presented the optimization method which was aimed at minimizing the number of evaluations of specific parts of queries. This method usually generates independent subqueries which can be further optimized by a proper method. The weakly dependent subqueries method is beneficial in each case even if the transformation does not generate independent subqueries. The algorithm of the method is not very complex, but efficient and very general. It makes rewrites

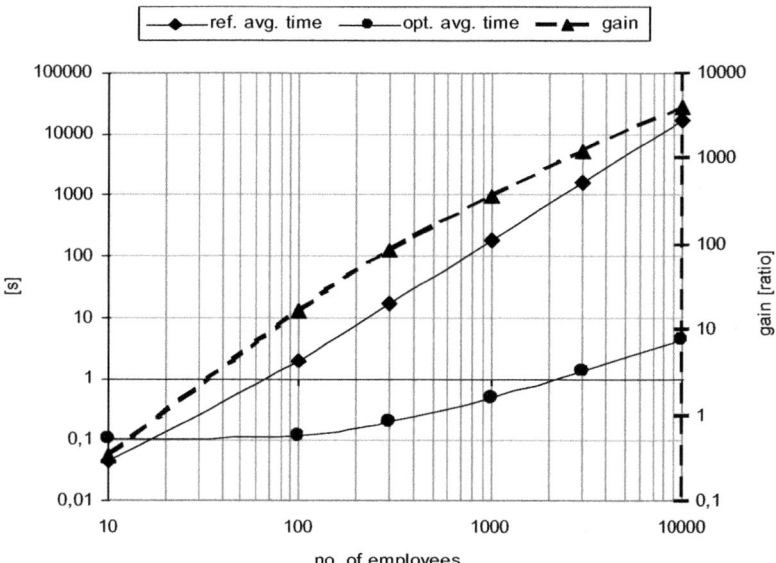

Fig. 4. Evaluations times and optimization gain for query (11)

for arbitrarily complex nested queries and does not depend on a kind a non-algebraic operator. In principle, the algorithm does not depend on a query cost model, however this is not sure and will be the subject of further investigations. The algorithm applied repeatedly detects and resolves all the possible weakly dependent subqueries in a query, including subqueries that are dependent on two or more names having enumerated types. The complexity of the algorithm is linear w.r.t. the query size.

In the future we are going to implement an algorithm that joins the method of weakly dependent subqueries with the method of independent subqueries. We observe that parts of both algorithms are very similar, hence can be based on the same code. Besides many experimental tests in real database applications are necessary to prove the efficiency of various variants of the algorithm.

We also plan to extend the method to dictionaries that are stored in databases. Indeed, the difference between dictionaries and enumerated types is secondary from the point of view of this method. For instance, instead of an enumerated type *jobPosition* we may have a dictionary of job positions that is supported by some integrity constraint. The only difference is that dictionaries can be updated, hence after such updates applications must be re-compiled and re-optimized.

A similar extension of the method concerns the case when a query involves very big and very small collections. For instance, assume there is 10 departments and 1000 employees. The query "Get employees together with the average salary in their departments" without optimization would require 1000 times of evaluation of the average salaries, while it is enough to evaluate them only 10 times. This extension will be the subject of further investigations and implementations.

References

1. Adamus, R., et al.: Stack-Based Architecture and Stack-Based Query Language. In: Proc. 1st ICOODB Conf., pp. 77–95 (2008)
2. Adamus, R., et al.: Overview of the Project ODRA. In: Proc. 1st ICOODB Conf., pp. 179–197 (2008)
3. Atkinson, M., Morrison, R.: Orthogonally Persistent Object Systems. The VLDB Journal 4(3), 319–401 (1995)
4. Bancilhon, F.: Understanding Object-Oriented Database Systems. In: Pirotte, A., Delobel, C., Gottlob, G. (eds.) EDBT 1992. LNCS, vol. 580, pp. 1–9. Springer, Heidelberg (1992)
5. Cattell, R.G.G., Barry, D.K., Berler, M., Eastman, J., Jordan, D., Russell, C., Schadow, O., Stanienda, T., Velez, F.: The Object Data Standard: ODMG 3.0. Morgan Kaufman, San Francisco (2000)
6. Cluet, S., Delobel, C.: A General Framework for the Optimization of Object-Oriented Queries. In: Proc. SIGMOD Conf., pp. 383–392 (1992)
7. Hryniów, R., Lentner, M., Stencel, K., Subieta, K.: Types and Type Checking in Stack-Based Query Languages. Institute of Computer Science PAS Report 984, Warszawa (March 2005),
   http://www.si.pjwstk.edu.pl/publications/en/publications-2005.html
8. Ioannidis, Y.E.: Query Optimization. Computing Surveys 28(1), 121–123 (1996)
9. Jarke, M., Koch, J.: Query Optimization in Database Systems. ACM Computing Surveys 16(2), 111–152 (1984)
10. Kowalski, T., et al.: Optimization by Indices in ODRA. In: Proc. 1st ICOODB Conf., pp. 97–117 (2008)
11. Lentner, M., Subieta, K.: ODRA: A Next Generation Object-Oriented Environment for Rapid Database Application Development. In: Ioannidis, Y., Novikov, B., Rachev, B. (eds.) ADBIS 2007. LNCS, vol. 4690, pp. 130–140. Springer, Heidelberg (2007)
12. ODRA (Object Database for Rapid Application Development) Description and Programmer Manual (2008),
    http://www.sbql.pl/various/ODRA/ODRA_manual.html
13. Płodzień, J., Kraken, A.: Object Query Optimization through Detecting Independent Subqueries. Information Systems 25(8), 467–490 (2000)
14. Płodzień, J.: Optimization Methods in Object Query Languages. Ph.D. Thesis, Institute of Computer Science, Polish Academy of Sciences, Poland (2000)
15. Płodzień, J., Subieta, K.: Static Analysis of Queries as a Tool for Static Optimization. In: Proc. IDEAS Conf., pp. 117–122 (2001)
16. Stencel, K.: Semi-strong Type Checking in Database Programming Languages (in Polish). Editors of the Polish-Japanese Institute of Information Technology (2006)
17. Subieta, K., Beeri, C., Matthes, F., Schmidt, J.W.: A Stack Based Approach to Query Languages. In: Proc. of 2nd Intl. East-West Database Workshop, Klagenfurt, Austria (1995)
18. Subieta, K.: Theory and Construction of Object Query Languages (in Polish). Editors of the Polish-Japanese Institute of Information Technology (2004)
19. Subieta, K.: Stack-Based Approach (SBA) and Stack-Based Query Language, SBQL (2008), http://www.sbql.pl
20. VIDE: Visualise All Model Driven Programming. European Commission 6th Framework Programme, IST 033606 STP (2009), http://www.vide-ist.eu/

Metamodelling with Datalog and Classes: ConceptBase at the Age of 21

Matthias Jarke[1], Manfred A. Jeusfeld[2], Hans W. Nissen[3],
Christoph Quix[1], and Martin Staudt[4]

[1] RWTH Aachen University & Fraunhofer FIT
Ahornstr. 55, 52074 Aachen, Germany
[2] Tilburg University, The Netherlands
[3] Cologne University of Applied Sciences, Germany
[4] Munich University of Applied Sciences, Germany
jarke@cs.rwth-aachen.de

Abstract. ConceptBase is a deductive object-oriented database system intended for the management of metadata. A distinguishing feature of the Telos language underlying ConceptBase is the ability to manage rules and constraints across multiple levels of instantiation in so-called meta formulas, thus offering uniform consistency management across heterogeneous notations or ontologies. Originally developed in the context of model-driven database design in the late 1980's, ConceptBase has been used in several thousand installations all over the world for numerous applications in areas such as requirements engineering, engineering information management, model management, eLearning, cultural information systems, and data warehousing. The internal representation is based on a quadruple object structure, combined with advanced Datalog engines, such that many optimization techniques in ConceptBase have pioneered ideas later pursued in the implementation of XML databases and ontology-based reasoning and data management engines.

1 Introduction

The large number of different modeling formalisms used in information systems engineering, semi-automated development techniques such as Model-Driven Design, but also the increasing richness of media handled by such systems beyond the traditional structured data, has renewed the interest in so-called metadata repositories and model management systems since at least the end-1990's. In standards such as the Information Resource Dictionary Standard IRDS [11] or OMG's meta object facility MOF [31], but also in many experimental and commercial systems such as, e.g., MetaEdit+ [20], Clio [10] or Rondo [24]. A shared feature of these standards is that not just data and their schema or other metadata are stored but also the metaschemas for these metadata and their relationships. In the typical heterogeneous environments, further metalevels may be necessary to manage the relationships between different metaschemas or modeling languages, such that a multi-level hierarchy of instance-class relationships

M.C. Norrie and M. Grossniklaus (Eds.): ICOODB 2009, LNCS 5936, pp. 95–112, 2010.
© Springer-Verlag Berlin Heidelberg 2010

ensues. It is surprising to see that, despite this obvious and increasing need, after more than 20 years, our ConceptBase system is apparently still the only one that offers full support for the syntax and semantics of such multi-level hierarchies with heterogeneity at all levels. This paper reviews some of the features of ConceptBase that made this possible as well as some of the many applications in research, teaching, and practice the system has enjoyed and continues to enjoy.

The development of ConceptBase was motivated by work in the European DAIDA project [15], in which an early version of what would now be called model-driven information systems development was developed, using a mapping from semi-formal requirements modeling languages [8] via the design language Taxis [25] to database programming languages. A repository was needed to document and maintain the developed artefacts as well as their relationships from a product, process, and design tool perspective, ensuring traceability and incremental design within and across multiple design versions. A version of the Telos information systems modeling language [26] formed the formal starting point for the ConceptBase development but the final version of Telos itself was also heavily influenced by the application domain of metadata repository management.

We started the development of ConceptBase in mid-1987, the first version became operational in late 1988 [16]. About a year later, a stable client-server version existed which was already used in 1989 as perhaps the first Internet-based knowledge base management system in a project on requirements traceability modeling across the Atlantic ocean, four years before the advent of the World Wide Web. Using innovative storage models similar to the ones nowadays used in XML stores, and extending optimization techniques for query and integrity processing in deductive databases for our case of a deductive object-oriented metadata manager, the performance of ConceptBase improved rapidly, leading to a stable and externally usable prototype by about 1993 [12]. In the rest of the 1990's, about 250 applications in various domains of research, teaching, and even industrial practice became known to us, some of them with our participation but many also completely independently.

In the new century, the user community of ConceptBase increased further, probably due to the broadened interest in model management and metadata management for multimedia data where our experiments were also brought into some of the multimedia metadata standardization committees. Dissemination was also helped by new system features and many further performance improvements, plus a robustness of the system that is now competitive with many commercial systems. At present, we know of over 1000 registered installations, probably a number of unregistered ones exist as well.

In [18], detailed descriptions of the meta modeling context, the ConceptBase systems, and some of the more influential applications are described, and a current version of the system is made available with many examples. In this short overview paper, we first review the most important language features of ConceptBase and then give an overview of the application domains and the impact experiments with ConceptBase have achieved in these domains. We end with some indications of ongoing work.

2   Language Features of ConceptBase

ConceptBase is an implementation of the object model O-Telos [17], a Datalog-based variant of Telos [26]; for simplicity, we use the name Telos in the sequel. We first give a general introduction to the Telos language features in general and then highlight some features that distinguish ConceptBase from similar systems or have been added to the system rather recently.

2.1   Basic Concepts

As in all deductive database models, Telos databases consist of an explicit and an implicit part. All explicit information as reified in the form of objects with object identity. This holds for regular objects (instance level), for classes, meta classes etc., but also for non-derived instantiation, specialization and attribution links. For example, any explicit attribute is also an object and can have attributes itself.

To make this very general object concept possible, the basic object is a proposition $P(o,x,l,y)$ in a kind of semantic network link labeled l with o is an object identifier (oid), x as the source oid and y as a target oid. Such a proposition has the dual role as a fact in the sense of deductive databases, and as an identifiable object in an object-oriented database, thus forming the elementary bridge within the deductive object-oriented approach of ConceptBase. It also allows ConceptBase to offer a textual syntax as well as an equivalent graphical syntax to the user. Both of them hide the object identifiers to the user and only work with the labels.

Note that this approach can be seen as a precursor to the very similar triple storage approach for XML or RDF [27], except that those do not work with object identifiers and thus offer a bit less flexibility. Among other things, this similarity implies that many of the storage and query optimization techniques developed for ConceptBase over the years can be evaluated for their applicability to semi-structured databases.

As special subkinds of propositions, Telos supports instantiation (instances, classes, meta classes, meta meta classes, etc.), specialization, and attribution. In the graphical syntax supported by the ConceptBase graph editor, these three kinds of links are typically indicated by graphical symbols, as shown, for example, in Fig 1. As shown in Sect. 2.2, the user can extend the collection of such subkinds by meta-objects which are given semantics through meta-formulas.

Deductive rules and integrity constraints can be defined for objects at any abstraction level. In the textual syntax of deduction rules and constraints (see Sect. 2.2 for examples), standard labels are used in literals for instantiation (x in C) and specialization ($C1$ isA $C2$) whereas, due to the greater variability of attribution link types, we offer the form (x m/l y) where x is the label of the source object, y is the label of the target object, l is the label of the link itself, and m is the label of the class of links to which the link belongs (also called the attribute category).

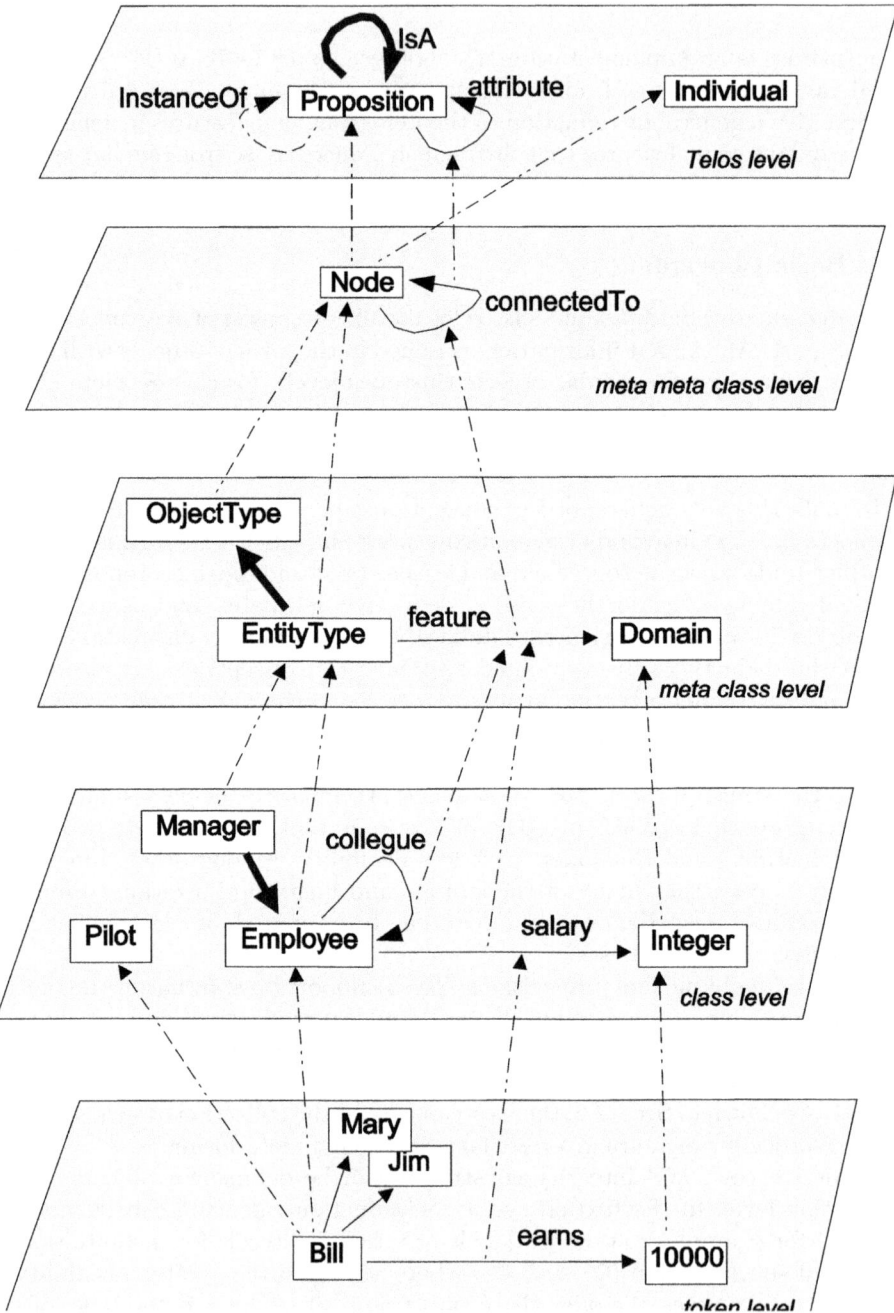

Fig. 1. A simple Telos knowledge base graph in five meta-levels: dashed lines indicate instantiation, bold lines isA, normal lines attribution; both nodes and links are objects in Telos

The external textual syntax of Telos is a frame syntax that groups a large number of propositions into a coherent and more easily understandable frame. It defines, for a given object, its classes (multiple instantiation is possible), its generalizations (not allowed for instances), and its attributes grouped by attribute categories. As a simple example, some of the objects in Fig. 1 can be described in frame syntax as follows:

```
Bill in Employee, Pilot with
   salary
      earns : 10000
   colleague
      col1 : Mary
      col2 : Jim
end

Employee in EntityType with
   feature
      salary : Integer;
      colleague : employee

Manager in EntityType isA Employee end
```

A collection of basic axioms comprising a number of facts, rules, and constraints defines the semantics of Telos used in ConceptBase. For example, the isA relationship between Manager and Employee means that instances of Manager can also have the features salary and colleague by inheritance. We refer to [18, Chap. 3] for more details.

The example also illustrates the perhaps most distinguishing feature of ConceptBase which will be elaborated in more detail in the next subsection: an in principle infinite hierarchy of instantiation relationships allows ConceptBase as a repository system of design knowledge to manage a complete hierarchy of example objects/scenarios, their classes, their meta classes, their meta meta classes, etc. in a uniform framework governed by a well-defined syntax of a deductive database.

Of course, such a uniform framework is only useful if it can be efficiently processed. This was achieved by the important result in Manfred Jeusfeld's thesis [17] that the collection of Telos axioms enforces a deductive database which can be mapped to Datalog with dynamically stratified negation, and thus processed with high efficiency by any good Datalog engine. Indeed, while the early ConceptBase versions were implemented on top of Prolog systems linked to data stores, recent versions since 2002 rely on dedicated Datalog engines, thus leading to very competitive performance and to by now commercial-level stability of the whole system with large data sets. For readers interested in deductive databases, it should be pointed out that achieving the dynamic stratification was by no means easy given the fact that we have essentially only one single stored relation (of Propositions) in ConceptBase. One of the key solution ideas was to replace the generic in relationship for instantiation by specialized in.C relationships to class C using partial evaluation—the same trick we shall use in Sect. 2.2 below for handling meta formulas efficiently.

In two further doctoral theses, supported by several master theses (too many to be mentioned here in detail), important practice-oriented extensions of the basic syntax and semantics of the language were achieved. Hans Nissen demonstrated that it is possible with just a few additional axioms and limited implementation effort, to add a module concept to ConceptBase. It allows, among other things, the team development and delayed consistency checking of large complex models [28]. With the concept of Query Classes, Martin Staudt invented a very flexible view mechanism which—like in SQL or (long after Concept-Base) XQuery—ensures closure in deductive repositories by making the results of queries ConceptBase objects; implementation of these objects nevertheless can adapt and extend all the ideas for efficient deductive query optimization, view maintenance, and integrity checking from the literature [34,35]. An interesting application was our idea of externally materialized views in which a query class is materialized outside control of the system itself but incrementally informed about necessary changes to the view. Such algorithms could, e.g., be used to maintain materialized views on mobile devices with uncertain linkage to their data sources. We shall give examples of query classes below.

2.2   Meta-formulas

In this subsection, we elaborate more how we accomplished the most distinguishing feature of ConceptBase—its handling of multiple instantiation levels as a pre-requisite for many model management applications in heterogeneous systems.

A deductive rule or integrity constraint typically ranges over exactly one abstraction level, i.e. it is defined at a certain level (e.g. the class level) and the variables range over objects at the next lower level (e.g. instance level). For example, a class Employee can have an attribute salary and a constraint that demands that the salary of an employee must be smaller than the salary of the Manager of his department. Another example is an integrity constraint that demands that instance of EntityType must have at least one attribute. Here, EntityType is a meta class and its instances are classes.

Meta-level formulas are formulas that range over objects from more than one abstraction level. For example, the key constraint in the relational data model is a formula expressed at the meta class level (the concept Relation is a meta class) but is evaluated against the database instance (instance level). The class level (database schema) is referred to by variables. Meta-level formulas are particularly useful for meta modeling, i.e. the specification of constructs of modeling languages.

As an illustrative example, consider a very simple process language, in which tasks have successor tasks. A task with more than one successor task is a 'predicate task' (condition). A task without successor is an end statement. A task that is not the successor of another task is a start statement. All other tasks are procedural tasks. Besides, tasks are executed by agents. We demand that there is a unique start statement and a unique end statement. We are interested in detecting loops. Moreover, we want to check whether there are agents who are executing two tasks t1 and t2, where t2 indirectly follows t1 but there is at least one task in between that is executed by another agent (execution split).

The structural part of this simple process language is defined in the Telos frame syntax as follows:

```
Task with
   attribute
      successor: Task
end
Agent with
   attribute
      executes: Task
end
```

To deal with the integrity constraints and the analysis queries, we need to be able to follow the successor link transitively. Since transitivity is frequently used, we specify it as a general construct with a meta-level formula:

```
Proposition in Class with
   attribute
      transitive: Proposition
   rule
      trans_R: $ forall x,y,z,R/VAR
                     AC/Proposition!transitive C/Proposition
                        P(AC,C,R,C) and (x in C) and (y in C)
                        and (z in C) and
                        A(x,R,y) and A(y,R,z) ==> A(x,R,z) $
end
```

Note that the relation R is a variable in the formula. It is the label of any attribute AC that is required to be transitive. In our class definition of Task, we now simply make the successor attribute transitive via

```
Task with
   attribute,transitive
      successor: Task
end
```

Some subclasses of Task do not require transitivity, e.g.

```
StartStatement in QueryClass isA Task with
   constraint
      c1: $ not exists link/Task!successor To(link,this) $
end

PredicateTask in QueryClass isA Task with
   constraint
      c1: $ exists s1,s2/Task A\_e(this,successor,s1) and
            A_e(this,successor,s2) and (s1 {\= s2) $
end
```

In a similar way, we can define end statements and join statements (more than one direct predecessor). The predicate A_e(x,successor,y) operates on explicit successor facts, whereas A(x,successor,y) also operates on facts derived via the transitivity rule

```
LoopTask in GenericQueryClass isA Task with
   parameter
      rep: Task
   constraint
      c: $ A(this,successor, rep) and
           A(rep,successor,this) and
           (exists s/Task A_e(rep,successor,s) and
                          A(s,successor,rep)) $
end
```

Hence, a task like this is a loop task for the loop represented by 'rep' if rep can be transitively reached from 'this' and rep can be reached from itself via at least one intermediate task s.

The execution split query is also exploiting the transitivity:

```
AgentWithSplitResponsibility in QueryClass isA Agent
with
   constraint
      c1: $ exists t1,t2,t/Task A(this,executes,t1) and
           A(this,executes,t2) and A(t1,successor,t) and
           A(t,successor,t2) and not A(this,executes,t) $
end
```

Figure 2 shows a graphical representation of the analysis of an example workflow defined by the query classes above. The queries are displayed as ovals. The answer to a query is the set of instances that fulfill the membership constraint of the query class. This derived instantiation is denoted by dotted links. Thus, InsuranceAgent is a derived instance of AgentWithSplit-Responsibility. A loop is detected as well featuring four loop tasks. The loop tasks checkPolicy and proposePayment are additionally classified as predicate tasks.

Note that the above query class definitions are sufficient to provide this functionality. Just by storing them in ConceptBase you get the desired analysis capability.

Meta-formulas are made for re-use. For example, we can define the concept of an organizational unit

```
OrgUnit with
   attribute, transitive, asymmetric
      subunit: OrgUnit
end
```

where asymmetry is defined as follows:

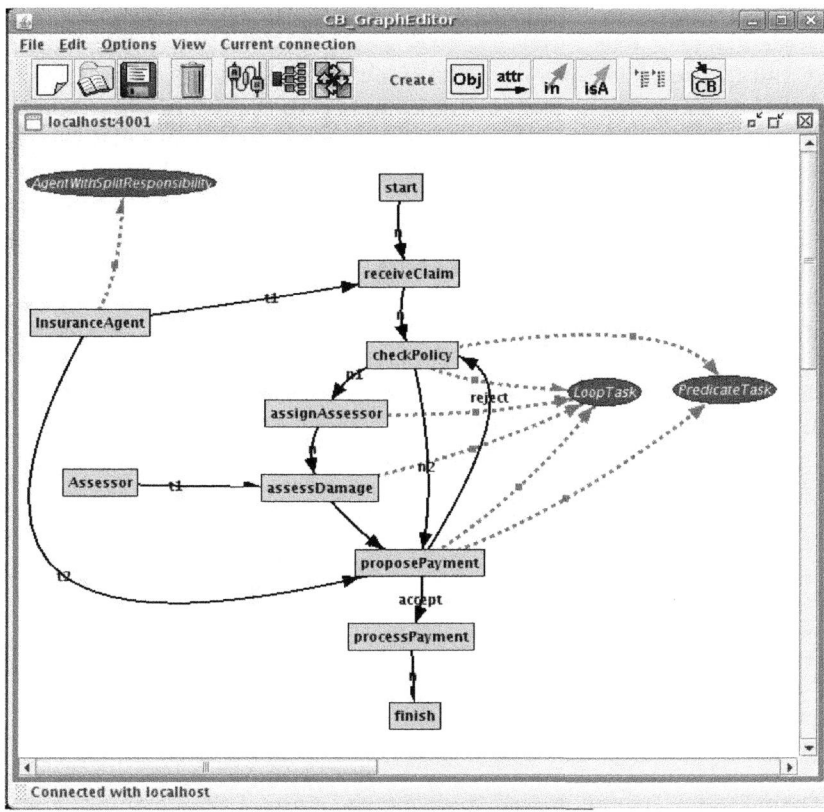

Fig. 2. Graphical analysis of a workflow model

```
Proposition in Class with
    attribute
        asymmetric: Proposition
    constraint
        asym_IC:  $ forall AC/Proposition!asymmetric
                    C/Proposition x,y,R/VAR
                    P(AC,C,R,C) and (x in C) and (y in C) and
                    A(x,R,y) ==> not A(y,R,x) $
end
```

ConceptBase comes with a library of pre-defined meta formulas (multivalued attributes, transitivity, symmetry, etc.) that can be extended and modified, as meta formulas are objects in ConceptBase that can be inserted to and deleted at any time. Other researchers have used this to investigate proposals for new basic abstraction mechanisms in information systems engineering such as materialization [4].

2.3   Active Rules

Active rules (also called event-condition-action or ECA rules) are triggered by
an event (e.g. an update), check a condition, and then execute the action part for
all variable instantiations of the condition part. They can be used for multiple
purposes, e.g. to set initial attribute values whenever an object is created for
the first time, or to call an external program upon certain database updates.
ConceptBase has a full implementation of active rules. We demonstrate here that
it allows to define the execution semantics of Petri nets. Petri nets have places
and transitions connected by directed links. Places have a positive number of
tokens. A transition is enabled if all input places have at least one token. Firing
a transition means to remove tokens from the input places of a transition and to
add them to all output places of the transition. The structural part of the Petri
net language is expressed in ConceptBase as follows:

```
Place with
   attribute
      sendsToken: Transition
   single
      tokenFill: Integer
end
Transition with
   attribute
      producesToken : Place
end
```

The `tokenFill` attribute is used to define the state of the Petri net. For conve-
nience, we define a function to return the token number of a given place. The
function is then used to define the concept of an enabled transition

```
TokenNr in Function isA Integer with
   parameter
      place: Place
   constraint
      c1: $ (place tokenFill this) $
end
EnabledTransition in QueryClass isA Transition with
   constraint
      c1: $ forall pl/Place (pl sendsToken this)
                  ==> (TokenNr(pl) \texttt{>} 0) $
end
```

A single ECA rule is sufficient to model the execution semantics of Petri nets. We
omit here the obvious definitions of auxiliary concepts such as `Connected-Place`
and `NetEffectOfTransition`:

```
ECArule UpdateConnectedPlaces with
   mode m: Deferred
   ecarule
```

```
      er: $fire/FireTransition tr/Transition pl/Place
          n,n1/Integer
   ON Tell (fire transition tr)
   IF (tr in EnabledTransition) and
        (pl in ConnectedPlace[tr]) and
        (n1 = TokenFill(pl)+NetEffectOfTransition(pl,tr))
   DO Retell (pl tokenFill n1)$
End
```

Figure 3 shows a Petri net visualized in the ConceptBase graph editor. The graph editor has been configured to display enabled transitions with a green color. Places with a token are visualized by circles with a corresponding number of black dots.

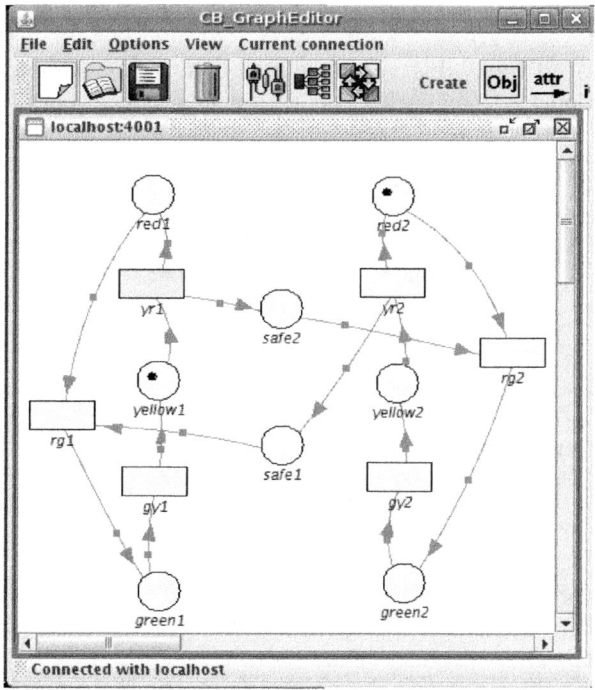

Fig. 3. Graphical display of a Petri net with ConceptBase

2.4   Function Definitions

The Petri net example illustrates the definition of a simple function TokenNr. Functions in ConceptBase are queries that return at most one result per input. As ConceptBase fully supports recursive Datalog, we can reuse this capability to support the recursive definition of certain simple functions. For example, the Fibonacci numbers can be computed by

```
fib in Function isA Integer with
   required,parameter
      n: Integer
   constraint
      cfib: $ (n=0) and (this=0) or
             (n=1) and (this=1) or
             (n>1) and (this=fib(n-1)+fib(n-2)) $
end
```

The definition employs double recursion. A naive evaluation would require exponential time to compute the result. As the second call can reuse the result of the first call, an optimized algorithm requires only linear time. Due to the bottom-up evaluation strategy of Datalog, ConceptBase requires only linear time, i.e. realizes the optimal algorithm with its Datalog engine.

A second example is the computation of the length of the shortest path between two nodes in a graph. This function is useful for a whole family of model metrics. In ConceptBase, this can be defined by a combination of a function and a query definition that call each other recursively:

```
sp in Function isA Integer with
   parameter x: Node; y: Node
   constraint
      csp: $ (x=y) and (this=0) or
             (x nexttrans y) and (x <> y) and
             (this = MIN(spSet[x,y])+1) $
End

spSet in GenericQueryClass isA Integer with
   parameter x: Node; y: Node
   constraint
      csps: $ exists x1/Node (x next x1) and
                (this=sp(x1,y)) $
End
```

So, the length of the shortest path between x,y is 0 iff x=y. Otherwise, it is the minimum of the length of all shortest path starting from a successor of x plus 1. The function sp can be used to define the concept of a node being on a shortest path between two given nodes. In Figure 4, nodes on a shortest path (except the start and end node) are displayed in yellow.

3   Application Experiences and Impact

ConceptBase has been used in a wide variety of application domains where meta modeling and metadata repository management in heterogeneous environments play a role. In most cases, individuals and organizations used ConceptBase to investigate or teach certain concepts, or to prototype ideas from which then code

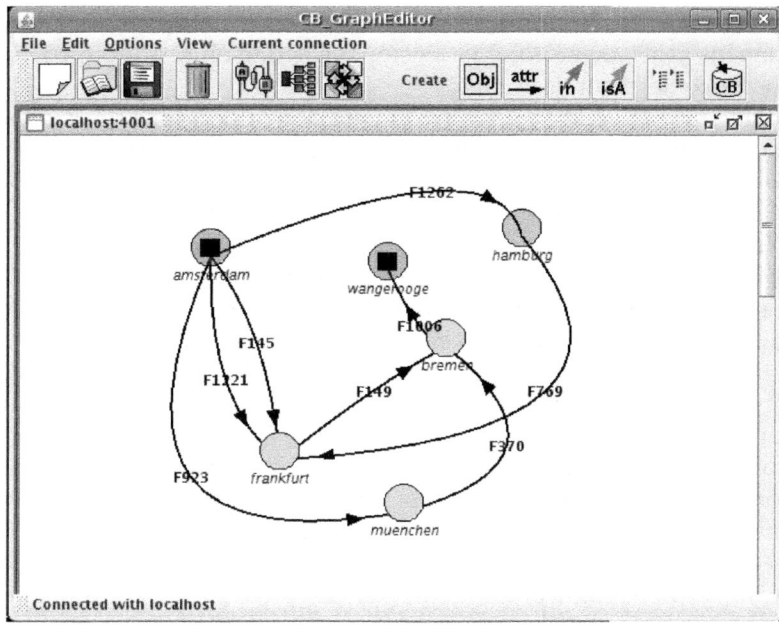

Fig. 4. Graphical representation of nodes on a shortest path

was derived—in a few cases even automatically generated—for commercial systems. Below, we summarize experiences in three broad application areas, namely IS engineering environments, requirements analysis, and the more recent multimedia community management. Detailed descriptions of several applications can be found in [18].

3.1 Repository Management of Heterogeneous Engineering Environments

The original motivation for the development of ConceptBase was the integrated management of requirements [8], Taxis database design specifications [25], and database programs in the European DAIDA project [15]. In a precursor of today's model-driven approaches, semi-automatic tools for the mapping from requirements to designs, and for the code generation from design specs were developed. An important goal was to make this process incremental such that small requirements changes would not lead to a complete repetition of the whole process. This required a meta meta model in which the design objects in the different formalisms, the human design decisions taken in the semi-automatic process, and the tool applications for automated parts of the process could be documented in a homogeneous manner. This meta meta model was defined and tested in early versions of ConceptBase. In an operational mode, this meta meta model then served as the basis for a query facility by which design tools could store retrieve repository objects under this schema, and by which implications of design changes could be roughly analysed. Constraints were used to prevent tools from inserting inconsistent or incomplete design objects, or to warn against non process-conformant decisions.

Especially the issue of traceability among design decisions spawned a major research initiative in this field which we conducted jointly with researchers in New York and later Monterey and Atlanta, in what was perhaps the worldwide first Internet-based knowledge base management system operating across the Atlantic. In large-scale empirical studies in the US, reference models for different degrees of maturity in traceability were developed using ConceptBase [33], and served as blueprints for the models underlying market-leading traceability tools by Anderson Consulting (now Accenture) and Texas Instrument. Other groups e.g. at the TU Munich used ConceptBase to model the structures of commercial software development environments such as HP's FUSION environment. In our cooperations with engineering groups at RWTH Aachen University, similar repository meta meta models were developed for engineering environments in industrial quality management and in chemical engineering design.

In the European DWQ project on Foundations of Data Warehouse Quality, ConceptBase was employed as an active metadata repository linking models of sources, integrators, data warehouses, and client data perspectives. The repository was used as a semi-shallow documentation mechanism for the inputs and results of description logic reasoners [23,14], and as a basis for generating code from the metamodel relationships using both local-as-view and global-as-view algorithms [9,22,32].

Since 2001, this early work also fed into research on model management conducted at Microsoft Research [1,2] and influenced our own recent projects on generic metamodels for model management in heterogeneous environments [21,22]. Such a more active role of the metadata repository was pioneered in a project for a large European software vendor in the mid-1990s where we were able to show that, using a notation-oriented meta meta model and related meta-formulas, the reverse engineering of complex relational databases into entity-relationship models, could be automatically supported to a large percentage with surprisingly little effort [19]. The same turned out to be true for the reverse code analysis of a significant part of one of the world's largest switching systems, Ericsson's AXE system.

3.2 Multi-perspective Requirements Engineering

Requirements elicitation and management (RE) is well known to be one of the most important and difficult tasks in information systems engineering. An early external example of ConceptBase usage in this field was a requirements analysis tool for Telecommunication Services (RATS) developed as a prototype at British Telecom [5]. Their meta model was quite elaborate, including aspects such as non-functional quality goals, use cases, and multiple domain models, all coming along with version histories. ConceptBase rules and constraints were used to give some guidance to the development process.

In our own work, we pursued a slightly different line of work. Practice experiences showed that one of the best ways to elicit requirements in complex systems is their capture from many different perspectives—different notations as well as different user task perspectives. Capture is interleaved with inconsistency analyses among these perspectives to spawn debate, thus clarifying mutual misunderstandings and bringing to light hidden assumptions and requirements. This approach which became popular as Viewpoint Analysis in the late 1990's [6,30], is of course a perfect application example for ConceptBase. Together with the German software and consulting firm USU, we developed a process analysis meta meta model focusing on task interrelationships and media breaks, which was applied successfully in numerous business and software requirements analyses [29]. This application was also the motivation for adding modules to ConceptBase [28].

In the last years, multi-perspective modeling has been extended to the analysis of inter-organizational networks and even of Internet communities, with particular emphasis on rich models of trust evolution in such networks [7].

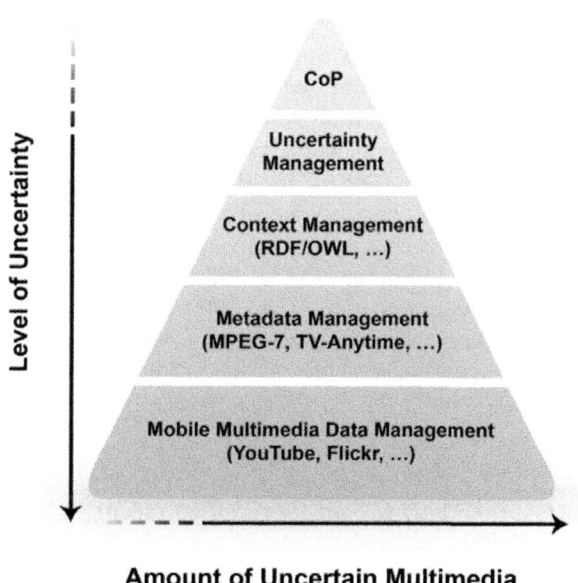

Fig. 5. Modeling perspectives on multimedia community metadata management

3.3   Multimedia Information Engineering

Since the late 1990's, the KBS Hyperbook project at TU Hannover [17, Chap. 5], pioneered the idea to use the metadata management facilities of ConceptBase for the structuring of eLearning environments. These experiments also formed a starting point for research in the well-known peer-to-peer learning environment Edutella [27].

In interdisciplinary cooperation with various kinds of media scientists, we have extended such approaches to various approaches to the analysis and support of multimedia communities of practice on the Internet in numerous fields of education and research, ranging from Judaic studies to movie sciences to general contributions to cultural reconstruction in former war areas, to multimedia metadata standards such as MPEG-7/21. Goal is supporting the interaction of communities across different types of media and under different negotiated cooperation regimes; social network analyses are augmented by aspects of media usage and by requirements engineering strategies. Figure 5 illustrates the number of different perspectives to be considered in such environments [3]. The closeness of many ConceptBase features to recent XML and RDF extensions keeps this work rather directly relevant even for people who are not using the system itself.

4   Summary and Outlook

With its distinguishing feature of powerful multi-level metamodel handling under the well understood and efficiently implemented Datalog semantics, ConceptBase has successfully preserved a niche from which some impact could be achieved in many application domains. We feel that the potential of meta-formula management for multi-language, multi-domain or multi-perspective engineering has still not yet been fully utilized. Ongoing work at Tilburg University shows that traceability can be defined as an extremely versatile ConceptBase attribute category which can then be used to automatically generate inconsistency management analyses across notations, ontologies, or tasks, thus automatically generating a surprising number of traceability tasks in engineering projects. ConceptBase is free software since summer 2009 and can be downloaded from http://conceptbase.sourceforge.net/.

References

1. Bernstein, P.A., Halevy, A.Y., Pottinger, R.A.: A Vision for Management of Complex Models. ACM SIGMOD Record 29(4), 55–63 (2000)
2. Bernstein, P.A., Melnik, S.: Model Management 2.0: Manipulating Richer Mappings. In: ACM SIGMOD Intl. Conf. on Management of Data, Beijing, China, pp. 1–12 (2007)
3. Cao, Y., Klamma, R., Jarke, M.: Mobile Multimedia Metadata Management for Virtual Campfire – The German Excellence Cluster UMIC (2009) (submitted for publication)
4. Dahchour, M.: Formalizing Materialization Using a Metaclass Approach. In: Pernici, B., Thanos, C. (eds.) CAiSE 1998. LNCS, vol. 1413, p. 401. Springer, Heidelberg (1998)
5. Eberlein, A., Halsall, F.: Telecommunication Service Development: A Design Methodology and Its Intelligent Support. Engineering Applications of Artificial Intelligence 10(6), 647–663 (1997)

6. Feather, M.S., Fickas, S.: Coping with Requirements Freedoms. In: Intl. Workshop on the Development of Intelligent Information Systems, Niagara-on-the-Lake, Ontario, Canada, pp. 42–46 (1991)
7. Gans, G., Jarke, M., Kethers, S., Lakemeyer, G.: Continuous Requirements Engineering for Organization Networks: A (Dis-)Trust-Based Approach. Requirements Eng. J. 8(1), 4–22 (2003)
8. Greenspan, S., Borgida, A., Mylopoulos, J.: A Requirements Modelling Language and Its Logic. Information Systems 11(1), 9–23 (1986)
9. Halevy, A.Y.: Answering Queries Using Views: A Survey. VLDB Journal 10(4), 270–294 (2001)
10. Hernandez, M.A., Miller, R.J., Haas, L.M.: Clio: A Semi-Automatic Tool for Schema Mapping. In: ACM SIGMOD Conf., Santa Barbara, CA, p. 607 (2001)
11. ISO/IEC International Standard Information Resource Dictionary System (IRDS) – Framework, ISO/IEC 10027 (1990)
12. Jarke, M., Eherer, S., Gallersdörfer, R., Jeusfeld, M.A., Staudt, M.: ConceptBase – A Deductive Object Base for Meta Data Management. J. Intelligent Information Systems 4(2), 167–192 (1995)
13. Jarke, M., Jeusfeld, M.A., Quix, C., Vassiliadis, P.: Architecture and Quality in Data Warehouses: An Extended Repository Approach. Information Systems 24(3), 229–253 (1999)
14. Jarke, M., Lenzerini, M., Vassiliou, Y., Vassiliadis, P.: Fundamentals of Data Warehouses, 2nd edn. Springer, Heidelberg (2003)
15. Jarke, M., Mylopoulos, J., Schmidt, J.W., Vassiliou, Y.: DAIDA – An Environment for Evolving Information Systems. ACM Trans. Information Systems 10(1), 1–50 (1992)
16. Jarke, M., Rose, T.: Managing Knowledge about Information Systems Evolution. In: ACM SIGMOD Conf., Chicago, IL, pp. 303–311 (1988)
17. Jeusfeld, M.A.: Update Control in Deductive Object Bases (in German). Ph.D. Thesis, University of Passau, Germany (1992)
18. Jeusfeld, M.A., Jarke, M., Mylopoulos, J. (eds.): Metamodeling for Method Engineering. MIT Press, Cambridge (2009)
19. Jeusfeld, M.A., Johnen, U.: An Executable Meta Model for Re-engineering of Database Schemas. Intl. J. Cooperative Information Systems 4(2-3), 237–258 (1995)
20. Kelly, S., Lyytinen, K., Rossi, M.: MetaEdit+ – A Fully Configurable Multi-User and Multi-Tool CASE and CAME Environment. In: Constantopoulos, P., Vassiliou, Y., Mylopoulos, J. (eds.) CAiSE 1996. LNCS, vol. 1080, pp. 1–21. Springer, Heidelberg (1996)
21. Kensche, D., Quix, C., Chatti, M.A., Jarke, M.: GeRoMe – A Generic Role Based Meta Model for Model Management. In: Spaccapietra, S., Atzeni, P., Fages, F., Hacid, M.-S., Kifer, M., Mylopoulos, J., Pernici, B., Shvaiko, P., Trujillo, J., Zaihrayeu, I. (eds.) Journal on Data Semantics VIII. LNCS, vol. 4380, pp. 82–117. Springer, Heidelberg (2007)
22. Kensche, D., Quix, C., Li, X., Li, Y., Jarke, M.: Generic Schema Mappings for Composition and Query Answering. Data & Knowledge Eng. 68(7), 599–621 (2009)
23. Lenzerini, M.: Data Integration: A Theoretical Perspective. In: 21st ACM Symp. Principles of Database Systems (PODS), Madison, Wisconsin, pp. 233–246 (2007)
24. Melnik, S., Rahm, E., Bernstein, P.A.: Rondo: A Programming Platform for Generic Model Management. In: ACM SIGMOD Intl. Conf. Management of Data, San Diego, CA, pp. 193–204 (2003)

25. Mylopoulos, J., Bernstein, P.A., Wong, H.K.T.: A Language Facility for Designing Interactive Database-Intensive Applications. ACM Trans. Database Syst. 5(2), 185–207 (1980)
26. Mylopoulos, J., Borgida, A., Jarke, M., Koubarakis, M.: Telos – Representing Knowledge about Information Systems. ACM Transactions on Information Systems 8(4), 325–362 (1990)
27. Nejdl, W., et al.: Edutella – A Networking Infrastructure based on RDF. In: Proc. 11th WWW Conf. Honolulu, Hawaii, pp. 604–615 (2002)
28. Nissen, H.W., Jarke, M.: Repository Support for Multi-Perspective Requirements Engineering. Information Systems 24(2), 131–158 (1999)
29. Nissen, H.W., Jeusfeld, M.A., Jarke, M., Zemanek, G.V., Huber, H.: Managing Multiple Requirements Perspectives with Metamodels. IEEE Software 13(2), 37–48 (1996)
30. Nuseibeh, B., Kramer, J., Finkelstein, A.: A Framework for Expressing the Relationships Between Multiple Views in Requirements Specifications. IEEE Trans. Software Eng. 20(10), 760–773 (1994)
31. Object Management Group: Meta Object Facility (MOF) Core Specification Version 2.0. OMG (2006)
32. Quix, C.: Metadata Management for Quality-Oriented Information Logistics in Data Warehouse Systems (in German). Ph.D. Thesis, RWTH Aachen University, Germany (2003)
33. Ramesh, B., Jarke, M.: Reference Models for Requirements Traceability. IEEE Trans. Software Eng. 27(1), 58–93 (2001)
34. Staudt, M., Jarke, M.: Incremental Maintenance of Externally Materialized Views. In: Proc. VLDB 1996, Mumbai, India, pp. 75–86 (1996)
35. Staudt, M., Jarke, M.: View Management Support in Advanced Knowledge Base Servers. J. Intelligent Information Systems 15(3), 253–285 (2000)

Unified Event Model for Object Databases

Michael Grossniklaus[1], Stefania Leone[2],
Alexandre de Spindler[2], and Moira C. Norrie[2]

[1] Dipartimento di Elettronica e Informazione, Politecnico di Milano
I-20133 Milano, Italy
`grossniklaus@elet.polimi.it`
[2] Institute for Information Systems, ETH Zurich
8092 Zurich, Switzerland
`{leone,despindler,norrie}@inf.ethz.ch`

Abstract. Most object databases offer little or no support for event-based programming over and above what is provided in the programming language. Consequently, functionality offered by traditional database triggers and event-condition-action (ECA) rules has to be coded in each application. We believe that a notion of triggers should be offered by object databases to facilitate application development and a clear separation of concerns. We present a general and flexible event model that unifies concepts from programming languages and database triggers. We describe an implementation of the model and how it can support the requirements of a rich variety of applications.

1 Introduction

Event-based programming is gaining in popularity and is a paradigm now used in a wide range of applications. The underlying concept of automatically invoking actions in response to pre-defined events is well-known in traditional databases under the term *triggers*. Triggers were first introduced into databases as a means of maintaining database consistency. Later, they were generalised into event-condition-action (ECA) rules capable of representing business logic and widely promoted in the active database community.

Most object databases offer little or no support for event-based programming over and above what is provided in the programming language. Consequently, functionality offered by database triggers and ECA rules has to be coded in each application, resulting in a duplication of programmer effort. Further, the event model offered by most object-oriented programming languages is more restrictive than that typically offered by database triggers and ECA rules. We therefore believe that object databases should offer a concept of triggers in order to facilitate the application development process and support a clean separation of concerns.

In this paper, we present a general and flexible event model for object databases that unifies concepts from programming languages and database triggers. The model is capable of supporting a rich variety of application requirements

M.C. Norrie and M. Grossniklaus (Eds.): ICOODB 2009, LNCS 5936, pp. 113–131, 2010.

common in emerging domains such as sensor databases as well as more traditional applications. Further, it also supports distributed triggers where an event in one database may trigger an action in another database.

Section 2 provides the background in terms of database triggers, ECA rules and support for event-based programming in object databases. We then present the core of our unified event model in Sect. 3 and a detailed discussion of event scopes in Sect. 4. The architecture of our event system and details of implementation are given in Sects. 5 and 6, respectively. To illustrate the use of our model, a small example application is presented in Sect. 7. Concluding remarks are given in Section 8.

2   Background

Database triggers were first developed as a mechanism to automate basic database management tasks such as integrity constraint enforcement, view maintenance and authorisation control. Once the potential of a mechanism to automatically invoke actions in response to pre-defined events was realised, triggers were generalised into the concept of ECA rules that could be used to represent business logic within the database and the field of active databases emerged. Active rules have also been used as the basis for version management and workflow control systems. Recent research in the management of data streams has seen a renewed interest in database technologies for event processing.

Active databases were an active area of research in the late 1980s and 1990s with approaches based on both relational [1,2,3,4,5,6,7,8] and object-oriented [9,10,11,12,13,14,15] database management systems. These approaches are compared and classified in [16]. While most of these systems provide a notion of ECA rules in different variations, the issue of rule component reuse has not been addressed in detail. In addition, publish-subscribe mechanisms as known from programming languages are not supported.

A number of architectures and frameworks for managing applications in distributed settings incorporate a notion of events. One of the earliest examples is CORBA where the event service allows for the decoupling of the communication between distributed objects. An example of more recent work is WebLogic Event Server [17] which manages event-driven, distributed applications with applications interacting by exchanging events. Applications are developed in Java combined with their own event processing language (EPL) which is an extension to SQL for querying streams of events. EPL rules can be dynamically changed and adapted at runtime. Applications are based on and composed of so-called event processing networks, a model based on Petri nets which represent an event flow graph including the event streams, producers and consumers. No details about how events are processed and the possible reuse of rules are given.

Other approaches introduce an event processing language for application development. For example, EventScript [18] is a language that processes events and the corresponding actions based on regular expressions. The language can be executed in a Java-based runtime and it is claimed that it is easy to integrate it with other runtime environments.

In [19], a rich event model is presented that incorporates concepts such as typing, inheritance and exheritance, dynamic type inferencing as well as extensibility and addressability. Event objects can be accessed using different methods, such as an event access expression, or using an event API in Java or C# or a tailored event expression language.

Support for event-based programming in object databases tends to be limited. For example, db4o offers Java developers a concept similar to that of triggers offered by most RDBMS. In order to introduce active behaviour, the classes of persistent objects must implement a so-called `ObjectCallBack` interface [20]. This interface declares a set of callback methods that correspond to the system-defined trigger hooks provided by most RDBMS, while their body represents the action to be taken. Actions can be executed upon one of the following: before/after object update, before/after object creation and deletion, and before/after object activation and deactivation. The action to be taken is implemented using Java and, since the interface is implemented by the class itself, the developer has access to the internals of that class. However, having to implement the desired set of methods of the interface for each and every class that should exhibit active behaviour can involve a lot of work. In addition, incorporating triggers and thus event processing into the persistent class itself inhibits any kind of reuse. Furthermore, event processing is not orthogonal to the persistent data but part of the domain class definition in the application logic. Note that the scope of db4o callback methods is always the class, i.e. the extent of objects of a given class that implements specific callback methods.

A more comprehensive approach is taken by the Java Versant API (JVI) for the Versant Object Database where events are propagated from the database to registered clients based on the JavaBeans event model. Four kinds of events—class, object, transaction demarcation and user-defined events—are supported by Versant and for each type of event a corresponding listener interface exists. The database and the clients communicate through so-called event channels that are persistent across client applications and serve to limit the scope of the monitored events. Class-based channels only propagate events of a certain class of objects, while object-based channels monitor a set of objects. Finally, query-based channels can be used to receive events related to the objects contained in the result set of the query. As a consequence, Versant overcomes some of the limitations regarding the scope of events present in db4o as mentioned above. Also, by separating the kind of events from the scope of monitored events, their approach is capable of supporting a higher degree of flexibility and reuse. As in the approach taken by db4o, event handlers are defined by the application logic and executed on the client side. In contrast to traditional database triggers that are part of the database logic and executed on the server side, this approach can lead to several problems. Events are often used to ensure the consistency of the database, i.e. to execute maintenance code when objects are created or deleted. If the event handling logic is defined by the client, different clients can produce different and even inconsistent database states. Another problem stems from the fact that if events are triggered on the server and handled on the client this results in an increased communication overhead that can have adverse effects on the performance of the system.

As another option, Java application developers can make use of the Observer-Observable pattern [21] offered by the Java API. The developer can create a class that extends the `Observable` class as well as a set of classes that implement the `Observer` interface. Objects of classes that implement the `Observer` interface can register themselves to observe objects of classes that extend `Observable`. However, this pattern and its Java implementation is not intended for persistent classes. As already mentioned, a class to be observed has to extend the Java class `Observable` and thus will maintain a list of registered observer objects. In the setting of persistent objects, the instances of the observable class are most likely to be made persistent. Since the `Observable` class is provided by the Java API, the application developer cannot declare that list of observers as transient and consequently has to store the observers implicitly with the object itself. Obviously, storing the list of observers along with an object can cause several problems upon retrieval, such as observers which no longer exist or double instantiation of the same observer object. In addition, the event handling is again not orthogonal to the actual persistent classes, since these classes have to extend the `Observable` class and manage the list of observers.

We believe that object databases need a well-defined event model that offers the generality and flexibility supported in active databases and modern event processing systems. By introducing the concept of event types and event handlers, event processing functionality can be made orthogonal to persistence, thereby ensuring that the goal of transparent persistence is not violated. The model should support user-defined as well as system-defined event types with a registration service that allows one or more handlers to be associated with the same event type, with handler selection depending on conditions of event activation. Further, the model should support reuse of event types and event distribution. With these goals in mind, we have designed and implemented such a model which we describe in the remaining sections of this paper.

3   Event Model

Our approach unifies concepts known from active databases with related ideas from object-oriented programming languages and notification systems. We introduced these concepts in the context of mobile databases in previous work [22] and now present how they can be adapted for object databases and their application domains in general.

We base our event model on the four concepts of *event triggers*, *event types*, *event handlers* and *event actions* shown in Fig. 1. In contrast to active databases where the single concept of a rule or trigger encapsulates a number of concepts, our approach separates the actors involved in event processing, namely, defining events, firing triggers upon event detection and processing. Defining and representing these concepts as entities in their own right leads to a higher potential

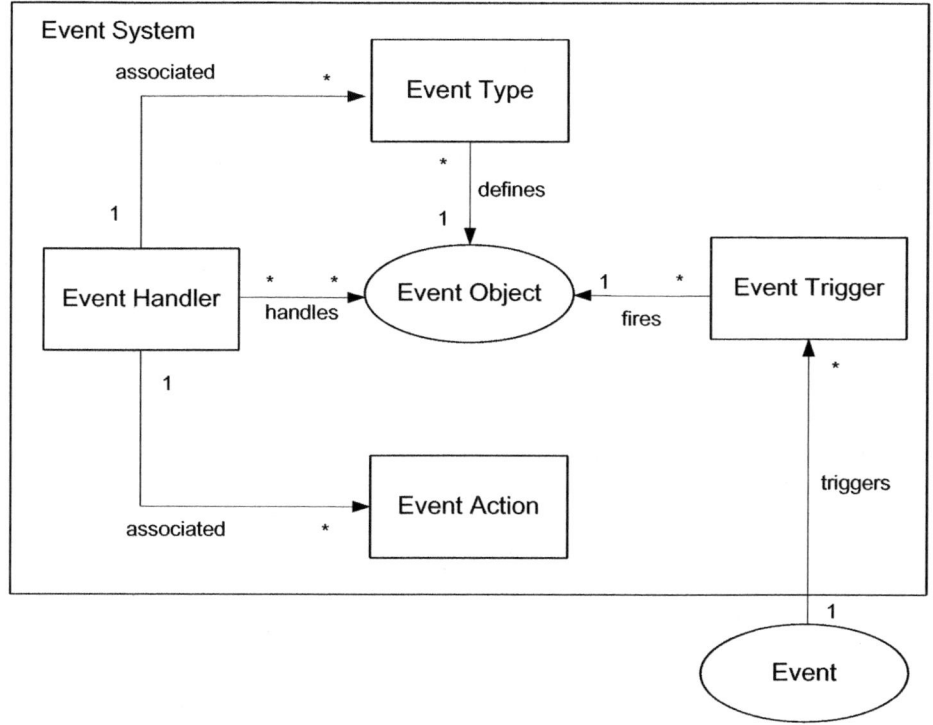

Fig. 1. Event system concepts

for reusability and provides the basis for specifying behaviour at a finer level of granularity.

An event type defines an operation and a scope. The operation is an activity upon which handlers should be notified. The scope denotes the source in which the activity should be detected, such as a single object, set or class of objects. For example, an event type `PersonCreation` could specify the `Person` class as the scope and the creation of a `Person` instance as the operation. We will discuss event scopes in detail in the next section.

An event action consists of a set of operations to be executed. Operations can include the execution of any database operation, notification of the application or firing of other events.

An event handler defines the entity that is registered to be notified upon the occurrence of an event of a certain type. An event handler is associated with an event type and action. As in active databases, the execution of the action can be guarded by a conditional expression. If it evaluates to true, the actions specified by the event handler are executed. To continue with our example, an event handler could be created and associated to the event type `PersonCreation` and to an action that should be executed upon that event. The action could consist of inserting the newly created instance into a given set of persons. Finally, an event handler may optionally specify a life cycle that governs when the handler can be invoked. The life cycle can be specified as a given point in time, a time span or a certain number of executions.

As can be seen in Fig. 1, event types and event actions can be associated to more than one event handler to allow for maximum reuse, while an event handler is always associated with exactly one event type and one event action. As in many notification systems, our model allows fallback actions to be defined that will be executed if the main event action fails. These are not included in Fig. 1 for the sake of simplicity. Note that fallback actions correspond to normal actions.

An event trigger is invoked as a result of the occurrence of an event, i.e. the detection of an activity within a source that matches an operation/scope combination specified by an event type. In our example, a trigger would be invoked whenever a new instance of the `Person` class is created. The trigger fires an event object that contains the scope object itself as well as all additional information needed for handling of the event. In our example, the scope object would be the newly created `Person` instance.

In summary, an event handler glues together an event type and an action. If an event of that type occurs, the trigger is invoked and fires an event object. The event object is handled by all handlers associated to the event type that defines the event object. Note that an event handler handles all event objects defined by its associated event type and that an event object may in turn be handled by a number of event handlers that are associated to that same event type.

Inspired by the concepts of observables in object-oriented programming languages, an event type describes a certain class of events and serves as a registration point for interested subscribers. Hence, an event type provides a way to explicitly specify what has been defined only implicitly in traditional databases by predefined events. Of course, these predefined database event types also exist in our model, but they are represented as system-defined event types and therefore provide full access to their metadata. As a result, the scope and its operations can be changed at runtime. In addition, this separation and publish-subscribe way of registering for event types also favours the handling of distributed events. Handlers can not only register to event types residing in their local database, but also to remote event types and, thus, react locally on remote events.

In contrast to database systems where events are exclusively triggered by the system, programming languages allow events to be defined and fired by user code. However, most programming languages still combine the definition of an event type and an event trigger in a single class that defines itself to be observable and then fires events whenever its internal state changes. Hence, a client of the class has no possibility to fire the events defined by the class. While this coupling might be appropriate sometimes for reasons of security, we have chosen to separate types and triggers for the sake of generality. Due to this separation, an event type also needs to specify a set of constraints that capture who is granted permission to fire events of that type and who can subscribe handlers for it. If the database object that fires the event has been granted access by the corresponding event type, the subscribed handlers are invoked and the specified parameters are passed along. By representing event triggers as a discrete concept, events can be fired by external processes such as the client application. Further, our system supports the definition of so-called multiple triggers. Instead of firing only once, a multiple trigger remains active in the system and repeatedly dispatches events at previously defined points in time.

4   Event Scopes

In Sect. 3, we introduced the notions of scope and operation as attributes of an event type definition. In this section, we take a closer look at these two concepts, introducing a classification of scopes and operations and showing how they can be combined in order to obtain a general and flexible means of defining event types and supporting reuse.

A scope can be a single object instance, a group of instances, a class of instances, a collection, a transaction or global. Thus, the granularity of an event type can be chosen according to specific application needs. A handler can be notified about an operation executed on a single instance, on any instance within a group of instances or an instance of a particular class. Depending on the scope, a set of operations can be chosen upon which the event is raised. The scopes and their corresponding operations are summarised in Tab. 1.

Table 1. Event scopes and triggering operations

Scope	Operations
Instance	Retrieve, update, delete
Set of instances	Retrieve, update, delete
Class extent	Create, retrieve, update, delete
Class	Schema evolution
Collection	Insert, remove object
Transaction	Begin, abort, commit
Global	Clock, external

The operations on scopes of single instances, groups of instances and instance classes are operations on an instance itself, such as the retrieval, update and deletion of an instance. Operations on the class extent additionally include the creation of new instances. Note that the scope of a class refers to the class as a structure and the corresponding operations include schema evolution activities such as altering a class definition and subclassing. The scope of a collection differs from a group of instances in that we refer to the concept of collection in the former and the actual member objects in the latter. This distinction becomes important since, for every scope, we have a different set of operations which can cause a trigger to be fired. While the scope of a collection is associated with operations such as insertion and removal of members, operations associated with the scope of a group of instances include retrieval, update and deletion of the instances. Operations on the scope of a transaction include begin, abort and commit and the global scope is associated with clock operations and any external operation such as user-defined operations.

A single instance is always a member of one or multiple class extents and can be a member of an arbitrary number of sets of instances. Similarly, a set of instances is always a subset of a class extent. Therefore, an activity that is detected on a single instance is also detected within the scope of the instance's class extent and any set to which the instance belongs. As a consequence, the set of scopes S is a partially ordered set where the partial order $\leq$ is given by { $instance \leq set\_of\_instances$, $instance \leq class\_extent$, $set\_of\_instances \leq class\_extent$, ... }.

Having the scope and operation stored in two separate attributes of an event type allows for maximum reuse. For example, an attribute write operation can be reused in the cases that the scope is a single instance, a set of instances or a class extent. However, a complete separation is not possible as some operations cannot be used with particular scopes and other operations are specific to a single scope. An attribute write operation cannot be used in combination with a collection scope while an insert operation can only be used with a collection scope.

We now further specify the operations outlined in Tab. 1 and show how this naturally leads to reusability. We introduce a minimal classification which consists of instance, extent, class, collection, transaction and global operations. For example, an instance operation is an attribute read or write, a method invocation, or the storage, retrieval or deletion of an instance. A collection operation is the insertion or removal of a member or access to a member. Table 2 summarises the main operations, their possible concrete operations and the scopes with which they can legally be associated in an event type.

An instance operation denotes all possible operations on a single instance such as reading or writing an attribute value, a method execution or its storage, retrieval and deletion. Together with the possible scopes which can be a single instance, a set of instances or a class extent, this operation spans a wide range

Table 2. Operatios

Operation Classes	Operations	Legal Scopes
Instance operations	Attribute read/write, method execution, store, retrieve, delete	Instance, set of instances, class extent
Class Extent operations	Create, store, retrieve, delete	Class Extent
Schema operations	Changes to attribute or method declarations	Class
Collection operations	Insert, access, remove	Collection
Transaction operations	Begin, abort, commit	Transaction
Global operations	Clock, external	–

of event types for which handlers can be registered. An extent operation can be either the creation of a new instance or the storage, retrieval or deletion of an instance of a particular class. Therefore, these operations may only be associated with a class scope. A schema operation includes changes made to class definitions, i.e. the addition, removal or update of an attribute declaration as well as changes to method signatures. Such operations must always be associated with a particular class. A collection operation comprises all possible operations on a collection as defined by common collection interfaces and is associated with a collection object. A transaction activity may be a begin, abort or commit operation and is associated with a transaction scope. Finally, global operations such as a clock or an external application raising an event are not associated with any particular scope object.

To represent an event type with which handlers can register to be notified when an attribute value of a particular instance has been changed, an event type with its scope attribute pointing to the instance of interest is associated with the instance operation `attribute write`. Alternatively, if a handler is to be notified upon the change of an attribute of any instance of a particular class extent, an event type with the scope attribute pointing to the particular class is associated with the same instance operation. In the case of an event type describing the insertion of members into a collection, the scope attribute is set to the collection of interest and the operation attribute to the insert collection operation.

5   Architecture

Figure 2 gives an overview of the system architecture. The event system is part of the DBMS and consists of several components. A monitoring service monitors the data in the database ①. On any operation defined by an event type, the monitoring service fires a trigger and thus initiates the event processing ②. The event processor ④ receives the trigger containing all the information required as described in Sect. 3 and retrieves all registered handlers for a given event type from the handler registry ③. For each of these retrieved handlers, their condition is first evaluated. If the condition is valid, the handler's action is executed. For this purpose, the corresponding action is retrieved from the action library. If the execution of the action fails, the fallback action is executed, which is in turn retrieved from the action.

As can be seen in Fig. 2, our approach aims for maximum reusability by providing an event type and an action library from which event types and actions can be reused when registering a new handler. In addition, new event types can be composed using existing event types. The system allows for runtime adaptivity in that new event types, new actions and new event handlers can be built as well as existing ones being manipulated and deleted.

If a new handler is to be registered, the following steps have to be taken. First, an event type has to be created, composed or selected from the event library. In addition, an action as well as a fallback action has either to be specified or

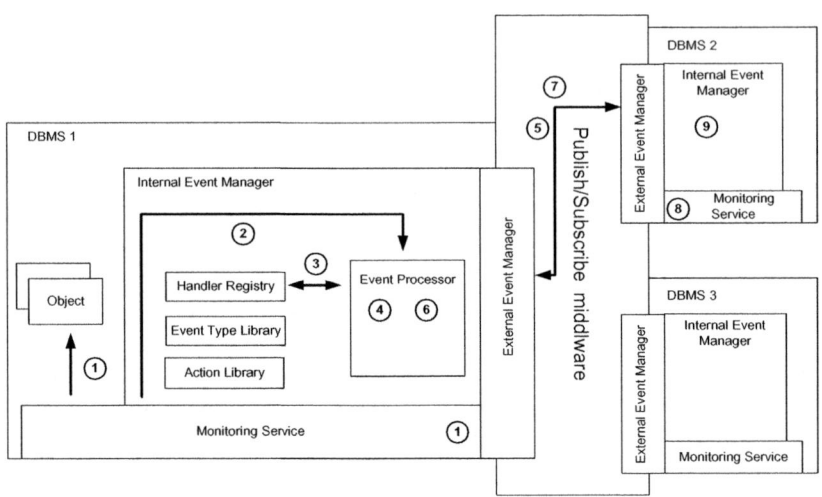

Fig. 2. Architecture

an existing one can be selected and reused from the action library. Finally, an optional condition can be defined to further constrain the action's execution.

Note that when creating and registering a handler, one can decide between creating a synchronous or asynchronous handler. If a trigger is fired and a synchronous handler is registered for that event, the handler is processed within the given transaction. If the base transaction is aborted, the operations performed as a result of the event handler executions are undone as well. An asynchronous handler is in general less time-critical. Therefore asynchronous handlers are processed when the transaction that created the trigger is being committed, i.e. in a separate transaction.

In addition, our approach also allows the distribution of events. Remote handlers can be registered for remote events. This implies that, when creating a handler, one can choose between creating a local or remote handler. Consider the case in Fig. 2 where we have three databases and one database would like to subscribe to events that happen in another database. For example, assume DBMS 2 should react to an event that happens in DBMS 1. To do so, a so-called remote handler that listens to events of a certain type residing in DBMS 1 has to be created and registered in DBMS 2. In contrast to a local handler, this remote handler is associated with an event type defined in DBMS 1 and an action defined in DBMS 2. In order to query the network for external event types, each DBMS exposes an external event manager, that, among other things, returns their internal event type libraries upon request.

In our example, a remote handler is created in DBMS 2 and registered in the handler registry of DBMS 2. The creation of a remote handler causes an additional handler to be created implicitly and registered in DBMS 1 where the event type of interest resides ⑤. This handler is associated with the requested event type and a special action that invokes the remote notification.

The notification process in that case works as follows. After a trigger for the subscribed event type has been fired in DBMS 1, the DBMS 1 event processor processes all handlers registered for that type of event ⑥ as discussed before, including the implicitly created handler. Note that the action of the handler in DBMS 1 corresponds to the publishing process, basically forwarding the trigger, including the scope object and other defined parameters, to DBMS 2. This is carried out by the external event managers of the two sites. In our case, the action of the handler in DBMS 1 forwards the trigger to the external event manager of DBMS 2 ⑦.

In DBMS 2, the external event manager acts as an external application and invokes a trigger to be fired by the monitoring service ⑧. That trigger is conceptually equivalent to the trigger fired in DBMS 1 and contains the scope object from DBMS 1 along with all other defined parameters. Consequently, all the handlers for that event type are processed ⑨, which includes the initially registered remote handler. As a result, DBMS 2 executes an action invoked by an activity in DBMS 1.

6   Implementation

The event manager serves as the main interface to the event system for an application developer. Figure 3 shows UML diagrams of the three components forming the manager interface. The event manager consists of two interfaces, `InternalEventManager` and `ExternalEventManager`. The internal event manager provides the methods to create, update and delete instances of the concepts introduced in Sect. 3, namely event types, handlers and actions. Note that triggers cannot be created explicitly. However, the `Monitor` interface provides a `fire(EventType, Object)` method, which causes a trigger to be fired. Trigger management is thus encapsulated by the `Monitor`. As a result, developers do not have to first create trigger objects and then fire them but only need to use one method call.

As part of the internal event management, the retrieval of handlers to be notified about the occurrence of a particular type of event plays an important role in the event processing. Once an event object has been fired — triggered by a particular operation within a given scope — all event types having this operation and scope must first be selected. Note that multiple event types may be selected as the scopes may directly match or include each other by means of their partial order. Second, when the event types have been selected, the handlers registered for these are retrieved and notified. This two-stage process is similar to the condition-action processing in active databases and [16] presents an overview of implementations of its subroutines.

An external event manager serves as an interface to the publish/subscribe middleware introduced in Sect. 5. It therefore allows for a list of existing event types to be retrieved, so that handlers residing on other databases can register

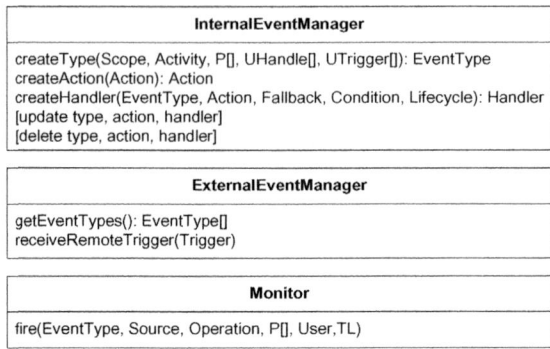

Fig. 3. API of the event manager

for them. It also declares a method `receiveRemoteTrigger` which is used by the middleware to notify the database about an event occurring in another database.

Having presented the event system API, we now describe the implementation of the event model. Figure 4 shows simplified UML diagrams of the main classes implementing the four core concepts of the event model, namely event type, handler, trigger and action.

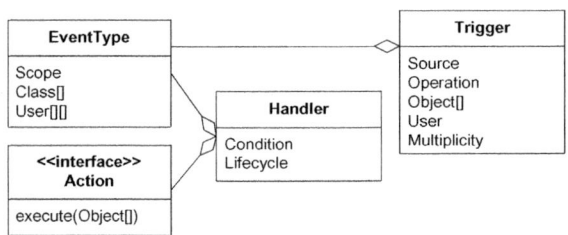

Fig. 4. Metamodel of the event system

An event type has attributes defining the scope, the list of parameters passed on to the handler and the two lists of users allowed to fire and handle events, respectively. The declaration of the parameters is simply implemented as a list of class objects denoting the type of each parameter. The scope attribute defines the source of an event as defined in Tab. 1. For each scope, there is a corresponding subtype of event type shown in Fig. 5. These subtypes declare an additional attribute specifying the operation related to their scope. Each of the six kinds of operations introduced in Tab. 2 is implemented as an enumeration where the members represent the concrete operation.

A handler is composed of a condition object and a lifecycle object. The condition object is an implementation of an interface defining an evaluation method. This method is declared to return a Boolean value which is true if the action

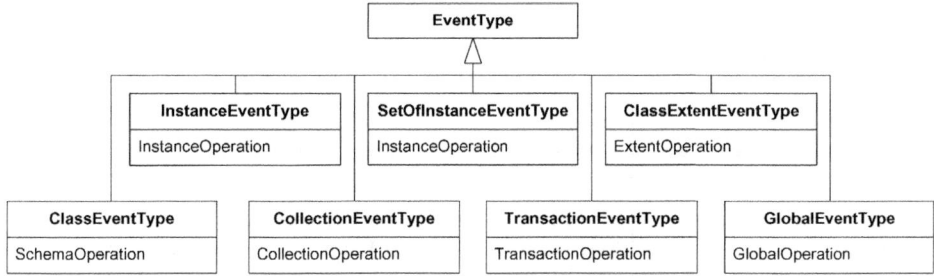

Fig. 5. Event type specialisations according to the scope

is to be executed and false otherwise. Note that for the implementation of this method, the entire system may be accessed as well as the parameters passed to the handler upon notification. The lifecycle object encapsulates the lifecycle definition assigned to the handler. Since a lifecycle can either be a time span, a point in time or a number of notifications, it is modelled as a root class `Lifecycle` with three subclasses `TimeSpan`, `PointInTime` and `NumberOf`, each declaring their specific attributes.

When a handler is notified, the condition method is evaluated and, if it returns true, the action is executed. The action object is of a class implementing the `Action` interface declaring the method to be executed. A second action object serves as a fallback method to be executed if the former method call fails. Consequently, when application developers create a handler, they must provide two instances of the action interface, the condition interface as well as instances of the lifecycle class.

Trigger objects contain the occurring operation, the object on which the operation has happened, a list of parameter objects passed to the handler and the user that executed the operation. Furthermore, a multiplicity attribute specifies whether this trigger is fired once or multiple times, and, in the latter case, with which period and for how many times or for how long. The multiplicity definition is realised using a class `Multiplicity` with an integer attribute representing the number of times the trigger should be fired.

7 Application

In order to outline the use of the proposed event system, we show how event types, handlers and actions are implemented for an online book store. We assume a simple application domain shown in Fig. 6 consisting of persons ordering books. A class `Person` represents customers who place an order. Instances of the `Order` class are associated with any number of ordered items represented as instances of the `Item` class. The status attribute of orders allows customers to be notified about whether an order has been processed, paid or shipped. As a first example, we want to configure the system to send an email to customers whenever the status of their orders has changed. As a first step, an event type is created.

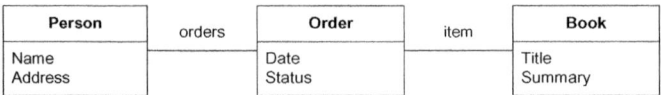

Fig. 6. Application domain of an online book store

```
EventType eventType = eventManager.createEventType(
    Order.class, InstanceOperation.ATTRIBUTE_UPDATE, null, null, null);
```

The event type is defined to fire an event whenever an instance of the `Order` class has changed its status attribute. Note that the first parameter passed to the handler is always the scope object on which the event has been triggered. Therefore, the scope is set to the class extent `Order` and the operation is an instance operation `ATTRIBUTE_UPDATE`. Since a handler processing such an event does not need any parameters, the `p[]` argument is set to `null`. Similarly, since we do not want to introduce any user rights, the two user lists are set to `null`.

Next, an action is created with an implementation performing the act of sending an email to a user whose order has changed its status. Then the action is registered with the system in order to be added to the action library and made available. As a fallback action, an action object is retrieved from the library which notifies the system administrator about a failure.

```
Action action = new Action(){
    public void execute(Object[] params)    {
        Order order = (Order) params[0];
        Person person = Queries.getPerson(order);
        Mailer.statusChangeMail(person, order.Status);
    }
};
eventManager.createAction(action);
Action fallback = eventManager.getAction(NotifySysadminAction);
```

Furthermore, a handler is created with the action previously defined and the condition that the updated attribute must be the one named `Status`. The condition is implemented as an anonymous class.

```
Condition condition = new Condition()    {
    public boolean evaluate(Object[] params)    {
        Field attribute = (Field) params[1];
        return attriute.getName().equals("Status");
    }
}
```

The handler's lifecycle parameter is set to `null` as the handler should behave as if having no particular lifecycle. If no lifecycle is specified, a handler executes its action whenever an event of a certain event type has been fired.

```
eventManager.createHandler(eventType, action, fallback, condition, null);
```

As a second example, customers may subscribe to be informed about special offers. For this purpose, a set of user instances is maintained containing those users to be informed. In what follows, we set the system to welcome any person who has been newly inserted into this group.

```
Set<Person> subscribedCustomers = new HashSet<Person>();
EventType eventType = eventManager.createEventType(
   subscribedCustomers, CollectionOperation.INSERT, null, null, null);
```

The scope of the event type is the collection assigned to the variable subscribed-Customers which contains all persons subscribed to be informed. The operation that fires the event is an insert collection operation. The action consisting of sending an email to the newly added person is defined and registered as follows.

```
Action action = new Action(){
  public void execute(Object[] params)   {
     Person member = (Person) params[1];
     Mailer.welcomeSubscribed(person);
  }
};
eventManager.createAction(action);
Action fallback = eventManager.getAction(NotifySysadminAction);
```

Finally, the handler is created and registered for the previously defined event type.

```
eventManager.createHandler(eventType, action, fallback, null, null);
```

In order to demonstrate the use of remote handlers, we assume that the book store has agencies located in particular countries and is handling orders from these countries. An agency manages its own physical stock by means of an inventory database. For this purpose, the domain model shown in Fig. 6 is extended with a map Map<Book, Integer> which maintains the number of books in stock. This map is kept up-to-date by a handler registered to be notified upon the change of an order status to *shipped*. The event type is defined as an attribute update on any object of class Order.

```
EventType orderStatusChanged = eventManager.createEventType(
   Order.class, InstanceOperation.ATTRIBUTE_UPDATE, null, null, null);
```

The action consists of updating the map. Given the order that has changed its status to *shipped*, all books it contains are retrieved. For each of these books, the inventory map is updated.

```
Action updateMap = new Action(){
   public void execute(Object[] params)   {
      Order order = (Order) params[0];
      Set<Book> books = order.getBooks();
      for (Book current : books)   {
         // update Map<Book, Integer>
      }
   }
};
eventManager.createAction(action);
```

The handler is set to only execute its action if the status has been changed to *shipped*. For this purpose, a condition is declared as follows.

```
Condition isShipped = new Condition()    {
   public boolean evaluate(Object[] params)    {
      Order order = (Order) params[0];
      Field attribute = (Field) params[1];
      return attriute.getName().equals("Status") &&
         order.getStatus().equals(Order.SHIPPED);
   }
}
```

Having defined all required parts, the handler is created.

```
eventManager.createHandler(orderStatusChanged, updateMap, fallback,
   isShipped, null);
```

Using remote handlers, a central database can be set to keep an account of the stock of each agency. Similar to the inventory database of the agency, a map `Map<Agency, Map<Book, Integer>>` is used. Whenever a new agency is created, a remote handler is registered for the event type `orderStatusChanged` defined in the database of the agency.

To do so, the method `ExternalEventManager.getEventTypes()` is used to retrieve all event types in the agency database. Once the `orderStatusChanged` event type is selected, the method `InternalEventManager.createHandler()` is used to create the handler. In the following code we assume that within the book shop network the connection details about the agency database are known as `host:port`. Furthermore, the selection of the particular event type leverages the fact that all event types have a name that can be used to query for them. Note that event type names have not been discussed in the scope of this paper due to space limitations.

```
ExternalEventManager agencyEventManager =
   new ExternalEventManager("zurich.bookstore.com:3927");
EventType orderStatusChanged =
   agencyEventManager.getEventType("OrderStatusChanged");
eventManager.createHandler(orderStatusChanged, updateMap, fallback,
   isShipped, null);
```

Note that the action must be changed in a way that it is able to handle the central map `Map<Agency, Map<Book, Integer>>` instead of the agency map `Map<Book, Integer>`.

8   Conclusions

In this paper, we have presented an event model for object databases that provides support for event-based programming required by many application domains. As object databases are situated in the intersection of database systems and object-oriented programming languages, our model unifies concepts that have originated in either of these domains. Additionally, the proposed event model clearly separates the concepts involved in event processing. It provides all the event processing functionality within the database and orthogonal to the data as well as support for event composition and distribution. In comparison to similar proposals, our approach is therefore better suited to distributed scenarios while at the same time offering a higher potential for code reuse.

An example of how code can be reused is the concept of the handler that allows for indirect event notification registration. For example, a developer could register two event handlers for the same event type, thereby reusing the event types in order to define different actions in response to a given event. The conditions associated with the event handlers will determine which actions are executed. By providing event and action libraries, we offer maximum reuse and flexibility for combining event types with actions.

A central contribution of our event model is the generalisation of the well-known concept of event scopes. The approach we have presented can be seen as an extension of the one taken by Versant discussed in Sect. 2. While their solution motivates the scope concept as a valid approach to building a flexible event model with a high potential for code reusability, Versant omits support for some scopes that we believe are important. Specifically, collection data structures and uniform access to metadata are important characteristics of most object databases and, therefore, we have included additional event scopes to deal with changes to collections as well as to the metadata, i.e. schema evolution. As a consequence, in our definition, the scope of an event can either be a single object, a group of objects, a collection of object or a class of objects as well as a transaction or the global scope.

We have also presented an architecture and implementation to support our event model in an object database, clearly detailing how the concepts of the model are realised in the setting of the Java language. As our model is a unification of concepts that originated in the domains of databases and software engineering, our architecture can be used to handle events both on the server and the client side. By default, events are processed within the database as they are part of the database logic. However, our event model also supports distributed event processing based on a publish/subscribe middleware and, therefore, events can also be handled on the client if required. Finally, we have discussed the implementation of a simple application scenario based on the programming interface of our unified event model.

References

1. Sellis, T.K., Lin, C.C., Raschid, L.: Implementing Large Production Systems in a DBMS Environment: Concepts and Algorithms. In: Proceedings of ACM SIGMOD International Conference on Management of Data, Chicago, IL, USA, June 1-3, pp. 404–423 (1988)
2. Stonebraker, M., Jhingran, A., Goh, J., Potamianos, S.: On Rules, Procedure, Caching and Views in Data Base Systems. In: Proceedings of ACM SIGMOD International Conference on Management of Data, Atlantic City, NJ, USA, May 23-26, pp. 281–290 (1990)

3. Stonebraker, M.: The Integration of Rule Systems and Database Systems. IEEE Transactions on Knowledge and Data Engineering 4(5), 415–423 (1992)
4. Hanson, E.N.: Rule Condition Testing and Action Execution in Ariel. In: Proceedings of ACM SIGMOD International Conference on Management of Data, San Diego, CA, USA, June 2-5, pp. 49–58 (1992)
5. Dewan, H.M., Ohsie, D., Stolfo, S.J., Wolfson, O., da Silva, S.: Incremental database rule processing in PARADISER. Journal of Intelligent Information Systems 1(2), 177–209 (1992)
6. Ghandeharizadeh, S., Hull, R., Jacobs, D., Castillo, J., Escobar-Molano, M., Lu, S.H., Luo, J., Tsang, C., Zhou, G.: On Implementing a Language for Specifying Active Database Execution Models. In: Proceedings of International Conference on Very Large Data Bases, Dublin, Ireland, August 24-27, pp. 441–454 (1993)
7. Simon, E., Kiernan, J., de Maindreville, C.: Implementing High Level Active Rules on Top of a Relational DBMS. In: Proceedings of International Conference on Very Large Data Bases, Vancouver, Canada, August 23-27, pp. 315–326 (1992)
8. Brant, D.A., Miranker, D.P.: Index Support for Rule Activation. In: Proceedings of ACM SIGMOD International Conference on Management of Data, Washington, D.C., USA, May 25-28, pp. 42–48 (1993)
9. Kotz, A.M., Dittrich, K.R., Mulle, J.A.: Supporting Semantic Rules by a Generalized Event/Trigger Mechanism. In: Proceedings of International Conference on Extending Database Technology, Venice, Italy, March 14-18, pp. 76–91 (1988)
10. Cacace, F., Ceri, S., Crespi-Reghizzi, S., Tanca, L., Zicari, R.: Integrating Object-oriented Data Modelling with a Rule-based Programming Paradigm. In: Proceedings of ACM SIGMOD International Conference on Management of Data, Atlantic City, NJ, United States, May 23-26, pp. 225–236 (1990)
11. Díaz, O., Paton, N.W., Gray, P.M.D.: Rule Management in Object Oriented Databases: A Uniform Approach. In: Proceedings of International Conference on Very Large Data Bases, Barcelona, Catalonia, Spain, September 3-6, pp. 317–326 (1991)
12. Beeri, C., Milo, T.: A Model for Active Object Oriented Databases. In: Proceedings of International Conference on Very Large Data Bases, Barcelona, Catalonia, Spain, September 3-6, pp. 337–349 (1991)
13. Schreier, U., Pirahesh, H., Agrawal, R., Mohan, C.: Alert: An Architecture for Transforming a Passive DBMS into an Active DBMS. In: Proceedings of International Conference on Very Large Data Bases, Barcelona, Catalonia, Spain, September 3-6, pp. 469–478 (1991)
14. Anwar, E., Maugis, L., Chakravarthy, S.: A New Perspective on Rule Support for Object-Oriented Databases. In: Proceedings of ACM SIGMOD International Conference on Management of Data, Washington, D.C., USA, May 25-28, pp. 99–108 (1993)
15. Kappel, G., Retschitzegger, W.: The TriGS Active Object-Oriented Database System – An Overview. ACM SIGMOD Record 27(3), 36–41 (1998)
16. Paton, N.W., Díaz, O.: Active Database Systems. ACM Comput. Surv. 31(1), 63–103 (1999)
17. White, S., Alves, A., Rorke, D.: WebLogic Event Server: A Lightweight, Modular Application Server for Event Processing. In: DEBS 2008: Proceedings of the Second International Conference on Distributed Event-based Systems, pp. 193–200 (2008)
18. Cohen, N.H., Kalleberg, K.T.: EventScript: An Event-processing Language based on Regular Expressions with Actions. In: LCTES 2008: Proceedings of the 2008 ACM SIGPLAN-SIGBED Conference on Languages, Compilers, and Tools for Embedded Systems, pp. 111–120 (2008)

19. Rozsnyai, S., Schiefer, J., Schatten, A.: Concepts and Models for Typing Events for Event-based Systems. In: DEBS 2007: Proceedings of the 2007 Inaugural International Conference on Distributed Event-based Systems, pp. 62–70 (2007)
20. Paterson, J., Edlich, S., Hörning, H., Hörning, R.: The Definitive Guide to db4o. Apress (2006)
21. Gamma, E., Helm, R., Johnson, R., Vlissides, J.: Design Patterns: Elements of Reusable Object-oriented Software. Addison-Wesley Professional, Reading (1995)
22. Grossniklaus, M., Norrie, M.C., Sgier, J.: Realising Proactive Behaviour in Mobile Data-Centric Applications. In: Proceedings of International Workshop on Ubiquitous Mobile Information and Collaboration Systems, Trondheim, Norway, June 11-12, pp. 561–575 (2007)

Multi-granular Spatio-temporal Object Models: Concepts and Research Directions[*]

Elisa Bertino[1], Elena Camossi[2], and Michela Bertolotto[2]

[1] CERIAS - Purdue University, 250 N. University Street West Lafayette, Indiana, USA 47907-2066
Phone: +1 765 496-2399; Fax: +1 765 494-0739
bertino@cs.purdue.edu
[2] School of Computer Science and Informatics - University College Dublin, Belfield, Dublin 4, Ireland
Phone: +353 (0)1 7162-944/913; Fax: +353 (0)1 2697-262
{elena.camossi,michela.bertolotto}@ucd.ie

Abstract. The capability of representing *spatio-temporal objects* is fundamental when analysing and monitoring the changes in the spatial configuration of a geographical area over a period of time. An important requirement when managing spatio-temporal objects is the support for multiple granularities. In this paper we discuss how the modelling constructs of object data models can be extended for representing and querying multi-granular spatio-temporal objects. In particular, we describe object-oriented formalizations for granularities, granules, and multi-granular values, exploring the issues of value conversions. Furthermore, we formally define an object-oriented multi-granular query language, and discuss dynamic multi-granularity. Finally, we discuss open research issues.

1 Introduction

Many relevant application domains, including homeland security, environmental protection, geological and agricultural sciences, require modelling and managing spatial data objects and monitoring their evolution according to time. The capability of representing *spatio-temporal objects* with respect to both their spatial layout and their temporal evolution, is fundamental when analysing and monitoring the changes in the spatial configuration of a geographical area over a period of time. An important requirement when managing spatio-temporal objects is the support for multiple granularities. For example, when tracing modifications to spatial areas, the history of the areas under observation has to be maintained and retrieved at multiple temporal granularities (e.g., years, months, decades). When analysing large spatial datasets, one may need to zoom-in and zoom-out

---

[*] Research presented in this paper was funded by a Strategic Research Cluster grant (07/SRC/I1168) by Science Foundation Ireland under the National Development Plan. The authors gratefully acknowledge this support. The work of Elena Camossi is supported by the Irish Research Council for Science, Engineering and Technology.

M.C. Norrie and M. Grossniklaus (Eds.): ICOODB 2009, LNCS 5936, pp. 132–148, 2010.

from the dataset under analysis according to different spatial granularities (e.g., meters, kilometres, feet, yards).

Granularities intuitively represent the units of measure of a dataset, and may be defined on all data dimensions (i.e., space and time for spatio-temporal data). For each dimension, a connected set of granularities must be defined, and the different sets are independent. The choice of proper granularities allows the system to store a minimal amount of data, according to the most appropriate levels of detail. In many applications different granularities may exist, neither of which is inherently better than the others. Therefore, a database system for such applications should support a wide range of granularities and allow the applications to define their own specific granularities. Moreover, because the selection of attribute granularities is based on a trade-off between application efficiency and modelling requirements and this trade-off may change over time, the model at hand should support the ability to dynamically set and change the spatio-temporal granularity. For example, in a spatio-temporal database for environmental monitoring, the collection of meteorological parameters like the amount of rainfall, the strength and direction of the wind, the value of atmospheric pressure, must be collected more frequently in the presence of exceptional events like hurricanes and storms. Furthermore, such a granularity modification may involve only specific geographical areas (e.g., those affected by the phenomenon), and is required for limited periods of time (e.g., the time when the phenomenon occurs), therefore the modification of the level of detail of data has to be spatio-temporally bounded.

However, even though research in the spatial and temporal data management systems has resulted in many spatial and temporal models, these models are in most cases extensions of the relational data model [1] and are unable to directly represent crucial modelling features of spatio-temporal data objects. As a result, the applications have to implement and maintain mappings between the spatio-temporal objects of interest and low-level data and are unable to efficiently support multiple object representations at different granularities in both space and time. We believe that an object DBMS (ODBMS), because of its modelling features such as complex data types and methods, is better suited for addressing such requirements. However, even with such a model, modelling and managing multiple granularities is not trivial and extensions are required. However, the natural extensibility of object models makes easier developing these extensions. The goal of this paper is to explore in details the notion of multiple granularities for spatio-temporal objects and show how the modelling constructs of an object data model can be extended for representing and querying these objects.

More specifically in the paper we discuss a number of issues, including:

- *The notion of granularities in space and time.* How do we represent them? How do we relate granularities and maintain a granularity lattice? How do we extend the granularity sets and, at the same time, preserve the relationships among granularities?
- *The notion of temporal, spatial, and spatio-temporal values.* How do we represent multi-granular spatio-temporal values? How do we support granularity conversions? How do we preserve data usability and reduce uncertainty

on converted values? Can we combine concepts like topologically consistent transformation, probability distributions, invertibility and quasi-invertibility properties to reduce uncertainty?

- *Navigating and querying through multi-granular data.* How does multi-granularity impact on object navigation and value comparison? How do we access to multi-granular spatio-temporal object values?
- *Dynamic multi-granular data.* How do we refine object attributes? Are conventional object specialization models adequate? How do we support object evolution with respect to the object state and the object granularities?

In the discussion, we will refer to the ST_ODMG and the ST^2_ODMGe object data models, which have been specifically defined for modelling and querying spatio-temporal objects with multiple dynamically varying granularities [2,3,31] and thus can illustrate solutions to some of the above challenges. Both models have been defined as extension of the ODMG model [4], the standard de facto for object-oriented databases; ST_ODMG has been recently extended for application to an object-relational data model [5].

The rest of the paper is organized as follows. We first discuss related work on modelling approaches for multi-granularity. We then illustrate how multi-granular spatio-temporal objects are represented and queried in the ST_ODMG model. In Sect. 5 we describe two different solutions for evolving multi-granular objects, i.e., attribute redefinition and dynamic objects. Afterwards, in Sect. 6 we discuss the issues of spatio-temporal multi-granularity. Finally, we conclude the paper illustrating future research directions.

2   Related Work

Spatio-temporal multi-granularity has been mostly investigated by separately considering the temporal and the spatial domains. The pioneering research work on temporal granularities is by Anderson [6]. A consensus among the different disciplines interested in temporal granularity representation is the formalization by Bettini et al. [7], who give a comprehensive discussion on temporal granularities for databases, data mining, and temporal reasoning. Granularity issues related to temporal databases have been investigated both for the relational and the object-oriented data models [8,9]. The introduction of multiple temporal granularities in an object-oriented data model poses additional issues with respect to the relational context, due to the semantic richness of such a model. Bertino et al. [10] investigate the impact of temporal granularities in an object-oriented model compliant with the ODMG standard.

The representation of data at multiple levels of details, that is, at multiple granularities, is a topic of relevant interest also in modelling spatial entities. In the context of Geographical Information Systems (GIS), much research addresses the development of data models for the multiresolution representation of geographic maps [11,12].

Research on multiple resolutions addresses in particular model-oriented generalization [13], which applies techniques used in cartography for representing spatial data at different levels of abstraction, by taking into account also the semantics of data and some notion of consistency to preserve data usability, as, for example, the preservation of topological relationships.

Other proposals address specifically the multi-granular representation of spatio-temporal data [14,2,15]. Claramunt and Juang [14] propose the application of nested hierarchies for modelling space and time to extract quantitative information about spatio-temporal relationships in a data set. Griffiths et al. [16] define the Tripod spatio-historical model. This model includes a definition of histories at different granularities. However, no operators are provided to convert multi-granular data, but the histories are always internally represented at the *chronon* [17] granularity. Katri et al. [18] define an annotation-model for the specification of spatio-temporal data at multiple granularities. Such a granularity formalization relies on the concepts of temporal indeterminacy [19] and spatial imprecision [20]. However, the resulting model and the granularity systems are effective only for data specification, because the conversion from a granularity to another is completely left to the user. The European project *MurMur* [21] addresses multiple resolutions through multiple representations, supporting *perceptions*, which include different points of view and spatial resolutions. Wang and Liu [?] adopt the same definition of spatial granularity as [2], addressing uncertain spatio-temporal regions. Belussi et al. [15] define spatio-temporal granularities as historical evolution of spatial granules, to search valid spatial granules in a given instant. Their approach relies on the mapping of spatial multiple granularities and granules onto graph structures (multidigraphs), which encompasses labelling functions for granules and their mutual (topological) relationships, disregarding value conversions.

3   Modelling Multi-granular Spatio-temporal data

The exploitation of multiple granularities for spatio-temporal data entails the definition of a multi-granular spatio-temporal type system and conversions to represent spatio-temporal data at different granularities. These elements are constructed relying on formal definitions for granularities, granules, and granular elements, and are the key components of a multi-granular algebra for representing and managing multi-granular spatio-temporal data. Relying on such an algebra, a multi-granular spatio-temporal query language, which will be discussed in the next section, may be designed as well.

In what follows, we discuss the formal definition of granularities, types, values, and multi-granular conversions we adopt in the design of ST_ODMG [2]. We refer the interested reader to [22] for a more complete discussion of granularity implementation challenges.

3.1   Spatial and Temporal Granularities

According to [7], temporal granularities may be formally represented as mappings from an ordered index set $\mathcal{IS}$ to the power set of the temporal domain (i.e., $\mathcal{TIME}$), which is totally ordered. Both Khatri et al. [18] and Camossi et al. [2] apply the same definition to spatial granularities, which are defined as mapping from an index set $\mathcal{IS}$ to subsets of $\mathcal{SPACE}$, the spatial domain. $\mathcal{SPACE}$ is two-dimensional (that is, subset of R^2). Spatial granularities may include 2-dimensional granules (e.g., units of area: *squaremeters*, *acres*, etc.; administrative boundaries classifications: *municipalities*, *countries*, etc.), or 1-dimensional granules (e.g., measures of length: *kilometers*, *miles*, etc.; map scales: 1 : 24000, 1 : 62500, etc.). For instance, *days*, *weeks*, *years* are temporal granularities; *meters*, *kilometers*, *feet*, *yards*, *provinces* and *countries* are spatial granularities.

Each subset of the temporal and spatial domains corresponding to a single granularity mapping is referred to as a temporal or spatial *granule*, i.e., given a granularity G and an index $i \in \mathcal{IS}$, $G(i)$ is a granule of G that identifies a subset of the corresponding domain. Granules are used to specify the *valid* spatio-temporal bounds on attribute values, as well as the temporal occurrence of database events. For instance, we can say that a value reporting the measure of the daily temperature in Rome is defined for the first and the second day of January. The granules of interest for this example can be identified by three textual labels: "01/01", "02/01", and "*Rome*", that respectively identify two temporal and one spatial granules. The interiors of different granules of the same granularity cannot overlap[1]. Moreover, non-empty granules of the same temporal granularity must preserve the order of the temporal domain.

Sets of temporal or spatial granules expressed at the same granularity are referred to as *temporal* or *spatial elements* [3], respectively. An element at granularity G is denoted as Υ^G. For instance, $\{1999, 2000, 2001\}^{years}$ is a temporal element at granularity *years*, and $\{\texttt{Rome, Berlin}\}^{municipalities}$ is a spatial element at granularity *municipalities*.

Different granularities provide different partitions of their domain of reference. The reason is that diverse relationships may hold among granularities, depending on the inclusion and the overlapping of granules [7]. For instance, in *ST_ODMG* [2] we assume that spatial and temporal granularities are related by the *finer-than* relationship: given two granularities G and H such that G is finer-than H, every granule g of G is properly included in a granule h of the coarser granularity H (cf. Fig. 1). If G is finer-than H, we also say that H is coarser-than G. For example, temporal granularity *days* is finer-than *months*, and granularity *months* is finer-than *years*. Likewise, spatial granularity *municipalities* is finer-than *countries*.

Relationships among different granularities are fundamental for enabling the comparison of multi-granular values in queries. For instance, in a query we might require to compare the values of seasonal sales of two similar products, one stored at spatial granularity *countries* and one at temporal granularity *provinces*, to decide which one to sell at a shop chain. To perform a meaningful comparison, these values have to be expressed at the same spatial granularity. In the following

---

[1] Temporal granules, according to the definition by Bettini et al. [23], do not overlap, while spatial granules can overlap on the granule boundaries.

Fig. 1. The *finer-than* relationship: G is finer-than H

sections we will describe granularity conversions supported by ST_ODMG for converting granular values at different temporal and spatial granularities related by finer-than. In this case, we observe that *provinces* is finer-than *countries*; therefore we may likely apply some conversions to these values (e.g., the value at granularity *countries* may be split among the different provinces of each country or viceversa). By contrast, if the granularities were, for instance, *feet* and *meters*, these values cannot be directly converted (being granules the basic units of measure, granule portions are meaningless); we may instead convert both values to a common representation, different from *feet* and *meters* (e.g., *μmeters*, which is finer-than both granularities). Therefore, given two multi-granular values, one at granularity G and one at granularity H such that G and H are not directly related by the finer-than relationship, such values may be compared if the two values may be represented (i.e., converted) at the same granularity K, that is finer-than G and H. K is chosen as the granularity that minimizes the number of conversions applied. If K is the coarsest, among the granularities finer-than G and H, K is referred to as the *greatest lower bound* *(GLB)* of G and H.

Furthermore, by relying on granularity relationships, we may design efficient representations for granularities. For instance, we may implement granules of temporal granularity *years* relying on the representation provided for *months* and exploiting the uniform relationship between these two granularities. Indeed, the mapping onto the temporal domain of a given granule of *years* may be obtained retrieving the mappings of the twelve *months* of that year. Iterating the same technique onto the set of temporal granularities, we map the representation of most granularities onto the most finer one the model assumes (e.g., *milliseconds*), and avoid the exhaustive mapping onto the temporal domain for most of the granularities (see [22] for further details).

3.2   Multi-granular Types, Values and Conversions

In addition to the conventional database values, a spatio-temporal database schema can include spatial, temporal, and spatio-temporal values. Multi-granular values in ST_ODMG are defined as partial functions from the set of granules of the corresponding granularity(ies) to the set of values of a conventional (i.e., literal or object types without any spatio-temporal capability) or geometric (i.e., two- and three-dimensional vector features) inner type. ST_ODMG provides two multi-granular parametric types: $Spatial_{SG}(\sigma)$ and $Temporal_{TG}(\tau)$, where SG and TG are a spatial and a temporal granularity, respectively; σ is a conventional or a geometric type; τ is a conventional or a *Spatial* type. These types may be

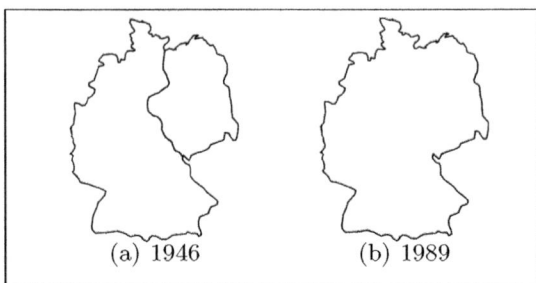

(a) 1946   (b) 1989

Fig. 2. A spatio-temporal geometric value

functionally combined to define multi-granular spatio-temporal types, as in the
following example.

Example 1. Suppose a class Europe is defined to describe geo-political properties
of European countries. The following is an example of a spatio-temporal value
storing some of the names of the Heads of Government of European countries.
Its type is $Temporal_{years}(Spatial_{countries}(\texttt{string}))$.

$$v = \{\langle 2007, \{\langle \texttt{France}, \texttt{'F. Fillon'}\rangle, \langle \texttt{Germany}, \texttt{'A. Merkel'}\rangle\}^{countries}\rangle,$$
$$\langle 2008, \{\langle \texttt{France}, \texttt{'N. Sarkozy'}\rangle, \langle \texttt{Germany}, \texttt{'A. Merkel'}\rangle\}^{countries}\rangle\}^{years}.$$

In Fig. 2, a value of type $Temporal_{years}(Spatial_{countries}(\texttt{set}\langle\texttt{Polygon}\rangle))$ illustrates the historical changes in the German political boundaries: each country
is represented through a polygon or a closed polyline.   □

To improve or reduce the level of detail of a multi-granular value, the value
has to be converted to a different granularity. To address this requirement, in
ST_ODMG we introduce *granularity conversions*, which include temporal and
spatial coercion [10] and refinement [24] functions. We note here that coercion
and refinement functions, that are basic notions in the object-oriented paradigm,
directly address the requirement of spatio-temporal value conversion from a conceptual point of view. However, in a spatio-temporal setting, these functions must
account for the additional semantics provided by granularities.

An important issue in the use of spatio-temporal coercion and refinement
functions is represented by data consistency. For instance, if one first coerces a
value v from a spatial granularity G into a value v' at a spatial granularity H,
one would expect the relationships v has with other spatial objects be preserved
by v'. To address this issue, model-oriented and cartographic map generalisation
operators that guarantee topological consistency [25,26], an essential property to
guarantee data usability, may be applied. For example, *merge* operators merge
adjacent features of the same dimension into a single one, while *splitting* operators subdivide single features in adjacent features of the same dimension. Other
operators perform *contraction* and *thinning* (whose inverse is *expansion*); *abstraction* and *simplification* (whose inverse is *addition*). Their application avoids
situations like the one shown in Fig. 3, where a non-topologically consistent line

simplification algorithm [27] is applied to coarse a coast line in a map (in black the original coast, in red the straight coarser one). Such a simplification would require a post-process revision, to correct the location of the island, which has been incorporated into the land, and of the city, which has been moved into the sea.

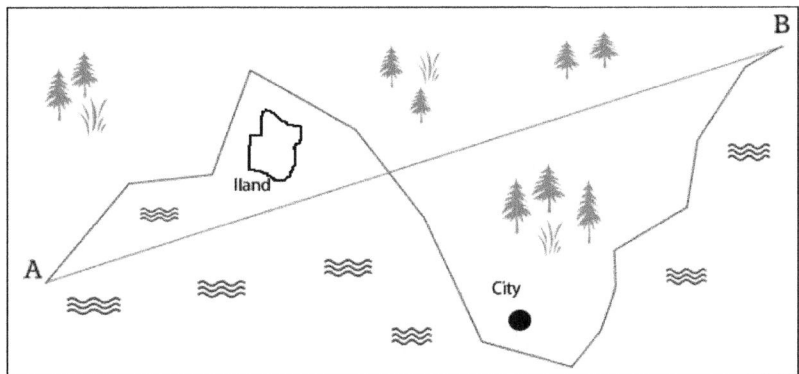

Fig. 3. Topologically inconsistent geometric transformation

The *ST_ODMG* model also provides operators for converting spatio-temporal quantitative (i.e., non-geometrical) attribute values. These operators perform *selection* (e.g., `projection`, `main`, `first`), and *aggregation* (e.g., `sum`, `average`) to convert values to a coarser representation; their inverse functions, *restriction* and *splitting*, convert attribute values to finer representations, according to downward hereditary property [28] or according to a probability distribution, respectively.

Granularity conversions in *ST_ODMG* have been proven to return legal values of the *ST_ODMG* type system [2]. Conversions that generalize geometric attribute values to coarser spatial granularities have been demonstrated to preserve the semantics of the spatio-temporal data represented [2]. Furthermore, the conversions we provided for converting spatio-temporal values at finer granularities address indeterminacy [19] and imprecision [20] that always affect this type of conversion (see also [24] for a more comprehensive discussion on *invertibility* and *quasi-invertibility* of multi-granular values).

4   Querying Multi-granular Spatio-temporal Data

A model for multi-granular spatio-temporal queries in *ST_ODMG* has also been defined [3]. The language extends the value comparison and object navigation paradigms of OQL [4] to support multi-granular spatio-temporal values. The key concept of the language is the *multi-granular spatio-temporal path expression* (*MST Path-Expr*), which extends the conventional notion of object-oriented path expression to multi-granular spatio-temporal values. In a *MST Path-Exprs* the access to multi-granular attribute values is specified by referring to portions of the spatio-temporal domain through the use of a specific operator ($\downarrow$).

References to the spatio-temporal domain are given explicitly through spatial and temporal *elements* we introduced in the previous section, as illustrated in the following example.

Example 2. Given the spatio-temporal value of Example 1, representing the name of European Heads of Government, the temporal path expression $v \downarrow \{2007\}^{years}$ returns the spatial value:

$\{\langle$France,'F. Fillon'$\rangle,\langle$Germany,'A. Merkel'$\rangle\}^{countries}$.

By contrast, the spatial path expression $v \downarrow \{\textbf{France}\}^{countries}$ returns the temporal value:

$\{\langle$2007,'F. Fillon'$\rangle,\langle$2008,'N. Sarkozy'$\rangle\}^{years}$. $\square$

In *MST Path-Exprs*, we also use multi-granular spatio-temporal *expressions* (*Exprs*), which are implicit representations of spatio-temporal elements. *Exprs* are given as conditions that are evaluated on database objects. They result in temporal and spatial elements, which intuitively represent *when* and *where* such conditions are satisfied. Conditions are specified through temporal and spatial variations of conventional comparison operators (e.g., $=_T$, $<>_S$) and binary topological relationships as defined by Egenhofer and Franzosa [29] (e.g., $equals_T$, $overlaps_S$).

Example 3. Given the spatio-temporal value of Example 1, the temporal expression $v =_T$ 'N. Sarkozy' returns the temporal element $\{2008\}^{years}$, whereas the spatial expression $v =_S$ 'N. Sarkozy' returns $\{\textbf{France}\}^{countries}$. $\square$

Queries have the usual OQL `select-from-where` form. *MST Path-Exprs* are applied in the target list to specify the data to retrieve, and in the where clause to express conditions against multi-granular spatio-temporal objects. Whenever *MST Path-Exprs* involve different granularities, granularity conversions described in the previous section are applied during the evaluation of these *MST Path-Exprs*.

Example 4. Given class `Europe` of Example 1, and given a class `Nation` describing the properties of interest for a single country, the following query retrieves the name of the Head of Government of West Germany in 1980:

```
select e.head_of_government ↓ {1980}^{years}
from Europe e, Nation n
where n.name ↓ {1980}^{years} = 'West Germany'.
```

It returns the name 'H. Shmidt'. By contrast, the following query retrieves when Angela Merkel was Head of Government of Germany:

```
select e.head_of_government =_T 'A. Merkel'
from Europe e, Nation n
where (n.name ↓ e.head_of_government =_T 'A. Merkel') = 'Germany'.
```

It returns the temporal element representing the period from 2005 and 2009. $\square$

5   Adaptive Spatio-temporal Multi-granular Models

Adaptivity support is a crucial requirement for almost all applications we may
think of. In a spatio-temporal setting with multiple granularities, an added dimension to the problem of adaptation is represented by the *evolution* of attribute granularity. To date this problem has not been much investigated. In
what follows, we discuss two preliminary solutions to adapt attribute granularities: object-oriented attributes redefinition, and evolution models. The first
approach, which is discussed in [30], provides a weaker granularity adaptability,
which is limited to attribute redefinition along the inheritance hierarchy; then,
granularity modifications are pre-arranged in the database schema. Conversely,
the ST^2_ODMGe model [31], which is described at the end of the section, adopts
a flexible solution by which run time evolutions may be specified and executed.

5.1   Multi-granular Attribute Redefinition

The idea behind multi-granular attribute refinement is that the granularity at
which an attribute value is stored can be changed in a sub-class, to better reflect
the application evolution needs. In the sub-class the attribute values may be
maintained at a coarser or at a finer level of detail. For instance, if at the super-
class only the monthly values are recorded, in the sub-class the daily changes
can be maintained, improving the level of detail for the attribute. By contrast,
we may reduce the detail coarsening the attribute value in the sub-class.

The most critical requirement in attribute refinement is to preserve object
substitutability. Whenever an object instance of a sub-class is found in a context
where a super-class object is expected, its attribute values must be converted
to the expected granularity, leaving the whole procedure completely transparent
to the user. Therefore, multi-granular conversions including both coercion and
refinement functions, such those described in Sect. 3.2, must be provided by a
multi-granular model. Supplying a variety of conversions with different semantics
enables to choose, for each attribute and situation, the conversion that better
reflects the attribute semantics.

Substitutability impacts both on attribute accesses and updates. In an object
access, granularity conversions are used to compute the value to consider in the
super-class, given the value of the attribute in the sub-class. By contrast, in case
of object updates, granularity conversions are applied to convert the value to
the granularity required in the sub-class.

Example 5. The following multi-granular spatio-temporal schema includes an
example of multi-granular attribute refinement[2]. We give a partial definition for
class `Nation`, reporting the specification of attribute `population`, which stores

---

[2] The syntax we use in this example has been first introduced in *ST*_ODMG: it ex-
    tends the ODMG Data Definition Language to spatio-temporal multi-granularity.
    The same syntax has been further extended in [30] to support attribute refinement.

the daily updates to the amount of population recorded in each municipality of a country.

```
class Nation (...) {
    attribute Temporal_days(Spatial_municipalities(int)) population;
    ...
};
```

Then, we define a class **NationStatistic**, which *extends* **Nation**, to collect statistical information on the countries in the database. In particular, attribute **population** is refined at temporal granularity *years* and at spatial granularity *countries*.

```
class NationStatistic extends Nation (...) {
    ref attribute Temporal_years(Spatial_countries(int)) population {
        ⟨ split_{countries→municipalities}, sum_{municipalities→countries} ⟩,
        ⟨ restr_{years→days}, avg_{days→years} ⟩}
    ...
};
```

Two pairs of granularity conversions are specified for this attribute: the first refers to the spatial refinement, whereas the second deals with the temporal refinement. In each pair of conversions $\langle af, uf \rangle$, af is the granularity conversion used to access the attribute value from an object that at compile time has type **Nation**: the attribute value has to be converted from the sub-class granularity (e.g., *countries*) to that used in the super-class (e.g., *municipalities*). In this example both the spatial and the temporal granularities have been refined in the sub-class, therefore we have two refinement conversion functions to use in the access: both **split** (i.e., split) and **restr** (i.e., restriction) granularity conversions have to be applied to the value, that is converted from granularities *years* and *countries* to finer granularities *days* and *municipalities*. uf conversions are applied when updating the attribute from an object whose run-time type is **NationStatistic**, while at compile time it has type **Nation**: in this case, the conversions **sum** and **avg** (i.e., average) are applied to coarser the finer value to granularities *years* and *countries*.   □

To guarantee data consistency, both compile and run-time checks may be applied. At compile time, the consistency of the database schema must be verified, checking first that the granularities in the super-class and in the sub-class are related by some granularity relationship. In *ST_ODMG* we consider the finer-than relationship, but other relationships may be applied as well. Then, we have to check that two *inverse* or *quasi-inverse* [24] granularity conversions have been specified, one to use for the access and one for the update of the attribute. However, at run-time we may allow one to apply a different granularity conversion for the attribute access, whenever the user needs a different conversion semantics, and also in this case the granularity conversion must be compliant with the attribute refinement.

5.2   Evolutions of Spatio-temporal Multi-granular Objects

Being able to dynamically adapt the spatial and temporal granularities to respond to dynamic events and situations and to reflect changes in data signif-
icance is crucial in many contexts: e.g., periodic phenomena, modifications to
attribute values, operation execution, data aging or privacy restrictions. Specific
operations required for supporting dynamic adaptation of granularity include:
1) *granularity evolution*, which aggregates existing detailed data at a coarser
granularity (e.g., older data that may be stored for future reference), or even
refines information at a finer granularity (e.g., in data analysis); 2) *granularity
acquisition*, which changes at run-time the granularity used when inserting new
values in the database; 3) *value deletion*, which removes attribute values from
the database, whenever they are no longer useful at a given granularity (e.g.,
detailed data).

The recently defined ST^2_ODMGe (Spatio-(Bi)Temporal ODMG supporting
Evolutions) [31] addresses these requirement by supporting the modification of
the granularities used in attribute definitions, and the deletion of attribute values at run-time. Evolutions have the form: ON *Event* [IF *Condition*] DO *Action*.
Example of events are: update, delete, etc., that is, occurrences that modify
the database state, including evolution actions, and may have a periodic or an
extemporary behaviour. Furthermore, references to the transaction time, both
periodic and extemporary, may be specified as events. Conditions are specified
against database attribute values, and include also periodic checks, evaluated
on valid time. Finally, evolution actions are sequences of operations that may
modify the attribute granularities and delete the attribute values.

Evolutions are defined and executed at run-time and conform to the execution
model of active databases. Given an instance of an ST^2_ODMGe database and
a set of evolutions specified for it, the database is continuously monitored. The
execution of database transactions modifies the database state and triggers the
evolutions whose events refer to such transactions. Therefore, the corresponding
conditions are evaluated. For those triggered evolutions whose conditions evaluate to TRUE, the corresponding actions are executed. As a consequence, the
database state (or schema, in case of granularity acquisition) may be modified.

Example 6. Given class Nation defined in Example 5, the following are two
examples of evolutions we may specify to periodically obtain summarized values
of the amount of population of the countries in the database.

```
ON update Nation.population < days, municipalities >
IF every 1^{years}_{VT}
DO evolve < days, municipalities > to < days, countries > using
   sum_{municipalities→countries}, split_{countries→municipalities};


ON update Nation.population < days, countries >
DO evolve < days, countries > to < years, countries > using
   avg_{days→years}, restr_{years→days};
```

The first evolution is triggered by updates to attribute population as originally defined in class Nation, i.e., at temporal granularity *days* and at spatial granularity *municipalities*. Once one year of values (i.e., $1_{\mathcal{VT}}^{years}$, where $\mathcal{VT}$ denotes valid time) has been recorded for this attribute, the evolution is executed, and the first time a new value is created for this attribute: specifically, a new *granularity level* (see [31]) at granularity *days* and *countries* is defined for attribute population. For each country, it stores the daily amount of population, given as the sum of the population of every municipality in the country. This evolution is executed periodically, every $1_{\mathcal{VT}}^{years}$. Every time this new granularity level is updated (i.e., once a year), the second evolution is triggered. It results in the creation of a new granularity level, at granularity *years* and *countries*, that stores the annual amount of population of the country. This value is obtained as the average of the daily amount stored in the previous granularity level.

Consequently to the execution of evolutions, the run-time type of population is $Temporal_{days}(Spatial_{municipalities}(int)) \times Temporal_{days}(Spatial_{countries}(int)) \times Temporal_{years}(Spatial_{countries}(int))$. Note that the last granularity level has the same type of attribute population we defined in class NationStatistic of Example 5. However, in this case the value is automatically computed, and belongs to the same object of type Nation it refers to. By contrast, in the case of Example 5, for each country at least two objects have to be created to maintain the same information.   □

After the execution of evolutions, the run-time type of the attribute values is a Cartesian product of multi-granular types as defined in Sect. 3. Therefore at run-time the state of objects in the database is no longer consistent with their class definition. We formally revisited the notion of object consistency, weakening the conditions on attribute values and on objects spatio-temporal lifespans to include the side-effects of evolutions. In particular, we require that each evolution specification includes a pair of *inverse* and *quasi inverse* granularity conversions among portions of the same attribute value expressed at different granularities.

Moreover, we take advantage of attribute run-time values at multiple granularities to enhance the access strategies to multi-granular values. We demonstrate that, under certain assumptions, object access is invariant to the execution of evolutions. In particular, the stored information may be preserved after the deletion of a value, because the same value may be present in the database at a different granularity, therefore it may be retrieved when needed. Furthermore, object access may benefit from evolutions with respect to both effectiveness and efficiency. The values resulting from the execution of granularity conversions are already materialized in the database, thus improving the performance of queries involving aggregates and granularity refinement. The existence in the database of values at different granularities makes possible to apply two different strategies for object access. Such strategies optimize, respectively, the *execution efficiency*, minimizing the retrieval time, and the *result accuracy*, minimizing the indeterminacy of granular values.

6   Open Research Challenges

Even though ST_ODMG and ST^2_ODMGe represent some important initial steps towards the problem of developing adaptive multi-granular spatio-temporal object models and systems, many open research challenges are still open. We briefly outline them in the following.

Foundations of formal models and type systems. Because of the complexity of an adaptive multi-granular spatio-temporal object model, it is crucial for formal definitions exist for both static and dynamic features of the model. Suitable type systems, that are also relevant for object-oriented programming languages manipulating spatio-temporal objects, need to be developed, perhaps as extension of conventional type systems. For example, when declaring a variable one may have to specify, in addition to the variable type, the spatio-temporal granularity of the variable. Assignments of a value to a variable must then take into account not only the types of the value and the variable, but also their spatio-temporal granularities. Static type checking of programs would then need to be extended by, for example, allowing such an assignment provided that a conversion function be defined for the granularities of the value and the variable, respectively. Consistency properties, such as assuring the correct combination of spatial and temporal type constructors, would also need to be devised, coupled with techniques for their analysis.

Analysis tools for evolutions. If evolution are formulated according to the active database paradigm, it is important not only that object-oriented models and systems be equipped with triggers, but also that tools for the analysis of these "evolution" triggers be supported to detect non-terminating executions and indeterministic executions. Note that such issues have been extensively investigated in the area of active DBMS and currently no satisfactory solution exists. However, since we deal with a specialized domain, that is, the evolution of granularities, effective solutions to these issues for this domain are more likely to be found.

Implementation strategies. Efficient and comprehensive implementations are crucial. Several alternatives can be investigated including implementation of the required features as class libraries on top of existing ODBMS and extensions to ODBMS engines. Both approaches have shortcomings. The first approach may enable the best execution performance, but it may be impractical if all the multi-granular features have to be implemented from scratch (e.g., think of evolution triggers). By contrast, the second approach may require extensive implementation efforts and may still not able to cover all required features, especially the ones depending on the application domain, like specialized spatial conversion operators. In our opinion, the best approach would be to extend the engine of an existing ODBMS with some basic functions, supporting for example the organization of value domains according to multiple granularities, and providing a basic support for triggers, by at the same time allowing the applications to define their own application-depending granularities and specialized conversion functions (e.g., through the use of object methods).

Multi-granular volumetric objects. The geographic information systems and spatial community is showing a growing interest in systems for managing three-dimensional (3D) data. This is demonstrated also by commercial GIS and Spatial DBMS products, that offer support for representing and analysing volumetric information. However, those products do not offer instruments for dealing with multi-granular information. One of the main issues in supporting multi-granularity for volumetric information is the definition of meaningful multi-granular conversions, able to preserve topological consistency. Moreover, because the computational complexity of the analysis and conversion algorithms is very high and the explicit storage of spatial relationships result in huge data sets, techniques are needed to optimize both temporal and storage costs.

Multi-granular exploitation of legacy data. When analysing existing data sets, one may require to make explicit the granularity according to which data are represented, in particular when integrating or matching data sets from heterogeneous sources. The automatic exploitation of the level of detail of a data set is a challenging problem that so far has not been investigated. Semantics driven methods that make use of both implicit and explicit semantics of data, such the ones discussed by Albertoni et al. [32] for the extraction of the levels of detail used in data representation, may provide valid solution to this problem.

7   Conclusions

In this paper we have discussed concepts and approaches for handling multi-granular spatio-temporal data. In our discussion we refer to recent work on spatio-temporal multi-granularity, and illustrate the design of the ST_ODMG and the ST^2_ODMGe models, which extend the ODMG model to provide multi-granular spatio-temporal support. In particular we have discussed the formal design for several key concepts encompassing: granularities, granules, multi-granular values, multi-granular conversions, multi-granular spatio-temporal querying, multi-granular attribute refinement and evolutions. Furthermore, we have discussed some open problems of interest for multi-granular spatio-temporal data management, including the definition of formal multi-granular models and type systems; the development of analysis tools for evolution models; the definition of implementation strategies; the design of multi-granular volumetric data models; the handling of legacy data. Many other challenges exist when considering different application domains. Addressing these challenges typically requires extensible data management systems, like provided by object DBMSs, that must however be equipped with specialized features in order to support complex application-specific object model, like the dynamic multi-granular spatio-temporal data we have discussed in this paper.

References

1. Codd, E.: A relational model of data for large shared data banks. Communications of the ACM 13(6), 377–387 (1970)
2. Camossi, E., Bertolotto, M., Bertino, E.: A multigranular object-oriented framework supporting spatio-temporal granularity conversions. International Journal of Geographical Information Science 20(5), 511–534 (2006)
3. Camossi, E., Bertolotto, M., Bertino, E.: Querying multi-granular spatio-temporal objects. In: Bhowmick, S.S., Küng, J., Wagner, R. (eds.) DEXA 2008. LNCS, vol. 5181, pp. 390–403. Springer, Heidelberg (2008)
4. Cattel, R., Barry, D., Berler, M., Eastman, J., Jordan, D., Russel, C., Schadow, O., Stanienda, T., Velez, F.: The Object Database Standard: ODMG 3.0. Morgan Kaufmann, Academic Press (2000)
5. Camossi, E., Bertolotto, M., Bertino, E.: Multigranular Spatio-temporal Models: Implementation Challenges. In: Proceedings of the 16th International Symposium on Advances in Geographic Information Systems, Irvine, CA, USA, November 5-7. ACM, New York (2008)
6. Anderson, T.: Modeling time at the conceptual level. In: Proceedings of the International Conference on Databases: Improving Usability and Responsiveness, pp. 273–297 (1982)
7. Bettini, C., Jajodia, S., Wang, X.: Time Granularities in Databases, Data Mining, and Temporal Reasoning. Springer, Heidelberg (2000)
8. Snodgrass, R.: The TSQL2 Temporal Query Language. Kluwer Academic Press, Dordrecht (1995)
9. Dyreson, C., Evans, W., Lin, H., Snodgrass, R.: Efficently Spporting Temporal Granularities. IEEE Transactions on Knowledge and Data Engineering 12(4), 568–587 (2000)
10. Bertino, E., Ferrari, E., Guerrini, G., Merlo, I.: T_ODMG: An ODMG Compliant Temporal Object Model Supporting Multiple Granularity Management. Information Systems 28(8), 885–927 (2003)
11. Jiang, B., Claramunt, C.: A structural approach to the model generalization of a urban street network. Geoinformatica 8(2), 157–171 (2004)
12. Stell, J., Worboys, M.: Stratified Map Spaces: A Fomal Basis for Multi-Resolution Spatial Databases. In: Poiker, T., Chrisman, N. (eds.) Proceedings of 8th International Symposium on Spatial Data Handling (International Geographical Union), pp. 180–189 (1998)
13. Weibel, R., Dutton, G.: Generalizing Spatial Data and Dealing with Multiple Representations. In: Longley, P., Maguire, D., Goodchild, M., Rhind, D. (eds.) Geographical Information Systems: Principles, techniques, management and applications. John Wiley, New York (1999)
14. Claramunt, C., Jiang, B.: Hierarchical Reasoning in Time e Space. In: Proceedings of 9th International Symposium on Spatial Data Handling, pp. 41–51 (2000)
15. Belussi, A., Combi, C., Pozzani, G.: Towards a Formal Framework for Spatio-Temporal Granularities. In: Proceedings of the 15th International Symposium on Temporal Representation and Reasoning, pp. 49–53. IEEE Computer Society, Los Alamitos (2008)
16. Griffiths, T., Fernandes, A., Paton, N., Barr, R.: The Tripod spatio-historical data model. Data Knowledge and Engineering 49(1), 23–65 (2004)

17. Jensen, C.S., Dyreson, C.E., Böhlen, M.H., Clifford, J., Elmasri, R.A., Gadia, S.K., Grandi, F., Hayes, P.J., Jajodia, S., Käfer, W., Kline, N., Lorentzos, N.A., Mitsopoulos, Y., Montanari, A., Nonen, D., Peressi, E., Pernici, B., Roddick, J., Sarda, N.L., Scalas, M.R., Segev, A., Snodgrass, R.T., Soo, M.D., Tansel, A.U., Tiberio, P., Wiederhold, G.: A Consensus Glossary of Temporal Database Concepts. In: Etzion, O., Jajodia, S., Sripada, S. (eds.) Dagstuhl Seminar 1997. LNCS, vol. 1399, pp. 366–405. Springer, Heidelberg (1998)
18. Khatri, V., Ram, S., Snodgrass, R., O'Brien, G.: Supporting User Defined Granularities and Indeterminacy in a Spatiotemporal Conceptual Model. Annals of Mathematics and Artificial Intelligence, Special Issue on Spatial and Temporal Granularity 36(1-2), 195–232 (2002)
19. Dyreson, C., Snodgrass, R.: Supporting Valid-time Indeterminacy. ACM Transactions on Database Systems 23(1), 1–57 (1998)
20. Dukham, M., Mason, K., Stell, J., Worboys, M.: A formal approach to imperfection in geographic information. Computer, Environment and Urban Systems 25, 89–103 (2001)
21. Parent, C., Spaccapietra, S., Zimányl, E.: The murmur project: Modeling and querying multi-representation spatio-temporal databases. Information System 31(8), 733–769 (2006)
22. Camossi, E., Bertolotto, M., Bertino, E.: Spatio-temporal Multi-granularity: Modelling and Implementation Challenges. University College Dublin, Technical report (2009)
23. Bettini, C., Dyreson, C., Evans, W., Snodgrass, R.: A Glossary of Time Granularity Concepts. In: Etzion, O., Jajodia, S., Sripada, S. (eds.) Dagstuhl Seminar 1997. LNCS, vol. 1399, pp. 406–413. Springer, Heidelberg (1998)
24. Bertino, E., Camossi, E., Guerrini, G.: Access to Multigranular Temporal Objects. In: Christiansen, H., Hacid, M.-S., Andreasen, T., Larsen, H.L. (eds.) FQAS 2004. LNCS (LNAI), vol. 3055, pp. 320–333. Springer, Heidelberg (2004)
25. Bertolotto, M.: Geometric Modeling of Spatial Entities at Multiple Levels of Resolution. PhD thesis, Università degli Studi di Genova (1998)
26. Saalfeld, A.: Topologically Consistent Line Simplification with the Douglas-Peucker Algorithm. Cartography and Geographic Information Science 26(1), 7–18 (1999)
27. Douglas, D., Peucker, T.: Algorithms fot the Reduction of the Number of Points Required to Represent a Line or its Caricature. The Canadian Cartographer 10(2), 112–122 (1973)
28. Shoham, Y.: Temporal Logics in AI: Semantical and Ontological Considerations. Artificial Intelligence 33(1), 89–104 (1987)
29. Egenhofer, M., Franzosa, R.: Point-set topological spatial relations. International Journal of Geographical Information Science 5(2), 161–174 (1991)
30. Bertino, E., Camossi, E., Guerrini, G.: Attribute refinement in a multigranular temporal object data model. CERIAS TR 2009-06, Purdue University, USA (May 2009)
31. Camossi, E., Bertino, E., Guerrini, G., Bertolotto, M.: Adaptive management of multigranular spatio-temporal object attributes. In: Mamoulis, N., Seidl, T., Pedersen, T.B., Torp, K., Assent, I. (eds.) Advances in Spatial and Temporal Databases. LNCS, vol. 5644, pp. 320–337. Springer, Heidelberg (2009)
32. Albertoni, R., Camossi, E., Martino, M.D., Giannini, F., Monti, M.: Semantic granularity for the semantic web. In: Meersman, R., Tari, Z., Herrero, P. (eds.) OTM 2006 Workshops. LNCS, vol. 4278, pp. 1863–1872. Springer, Heidelberg (2006)

Mapping XSD to OO Schemas

Suad Alagić and Philip A. Bernstein

Microsoft Research
One Microsoft Way, Redmond, WA, USA
alagic@usm.maine.edu, philbe@microsoft.com

Abstract. This paper presents algorithms that make it possible to process XML data that conforms to XML Schema (XSD) in a mainstream object-oriented programming language. These algorithms are based on our object-oriented view of the core of XSD. The novelty of this view is that it is intellectually manageable for object-oriented programmers while still capturing the complexity of the core structural properties of XSD. This paper develops two mappings based on this view. The first one is specified by a set of rules that map a source XSD schema into its object-oriented schema. The second one maps XML instances that conform to an XSD schema to their representation as objects. In addition to mapping elements and attributes, these mappings reflect correctly the particle structures including different types of groups, and type derivation by restriction and extension. The structural properties of identity constraints are also mapped correctly. Formally defined mappings or algorithms of this sort have not been available so far, and existing industrial tools typically do not handle the level of complexity of XSD that our mappings do.

1 Introduction

XML Schema (XSD for short) is a standard for specifying structural features of XML data [17]. In addition, XSD allows specification of constraints that XML data is required to satisfy. Application programmers are faced with the problem of processing data that conforms to XSD in a general-purpose object-oriented programming language. For this to be possible, an object-oriented interface to XML data must be available to application programmers.

To enable this scenario we need a schema mapping that translates each XSD schema X into a corresponding object-oriented schema O. The schema mapping from X to O creates the object-oriented interface for application programmers. We also need an instance mapping between instances of X (i.e., XML documents) and instances of O (i.e., sets of objects). The instance mapping is used to translate XML documents into objects that can be manipulated by applications, and to translate objects that are created or modified by applications back into XML documents. Developing such translations poses nontrivial problems due to the mismatch of the core XSD features and the features that are expressible in type systems underlying mainstream object-oriented languages. All object-oriented interfaces to XML suffer the implications of this mismatch [10].

M.C. Norrie and M. Grossniklaus (Eds.): ICOODB 2009, LNCS 5936, pp. 149–166, 2010.
© Springer-Verlag Berlin Heidelberg 2010

The starting point is a user's XSD schema. An off-the-shelf XSD schema compiler is used in our approach to translate the user's schema into an object-oriented representation, such as .NET's XML Schema Object Model (SOM) [15]. The schema mapping rules translate the user's XSD schema into object-oriented interfaces. These interfaces comprise the user's programming model. They are a combination of predefined interfaces that are based only on XSD itself and user-schema-specific interfaces that are generated from a user's XSD schema. A program can use these interfaces to access pieces of an XML document that conforms to the XSD schema. Enabling this access requires that there be a mapping that translates an XML document into objects whose classes implement the generated XSD interfaces.

The main research contributions of this paper are as follows:

- We specify the structural core of XSD (Sect. 3)
- We specify the syntax for the XSD core (Sect. 3.1).
- We specify the rules for mapping an XSD core schema to its corresponding OO schema (Sect. 4).
- We specify an algorithm for mapping instances that conform to a source XSD core schema to their OO counterparts (Sect. 5).

Formally defined mappings or algorithms of this sort have not been available so far, and existing industrial tools typically do not handle the level of complexity of XML Schema that our mappings do.

2   Motivating Example

To motivate some of the detailed problems that need to be solved by such a system, let us consider how to map an example XSD schema into object-oriented (OO) interfaces. Consider the complex type `DictionaryType` defined in the XSD schema below. The structure of this type is defined as a sequence group where the number of elements in the sequence ranges from zero to an arbitrary and unspecified natural number. An OO representation of this type will obviously be based on a parametric type of sequence or list. However, as soon as we specify a type `SmallDictionaryType` that is derived by restriction from `DictionaryType`, we encounter a nontrivial problem.

```
<xsd:schema id="XMLDictionarySchema"
    xmlns:xsd="http://www.w3.org/2001/XMLSchema">

 <xsd: complexType name="DictionaryType"/>
  <xsd: sequence>
   <xsd:element name="item" type="ItemType"
           minOccurs="0" maxOccurs="unbounded"/>
  </xsd:sequence>
 </xsd:complexType>
 <xsd:complexType name="ItemType">
    <xsd:sequence>
```

```
          <xsd:element name="typeOfEntity"
                       type="EntityType" />
      </xsd:sequence>
      <xsd:attribute name="key" type="xsd:string" />
  </xsd:complexType>
  <xsd:element name="dictionary"
               type="DictionaryType">
        <xsd:key name="searchKey">
          <xsd:selector xpath="item"/>
          <xsd:field xpath="@key"/>
        </xsdkey>
  </xsd:element>
  <xsd:complexType name="SmallDictionaryType"/>
    <xsd:restriction base= "DictionaryType"/>
      <xsd:sequence>
        <xsd:element name="item" type="ItemType"
                     minOccurs="1" maxOccurs="1000"/>
      </xsd:sequence>
    </xsd:restriction>
  </xsd:complexType>
  <xsd:complexType  name="AddressType"/>
    <xsd:extension base="ItemType"/>
      <xsd:sequence>
        <xsd:element name="firstName"
                     type="xsd:string"/>
        <xsd:element name="lastName"
                     type="xsd:string"/>
        <xsd:choice>
          <xsd:element name="POboxAddress"
                       type="xsd:string"/>
          <xsd:element  name="streetAddress"
                       type="streetAddressType"/>
        </xsd:choice>
      </xsd:sequence>
    </xsd:extension>
  </xsd:complexType>
</xsd:schema>
```

XSD type derivations are represented in the OO schema by inheritance. But in this case, the structural specification of DictionaryType and SmallDictionaryType is identical. What is different is that the range-of-occurrences constraint has been strengthened. OO type systems cannot represent this constraint and hence cannot represent type derivation by restriction in XSD. Well-known OO interfaces to XSD typically lack any suitable representation of this type of construct and of type derivation by restriction as defined in XSD.

Consider now an actual dictionary specified as an XSD element. This element type will also be represented as an object type (a class or an interface). One problem of existing OO interfaces to XML is not distinguishing between two type hierarchies in XSD as in [13]. One hierarchy represents the actual instances, starting with elements. But an element has a name (i.e., a tag) and a value. The value of an element may be simple or complex, and hence belongs to a type that is defined in a different hierarchy of XSD types, all of which are derived from the root type `anyType`.

Yet another subtlety in this example is that a dictionary element is equipped with a key constraint, a typical database constraint that captures the essential semantics of a dictionary. Well-known OO interfaces to XML do not consider representation of this constraint. In fact, key constraints are not representable in OO type systems.

Now consider `ItemType`, which is the type of dictionary elements. Its complex structure is specified as a sequence group. In addition, this type is equipped with an attribute key. In the most straightforward representation of `ItemType` its corresponding object type will have properties `typeOfEntity` and `key`. This seems to be a preferred OO user view of `ItemType`[13]. However, it comes with nontrivial problems.

The first problem is the lack of distinction between elements and attributes. The second is that in XML two elements or an element and an attribute may have the same name. In those situations the straightforward representation does not work because the names of elements and attributes cannot be the property names in the corresponding object type, as they must be unique.

Consider now a specific item type `AddressType` of a dictionary. This type will be specified in XSD as derived by extension from the type `ItemType`. This type derivation has a fairly accurate representation by inheritance. The extension is specified as a sequence group with one subtlety. The third component of the sequence is specified as a choice-group, so an XML instance has either `POboxAddress` or `streetAddress` but not both.

XSD choice represents a major problem for OO interfaces to XML. Specifying a fixed number of subtypes of a type is contrary to the core features of the OO model. Because of the lack of a suitable representation for choice, some OO interfaces use the same representation for choice and sequence groups. This representation has nontrivial implications because these two types of groups have different semantics. In fact, widely known OO interfaces to XML do not have a suitable representation of XSD groups and its three subtypes (i.e., sequence, choice, and all groups).

To see the implications of structural misrepresentation of an XSD schema in its corresponding OO schema, assume that we have a database that conforms to an XSD schema. Suppose that application programs will be developed in an OO language and will be based on the OO representation of XSD schema. Manipulating OO representations of XSD instances will now lead to object structures that do not reflect the structure of XSD instances. Installing the updated XSD instances presents a huge challenge because of this structural mismatch. This is why our goal is to produce an OO representation of XSD that is as structurally accurate as possible, so that manipulating OO instances does not violate structural and semantic constraints of XSD.

3   XML Schema Core

3.1   Syntactic Specification

In this section we define a subset of XSD, which we call the XSD core [1]. It is comprised of features that we regard as essential to XSD and is the focus of our mapping from XSD schemas to OO interfaces.

In the XSD core, attributes and elements are specified as (Name, Type) pairs. Name stands for the tag and Type for the type of the associated value. The type of an attribute is required to be simple, and the type of an element may be either simple or complex.

Attribute ::= Name simpleType
Element ::= Name Type

The key notion of the XSD core is that of a *Particle*, which is a term followed by the range of occurrences. A term is either an *Element* or a *Group*. So a particle is a sequence of repeated terms where the number of occurrences of the term is between *minOccurs* and *maxOccurs*.

Particle := Term Range
Term := Element | Group
Range := [minOccurs][maxOccurs]

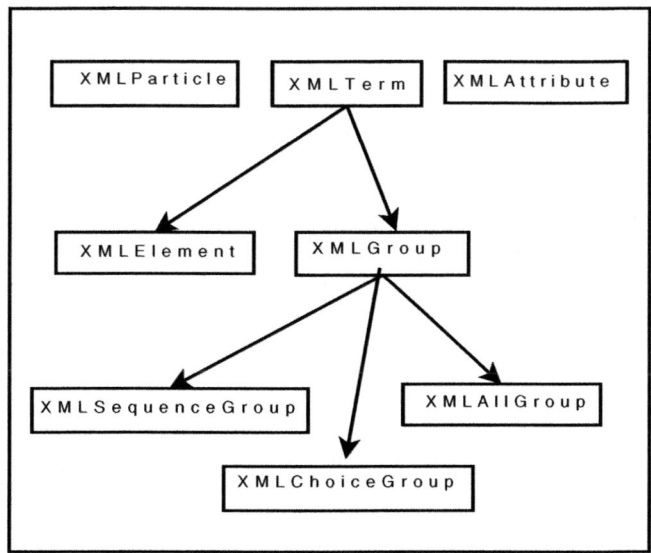

Fig. 1. XSD particle hierarchy

There are three types of groups in the core: sequence-groups, choice-groups and all-groups. A sequence-group is specified as a sequence of particles. The same applies to a choice-group, but its semantics is different. In a sequence-group all particles must be present, while in a choice-group exactly one of them must be present in a document fragment that conforms to the group definition. Particles of an all-group are of a particular type: they are elements. In the syntax, sets and sequences are represented as sequences, but in fact the ordering of elements in an all all-group is irrelevant.

$Group := Sequence \mid Choice \mid All$
$Sequence ::= Particle\{Particle\}$
$Choice ::= Particle\{Particle\}$
$All ::= Element\{Element\}$

A type is either simple or complex.

$Type ::= [Name]\ simpleOrComplexType$
$simpleOrComplexType ::= simpleType \mid complexType$

A simple type either is a built-in type or is derived from another simple type (its base) by simple type restriction.

$simpleType ::= builtInType \mid simpleType\ simpleTypeRestriction$

A simple type restriction is specified by a sequence of facets.

$simpleTypeRestriction ::= facet\{facet\}$

Facets include direct enumeration, specification of ranges of values, and specification of patterns of regular expressions. All of these facets specify the values belonging to the restricted type.

$facet ::= enumeration \mid range\mid regExpression$

A complex type is derived from its base type (denoted by Type below) by a complex type derivation:

$complexType ::= Type\ complexTypeDerivation$

There are three kinds of complex type derivation:

$complexTypeDerivation ::= simpleTypeExtension \mid$
$\qquad\qquad\qquad complexTypeExtension \mid complexTypeRestriction$

Simple type extension applies to complex types with simple content. Since the content is simple, the only allowed extension is adding attributes. Hence, this form of type derivation by extension is specified by a sequence of additional attributes.

$simpleTypeExtension ::= \{Attribute\}$

Complex type extension includes both extending the set of attributes and extending the particle structure of the base type. The extended particle structure is specified by a group. This group is obtained by forming a sequence-group of the base type particle of the complex type and appending additional particles specified in the complex type derivation.

$complexTypeExtension ::= \{Attribute\}\ Group$

Complex type restriction allows restriction of the base type by a set of facets, making changes in the set of attributes of the base type, and restricting the constraints in the particle structure of the base type. The particle structure may omit optional elements. Otherwise it remains the same, hence it is repeated, but the constraints will be different. An exception is omitting optional elements. The particle structure obtained this way is specified as a group.

complexTypeRestriction ::= {*Facet*}{*Attribute*} *Group*

There are three types of identity constraints in XSD: uniqueness, key and referential integrity (foreign key) constraints. An identity constraint consists of a specification of the key fields along with the scope to which the constraint applies. This scope is specified by an *XPath* expression.

identityConstraint ::= *Name field* {*field*} *path*

In addition, a referential integrity constraint contains specification of the key constraint to which it refers.

Specification of a schema includes its name and sets of global elements, types, attributes, groups and identity constraints:

Schema ::=
   Name Element{*Element*}{*Type*}{*Attribute*}{*Group*}{*identityConstraint*}

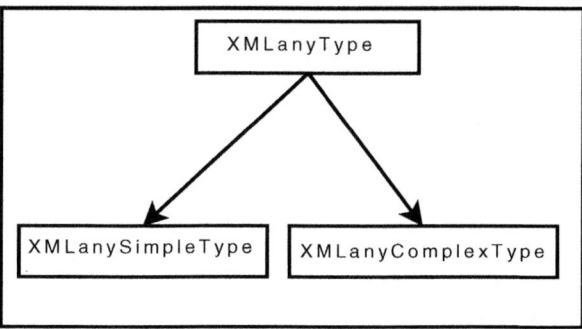

Fig. 2. XSD type hierarchy

3.2   Core Interfaces

The library of predefined interfaces includes the two type hierarchies presented by the diagrams in figures 1 and 2. Figure 1 represents the particles as defined in XSD. Since the range constraint may be associated with any type of a term, in a slightly simplified representation that follows SOM [15], elements and groups are viewed as subtypes of the particle type. Specific types of groups are defined as subtypes of the group type. The range constraints are specified by methods `minOccurs` and `maxOccurs` of the particle interface. Full specification is given in [1] along with a representative collection of LINQ queries with respect to object-oriented schemas specified according to XSD core.

All types are derived from XSD `anyType` denoted `XMLanyType` in Figure 2. We specify two subtypes of `anyType` that stand for simple and complex types.

Specific simple and complex types will be derived from those. The above two hierarchies are related. Since a complex type will in general be equipped with a set of attributes and a particle structure, it will in general refer to the types specified in the particle hierarchy.

The third type hierarchy represents XSD identity constraints, shown in Figure 3. In this paper we do not consider the implications of using a constraint language such as JML or Spec# as in [5], so that the representation of constraints is necessarily structural.

4   Mapping Schemas

This section presents an algorithm for mapping XSD schemas to OO interfaces. The algorithm assumes that the source XSD schema is valid. Its representation could be of any form, as long as its XSD schema components are available via correctly typed expressions such as: *XMLElement(elementName, typeName)*. This expression indicates that the source XSD schema contains an element type whose name is *elementName* and the type of its value is *typeName*.

The source XSD schema contains global elements, attributes, types, groups, etc. The algorithm is a set of mapping rules, each of which specifies how to map one of these source constructs to its OO representation. For each rule, we specify the typing assumptions under which the rule applies. The typing assumptions follow from our assumption that the XSD schema is valid. They are specified as typing rules with respect to a typing environment of mainstream object-oriented languages such as C# and Java. The rules are more closely tied to C#.

The typing environment, denoted by $\mathcal{T}$, includes facts about the types in an XSD schema. In particular, it includes a mapping from names to types and subtyping relationships. The fact that an identifier *id* has a type *typeName* in the environment $\mathcal{T}$ is expressed as

$\mathcal{T} \vdash id : typeName.$

Since the inheritance relationships are identified with subtyping in mainstream object-oriented languages, we will use the subtyping symbol $<:$ in the typing rules. So if *typeName* is the name of an XML type, the typing environment will allow the following deduction, which says that the XML type *typeName* is a subtype of *XMLanyType* in $\mathcal{T}$:

$\mathcal{T} \vdash typeName <: XMLanyType$

The typing environment is initialized with the core interfaces such as *XML-Element, XMLAttribute, XMLParticle, XMLGroup, XMLSequenceGroup, XML-ChoiceGroup, XMLAllGroup, XMLanySimpleType, XMLanyComplexType*, etc. We present some of the most important mapping rules. A complete set is given in [2].

First consider mapping element types and attribute types from the source XSD into OO interfaces. If *typeName* stands for an object representation of an XML type, and *elementName* is a valid name, then the expression

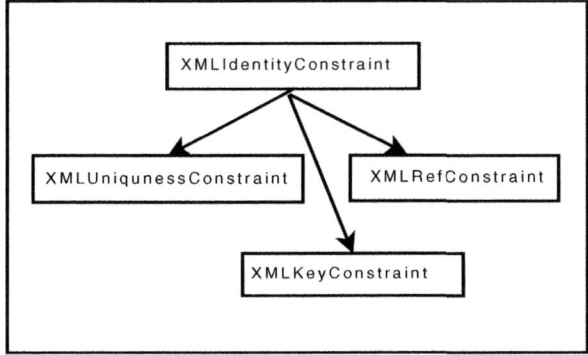

Fig. 3. XSD constraints hierarchy

XMLElement(elementName, typeName) is well typed and its type is *XMLElement*:

$$\mathcal{T} \vdash typeName <: XMLanyType,$$
$$\mathcal{T} \vdash elementName : NameType$$

$$\mathcal{T} \vdash XMLElement(elementName, typeName) : XMLElement$$

The above conditions summarize the typing assumptions about an element type in the source XSD schema. The conditions are the consequence of the fact that the source XSD schema has been validated. If e is a well typed expression *XMLElement(elementName,typeName)*, then its object-oriented image is map(e):

$$e = XMLElement(elementName, typeName)$$

$$map(e) = interface\ elementName : XMLElement\ \{$$
$$NameType\ name(); typeName\ value()\}$$

The typing and mapping rule for the attribute types follows the same pattern except the value of an attribute must be of a simple type so that we would have the following in the corresponding typing rule:

$$\mathcal{T} \vdash typeName <: XMLanySimpleType$$

If the source XSD schema contains a specification of an XML simple type whose name is *typeName*, then this type will in general be derived by restriction from its base type which is also simple. The set of constraining facets must also be specified in the source schema. Hence the information about a simple type in the source schema is summarized in an expression of the form
XMLanySimpleType(baseTypeName, typeName,facets).

The conditions under which
XMLanySimpleType(baseTypeName,typeName,facets) is a well typed expression of type *XMLanySimpleType* that are based on the assumed validation are as follows:

$$T \vdash baseTypeName <: XMLanySimpleType,$$
$$T \vdash typeName : NameType,$$
$$T \vdash facets : XMLSet < XMLFacet >$$

$$T \vdash XMLanySimpleType(baseTypeName, typeName, facets) :$$
$$XMLanySimpleType$$

If T is a well-typed expression
XMLanySimpleType(baseTypeName, typeName, facets)
then its object-oriented image $map(T)$ is:

$$T = XMLanySimpleType(baseTypeName, typeName, facets)$$

$$map(T) = interface\ typeName :\ baseTypeName\ \{$$
$$XMLSet < XMLFacet >\ facets()\}$$

In the most complex specification of an XML complex type, the base type is complex, and the type derivation includes a set of attributes and a new particle structure obtained either by extending the particle of the base type or restricting its range constraints. If the type is derived by restriction, a set of facets is also specified. So the information about a complex XML type coming from the source XSD schema is assumed to have the form of an expression *XMLany-ComplexType(baseTypeName, typeName, attributes, facets, particleType)*. The typing constraints for this expression that follow from its validation are:

$$T \vdash baseTypeName <: XMLanyType,$$
$$T \vdash typeName : NameType,$$
$$T \vdash attributes : XMLSet < XMLAttribute >,$$
$$T \vdash facets : XMLSet < XMLFacet >,$$
$$T \vdash particleType <: XMLParticle$$

$$T \vdash XMLanyComplexType(baseTypeName, typeName,$$
$$attributes, facets, particleType) : XMLanyComplexType$$

If T is a well typed expression
XMLanyComplexType(baseTypeName, typeName, attributes, facets, particleType), then its object-oriented image $map(T)$ is:

$$T = XMLanyComplexType(baseTypeName, typeName,$$
$$attributes, particleType)$$

$$map(T) = interface\ typeName :\ baseTypeName\ \{$$
$$XMLSet < XMLAttribute >\ attributes();$$
$$XMLSet < XMLFacet >\ facets();$$
$$particleType\ particle()\}$$

If the source XSD schema contains a group, the first piece of information that is available is the type of the group. In addition, a group specifies a sequence of particles, which in the case of an all-group are elements. In the rules for groups we assume that a group has a name (as global groups do) so that information from the source for a sequence-group has the form of an expression *XMLSequenceGroup(groupName, particles)*. The typing constraints for an expression *XMLSequenceGroup(groupName, particles)* that follow from the assumed validation are:

$$\mathcal{T} \vdash groupName : NameType,$$
$$\mathcal{T} \vdash particles : XMLSequence < XMLParticle >$$

$$\mathcal{T} \vdash XMLSequenceGroup(groupName, particles) : XMLSequenceGroup$$

If g is a well typed expression *XMLSequenceGroup(groupName, particles)* then its object-oriented image $map(g)$ is:

$$g = XMLSequenceGroup(groupName, particles)$$

$$map(g) = interface\ groupName : XMLSequenceGroup\ \{$$
$$XMLSequence < XMLParticle >\ particles()\}$$

A choice-group is also specified in the source XSD schema as a sequence of particles but its interface will be derived from *XMLChoiceGroup*. The only difference in the specification of an all-group is that in its sequence of particles, the particles must be elements.

The above developed mapping framework allows specification of mapping rules for the XSD identity constraints, a feature missing in just about all other approaches. The approach presented in this paper cannot express the semantics of the identity constraints, but it makes it possible to map their structural specification. The typing information about an identity constraint coming from a validated specification of such a constraint in the source XML schema is summarized in the rule given below:

$$\mathcal{T} \vdash name : NameType,$$
$$\mathcal{T} \vdash fields : XMLSequence < XMLPath >,$$
$$\mathcal{T} \vdash path : XMLPath$$

$$\mathcal{T} \vdash XMLIdentityConstraint(Name, fields, path) : XMLIdentityConstraint$$

The corresponding mapping rule that maps a constraint c into its corresponding object-oriented interface is:

$$c = XMLIdentityConstraint(Name, fields, path)$$

$$map(c) = interface\ Name : XMLIdentityConstraint\ \{$$
$$XMLSequence < XMLPath >\ fields();$$
$$XMLPath\ path()\}$$

The above rules apply to the uniqueness and key constraints. A referential integrity constraint is trivially more complex as it contains specification of a key constraint to which it refers.

5   Mapping Instances

The mapping rules for schemas and documents are clearly independent of the underlying implementation platform. But the XSD core may be viewed as an abstraction on top of SOM [15] as an implementation platform. Given an XSD schema, SOM will process it and make its OO representation available. This is why in the algorithm for mapping instances we assume that the source schema has been mapped to the target OO schema according to the rules in Sect. 4. We also assume that the source XML instances have been validated with respect to the source XSD schema. So the presented algorithm implements the map from XML instances to their corresponding OO instances according to figure 4.

Since the source schema has been mapped to the OO schema, the algorithm will consult the OO schema for the schema information required to correctly map the source XML instances to the corresponding objects. The information in the core interfaces in Sect. 3.2 is available both at the schema level and in the programming language interface. The distinction between the two levels will be indicated by the prefix Schema for the interfaces at the schema level. The complete algorithm is given in [2] and here we present its core features.

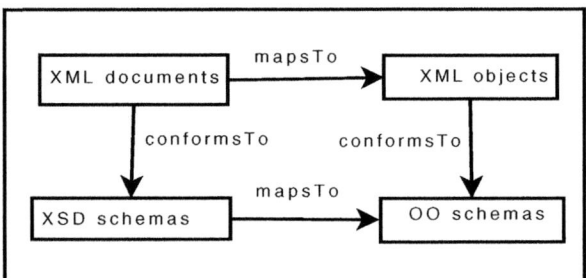

Fig. 4. Mapping schemas and objects

A given object instance will in general represent a particle object. A whole document will be represented as an element object. The complete structural representation is available using reflection. From a particle object one can get all the information required to generate a valid XSD particle recursively from a sequence of sub-particles. The recursion terminates when a particle of type element whose type is simple is reached. For a particle object that represents an element, the name and the type will be available from the element object. If the type of an element is derived from XML complex type, the actual complex particle structure of the element will be discoverable from the corresponding object type information. The object type representing an XML complex type contains a specification of the underlying particle structure which is how the algorithm gets invoked recursively.

The source XML instance is assumed to be available via a collection of methods of the class Input. The tag of the input element is used to access the schema information. The type of the element value is looked up in the schema. If the type is simple, the value of the element is taken from the input. If the type is complex, then an object of the type XMLAnyComplexType will be created as the element's value. This is accomplished by invoking the method createComplexValueObject which parses the complex structure of the input element.

```
XMLElement createElementObject(string tag) {
    Schema.XMLanyType type = Schema.lookUpType(tag);
    if type  <:  Schema.XMLAnySimpleType then
    XMLAnySimpleType value = (XMLAnySimpleType)Input.getValue();
    else  XMLanyComplexType value =
            createComplexValueObject((Schema.XMLanyComplexType)type);
    return newInstance(getClass("XMLElementClass"),[]Object{tag,value});
}
```

Mapping an attribute instance follows a similar logic, but it is much simpler because the value of an attribute is of a simple type.

The method createComplexValueObject has a complex schema type as its argument. The newly created instance will have two components: a set of attributes (which we represent as a sequence) and a particle structure. These two components are created invoking the methods createAttributesObject and createParticleObject, and then the object representing complex element value will be created.

```
XMLanyComplexType  createComplexValueObject(
                            Schema.XMLanyComplexType type){
 XMLSequence<XMLAttribute> attributes =
                    createAttributesObject(type.attributes());
 XMLParticle particle = createParticleObject(type.particle());
 return newInstance(getClass("XMLanyComplexType"),
                        []Object{attributes, particle})
}
```

The second component of a complex value object is a particle object that conforms to the XMLParticle type. This object is constructed by invoking the method createParticleObject which takes an argument of type Schema.XMLParticle so that it will have the source schema specification of the particle that is coming up in the input. An object of type XMLParticle will have the range specified by minOccurs and maxOccurs according to the schema information, and a sequence of particles coming up in the input whose number of occurrences will be determined by minOccurs and maxOccurs. Since each one of those particles appears as a sequence of particles, its particle sequence must be correctly recognized in the input and its sequence of particle objects constructed. This is possible only by looking at the schema information about the type of the particle under consideration

```
XMLParticle  createParticleObject(Schema.XMLParticle particle){
 XMLSequence<XMLParticle> particles = new XMLSequence<XMLParticle>;
 for (int i=1; i < particle.minOccurs; i=i+1){
    particles.Append(getParticleSequence(particle.particles(i)))};
 for (int  i = particle.minOccurs; i < particle.maxOccurs; i=i+1) {
  particles.Append(getParticleSequence(particle.particles(i)))};
  return newInstance(getClass("XMLParticleClass"),
         []Object{particle.minOcccurs,particle.maxOccurs,particles})
}
```

The method `getParticleSequence` tests the type of the particle as specified in the source XSD schema and returns a particle sequence that corresponds to each particular type of a particle.

Consider a sequence of particles appearing in the input that corresponds to a sequence group. The argument of the method `sequenceGroupParticles` is a sequence group in the source XSD schema and hence it contains a specification of a sequence of particles. For each particle in the sequence, the type of particle is tested to see whether it is an element. If so, the element tag is read from the input, an element object is constructed and appended to the output particle sequence. If the type of the ith particle as specified in the source schema is not an element, then the method `createParticleObject` is invoked recursively.

```
XMLSequence<XMLParticle> sequenceGroupParticles(
                                  Schema.XMLSequenceGroup seqGr)
{ XMLSequence<XMLParticle> particleSeq =
                                  new XMLSequence<XMLParticle>;
  for( int i = 1; i <  seqGr.particles().high(); i=i+1)
  { ithParticle = seqGr.particles()(i);
    if ithParticle instanceOf Schema.XMLElement
    then {string tag = Input.getTag();
          XMLElement newElement = createElementObject(tag);
          particleSeq.append(newElement) }
    else {XMLParticle newParticle = createParticleObject(ithParticle);
          particleSeq.append(newParticle) };
  return particleSeq
}
```

If the type of a particle is a choice group, the schema will still contain a specification of a sequence of particles, but only one of them will appear in the input. Which one is determined by the first tag that appears in the input particle. This is why we need a method `getFirstElementTag`.

The result of the `getChoiceGroupParticle` method is a sequence of particles because of type compatibility, but it will contain a single particle. The sequence of particles in the schema representation of the choice group is accessed and for each one of them the input tag is compared with the first element tag of the ith particle. When those are equal, the ith particle description in the schema will be taken as the valid description of the input particle.

```
XMLSequence<XMLParticle> getChoiceGroupParticle(
        Schema.XMLSchemaChoiceGroup choiceGr) {
XMLSequence<XMLParticle> particleSeq = new XMLSequence<XMLParticle>;
string tag = Input.getTag();
 for (int  i=1; i < choiceGr.particles().high(); i=i+1)
 {ithParticle = choiceGr.particles()(i);
  if tag = getFirstElementTag(ithParticle) then
    {particleSeq.append(ithParticle);
     return(particleSeq)}
}
```

Constructing a particle sequence of an all group follows the above logic with one simplification. We know that a sequence of particles in the input should be interpreted as a sequence of elements of an all group.

6 Related Work

One of the first OO models of XML was DOM [7]. Although it is a part of W3C activities, DOM predated XSD and hence has very limited in its support of XSD. It contains interfaces such as Element and Attribute which are subtypes of the interface Node. The DOM model has a variety of other XSD-specific features. However, it is far from capturing the structural complexity of XSD. A tool that works with DOM and its Java version JDOM is JAXP [9] which is a Java API for XML processing.

LINQ to XML is an OO interface to XML data that is based on the assumption that an XML schema is not available [12]. LINQ to XML has a fixed collection of classes such as XElement, XAttribute, XNode, XContainer, etc. An input XML document is parsed and viewed through the methods available in these classes. This approach requires extensive type casting and hence dynamic type checking. LINQ to XML supports LINQ queries, but the above typing issues apply to queries just as well.

LINQ to XSD takes a different approach in which specific classes are specified for specific element types that appear in the source XSD schema [13]. It has a variety of techniques for representing some structural features of XSD such as sequence groups, type derivation by inheritance etc. However, the representation model, as appealing as it may be, is too simple to represent XSD accurately. In particular, LINQ to XSD does not distinguish between elements and attributes, has nontrivial problems when the names of elements are repeated, does not represent the notion of a particle with range constraints, does not represent identity constraints, and cannot represent type derivation by restriction because this form of type derivation in XSD is based on constraints.

Paper [16] presents a view of the essence of XSD but it is not object-oriented. This model is limited to well-established and well-understood constructs in type systems. However, some of those constructs are actually not available in mainstream OO languages. Since this approach is based on what is expressible in type systems, it cannot represent particle structures with general range constraints, type derivation by restriction in general, or identity constraints.

The .NET Schema Object Model (SOM) is the most accurate and OO representation of XSD that we know of [15]. Given an XSD schema SOM produces its OO representation which we use in our approach. However, the complexity of SOM is prohibitive for typical application programmers. This is why we develop an OO interface that represents a correct abstraction over XSD, but is intellectually manageable [1]. We also use some more recent features of type systems of mainstream OO languages such as parametric polymorphism, which SOM does not have. Lack of such typing features in SOM creates undesirable representation problems for SOM which we do not have.

Data Contracts in .NET is the only system we know of that supports both schema level and instance level mappings in both directions: from XSD to OO and the other way around [6,11]. This system relies on SOM. Data Contracts has nontrivial limitations as to what kind of XSD schema features it can handle. For example, it cannot handle attributes. In the other direction, Data Contracts can handle only certain object types whose structure is such that this system can map them to XSD types.

An analysis of the mismatch between XML and OO languages is presented in [10]. LINQ to XSD in fact follows some of the representation options from [10]. The main difference between our work [1,2] and [10] is that we represent explicitly and accurately the structural core of XSD, its particle (elements and groups) and type hierarchies. In addition, we represent accurately the complex structure of content models, type derivations, and the identity constraints which are missing in all other approaches except in SOM.

XML Data Binder [18] also maps XSD schemas into a collection of classes that could be in Java, C#, C++ and VB. In fact, XML Data Binder generates code for those classes for access and update methods, as well as for some checks. Based on what is available from the XML Data Binder web site [18] we could not see evidence that that XML Data Binder will handle correctly the complexity of XML Schema. This specifically applies to representation of general particle structures and the XML Schema type hierarchy with type derivations by restriction and extension. As in most other approaches XML Data Binder has no way of representing range of occurrences constraints of a general form. It deals only with special cases. We assume that XML Data Binder can represent type derivation by extension using inheritance, but there is no indication that it will somehow represent type derivation by restriction in general when range constraints are involved. Just like most other approaches, mapping the identity constraints (keys, referential integrity) in XML Schema is not addressed.

XML Beans [19] seems to have a more elaborate and more accurate representation of XML Schema in comparison with XML Data Binder. For example, this applies to representation of XML Schema groups and XML Schema types. XML Beans also has a structural representation of the identity constraints, similar to ours. However, XML Beans will have the same problems as XML Data Binder in representing the ranges constraints or type derivation by restriction in general.

In all the industrial systems that we have seen there is no specification of the mapping rules from XML Schema to its object-oriented representation. Because of that it is hard to see what is actually correctly represented and how. Likewise, there is no published algorithm for mapping instances, i.e., input XML documents into their object-oriented representation. Explicit specification of the schema mapping rules and the instance mapping algorithm is a major distinction between our work and the other published results.

The only work we know of that goes beyond the limitations of type systems is [3,4,5]. This research is based on OO constraint languages such as the Java Modeling Language [8] or Spec# [14]. It is thus able to represent all the XSD constraint-related features such as general range constraints for particles, type derivation by restriction, semantics of different types of groups (sequence versus choice), and identity constraints (keys and referential integrity). This approach is also equipped with a prover to verify constraint-related features and transaction safety with respect to the schema integrity constraints. The overall technology is considerably more sophisticated and more complex than the technology based on type systems, mostly because of the prover which requires sophisticated users.

7   Conclusions

Our first contribution is to show that in spite of the complexity of XML Schema, it is actually possible to define its structural core and specify it formally in terms of the syntactic and typing rules commonly used for mainstream object-oriented programming languages. This makes it possible to present to object-oriented programmers a well-defined core of XSD that is intellectually manageable and a solid basis for complex object-oriented applications that process XML data. This is important because most object-oriented programmers have a limited understanding of XML Schema and are not willing to get involved in deciphering its complexity.

Our second contribution is in the algorithm for mapping XSD schemas to object-oriented schemas. This algorithm is specified through a collection of rules that includes the typing assumptions under which the rules apply. Our rules for mapping XSD schemas into object-oriented schemas are the first such rules ever specified in an explicit and formal manner. One novelty in these rules is that they have two important properties: (i) they are lossless for the XSD core; and (ii) they produce object-oriented interfaces that conform to the rules of object-oriented type systems of mainstream object-oriented languages.

The rules are lossless in the sense that the mapping from the XSD-core structures of an XSD schema to object-oriented types preserves the core structural features which include particle structures (elements and different types of groups) and the type hierarchy based on type derivations by extension and by restriction. The structural specifications of range constraints and identity constraints are also preserved. We conjecture that the mapping can be proved to be lossless in a precise mathematical sense—a subject for future work.

Our third contribution is the first algorithm for mapping XML instances conforming to a given source schema to their object-oriented representation. The existing object-oriented interfaces to XML have underlying algorithms that are neither visible nor published.

The framework for the mapping rules allows mapping identity constraints of the source XSD schema into their object-oriented representation. Although this representation is necessarily structural, it is critical to avoid losing the integrity constraints of the source schema, as they are in just about all other approaches. The implications on data integrity are obvious and nontrivial.

References

1. Alagić, S., Bernstein, P.: An object-oriented core for XML Schema, Microsoft Research Technical Report MSR-TR-2008-182 (December 2008),
   http://research.microsoft.com/apps/pubs/default.aspx?id=76533
2. Alagić, S., Bernstein, P.: Mapping XSD to OO schemas, Microsoft Research Technical Report MSR-TR-2008-183 (December 2008),
   http://research.microsoft.com/apps/pubs/default.aspx?id=76534
3. Alagić, S., Royer, M., Briggs, D.: Verification theories for XML Schema. In: Bell, D.A., Hong, J. (eds.) BNCOD 2006. LNCS, vol. 4042, pp. 262–265. Springer, Heidelberg (2006)
4. Alagić, S., Royer, M., Briggs, D.: Program verification techniques for XML Schema-based technologies. In: Proc. of ICSOFT Conf., vol. 2, pp. 86–93 (2006)
5. Alagić, S., Royer, M., Briggs, D.: Verification technology for Object-oriented/XML Transactions. In: Proceedings of ICOODB 2009 (International Conference on Object-Oriented Databases) (2009)
6. Data Contracts, http://msdn2.microsoft.com/en-us/library/ms733127.aspx
7. Document Object Model (DOM), http://www.w3.org/TR/REC-DOM-Level-1/
8. Java Modeling Language, http://www.eecs.ucf.edu/~leavens/JML/
9. All about JXAP, http://www.ibm.com/developerworks/java/library/x-jaxp/
10. Lammel, R., Meijer, E.: Revealing the X/O impedance mismatch. In: Backhouse, R., Gibbons, J., Hinze, R., Jeuring, J. (eds.) SSDGP 2006. LNCS, vol. 4719, pp. 285–367. Springer, Heidelberg (2007)
11. Microsoft Corp., Using Data Contracts,
    http://msdn.microsoft.com/en-us/library/ms733127.aspx
12. Microsoft Corp., LINQ to XML,
    http://msdn.microsoft.com/en-us/library/bb387098.aspx
13. Microsoft Corp., LINQ to XSD Alpha 0.2 (2008), http://blogs.msdn.com/xmlteam/archive/2006/11/27/typed-xml-programmer-welcome-to-LINQ.aspx
14. Microsoft Corp., Spec#, http://research.microsoft.com/specsharp/
15. Microsoft Corp., XML Schema Object Model (SOM),
    http://msdn2.microsoft.com/en-us/library/bs8hh90b(vs.71).aspx
16. Simeon, J., Wadler, P.: The Essence of XML. In: Proceedings of POPL 2003, pp. 1–13. ACM, New York (2003)
17. W3C: XML Schema 1.1, http://www.w3.org/XML/Schema
18. XML Data Binder,
    http://www.liquid-technologies.com/XmlStudio/Xml-Data-Binder.aspx
19. XMLBeans, http://xmlbeans.apache.org

Author Index

GPSR Compliance

*The European Union's (EU) General Product Safety Regulation (GPSR)
is a set of rules that requires consumer products to be safe and our
obligations to ensure this.*

*If you have any concerns about our products, you can contact us on
ProductSafety@springernature.com*

In case Publisher is established outside the EU, the EU authorized
representative is:

Springer Nature Customer Service Center GmbH
Europaplatz 3
69115 Heidelberg, Germany

Batch number: 09478804

Printed by Printforce, the Netherlands